Reasoning from the Scriptures
with
MASONS
Ron Rhodes

HARVEST HOUSE PUBLISHERS
Eugene, Oregon 97402

Cover by Terry Dugan Design, Minneapolis, Minnesota

REASONING FROM THE SCRIPTURES WITH MASONS
Copyright © 2001 by Ron Rhodes
Published by Harvest House Publishers
Eugene, Oregon 97402

Library of Congress Cataloging-in-Publication Data

Rhodes, Ron.
  Reasoning from the scriptures with Masons / Ron Rhodes
    p. cm.
  Includes bibliographical references and index.
  ISBN: 0-7369-0467-0
    1. Freemasonry—Controversial Literature. 2. Freemasonry—Religious Aspects—
Baptists. I. Title.

HS459 .R44 2001
366'.1—dc21   00-047126

Printed in the United States of America

01 02 03 04 05 06 07 / BC-MS / 10 9 8 7 6 5 4 3 2 1

To pastors everywhere
who are bold enough to speak the truth in love
to those in their congregations
who have been deceived by the Masonic Lodge.

Acknowledgments

Kerri, David, and Kylie—
you are the greatest blessings in my life!
I couldn't do my work of ministry without you.
You are deeply, deeply appreciated.

Contents

The Masonic Lodge

Masonry is a centuries-old fraternal order and secret society that is deeply entrenched in symbolism, secret oaths, and secret rituals. Key themes, according to Masons themselves, include the universal fatherhood of God and the brotherhood of man.

Some very famous people have been Masons throughout American history: 14 presidents (including George Washington), 18 vice presidents, five chief justices of the Supreme Court, General Douglas MacArthur, John Philip Sousa, John Wayne, Clark Gable, Norman Vincent Peale, Ernest Borgnine, Cecil B. DeMille, W.C. Fields, Henry Ford, Barry Goldwater, J. Edgar Hoover, Harry Houdini, J.C. Penney, Roy Rogers, and Red Skelton. In earlier days, people from all over the world were masons, including: Benjamin Franklin, James Monroe, Alexander Hamilton, Oscar Wilde, Mark Twain, Wolfgang Amadeus Mozart, Francois Voltaire, Franz Joseph Haydn, and Paul Revere.[1] The majority of the 56 signers of the American Declaration of Independence were Masons.[2] Most of the American generals in the Revolutionary War were Masons.[3] Many people have assumed that with such intelligent and respectable people joining a Masonic Lodge, there must not be anything wrong with such membership.

Today, millions of people are involved in the various orders within Freemasonry. There are approximately 3 million Masons in the Blue Lodge, over a quarter of a million in the York Rite, close to a million in the Scottish Rite, and perhaps another million in the various other orders.[4] There are presently 33,700 Masonic Lodges (meeting places for Masons) in 164 countries in the world, with approximately 15,300 of these in the United States. Bible apologists John Ankerberg and John Weldon provide these details:

> In the Philippines there are 211 Lodges and 15,037 Masons. England has more than 8,000

Lodges with a membership of more than 600,000. West Germany has 388 Lodges with 21,000 members, and Italy has 562 Lodges with 24,000 members. Even communist Cuba has 324 Lodges and 19,728 members! In Canada, there are 183,000 members in 1,600 Lodges, and the U.S. boasts at least 4 million Masons in 15,300 Lodges. More Masons live in California (188,535) than in Canada. There are 90,000 Masons in Georgia, 83,000 in Florida, 146,000 in Illinois, 88,000 in Massachusetts, 111,000 in Michigan, 220,000 in Ohio, 206,000 in Pennsylvania, 75,000 in South Carolina, 206,000 in Texas, and 96,000 in Tennessee.[5]

In view of such staggering statistics, it is not surprising that some 80,000 Masonic books have been published in Europe and 20,000 in America.[6] This is obviously a subject of great interest to many people. Indeed, as Michael Baigent and Richard Leigh put it in their book *The Temple and the Lodge*: "One need only pronounce the word 'Freemasonry' in a pub, restaurant, hotel lobby or other public place to see heads twitch, faces swivel attentively, ears fine-tune themselves to eavesdrop."[7]

People seek membership in a Masonic Lodge for a variety of reasons. Some like the idea of belonging to a secret society where they are privileged to learn secret mysteries rooted in ancient times. Some are fascinated by all the rich symbolism. Some people join because they appreciate the emphasis on the brotherhood of man and the accompanying humanitarianism (such as involvement in various charities, including burn centers for children). Many join because they think it is a good place to network and make business contacts.[8] Still others join simply because a relative or acquaintance they know and respect is a Mason. Researcher Ron Campbell observes:

Most men do not join lodges of Freemasonry
with the thought that it is anything less than good
and right. In fact, most men know little about the
Lodge when they join. They are simply convinced by friends, fathers, fathers-in-law, uncles
or grandfathers that it is a good thing and would
benefit them greatly.[9]

The Origin of Freemasonry

The origin of Freemasonry is shrouded in deep mystery and
wild legends. Some Masons have claimed that Freemasonry goes
back to the time of Adam and Eve, arguing that the fig leaves ref-
erenced in Genesis 3:7 were actually the first Masonic "aprons"
(which are used in Masonic initiatory ceremonies).[10] It is sometimes argued that Moses was a Grand Master who often mar-
shaled the Israelites into a regular and general lodge while in the
wilderness.[11] Other Masons claim Freemasonry dates back to the
time of Solomon, who utilized the skills of stone masons in
erecting the temple in Jerusalem.[12] Solomon is said to have been
Grand Master of the lodge at Jerusalem.[13]

Contrary to such claims, history reveals that Freemasonry formally began in London, England, in 1717, due to the efforts of
James Anderson, George Payne, and Theopholis Desaguliers.[14]
The earliest recorded minutes of a Masonic meeting date back to
1723.* It was just a matter of time before new lodges sprang up
across England, Ireland, Scotland, Holland, Germany, France,
and other European countries.[15] This movement spread rapidly.
Freemasonry arrived on American soil by 1733, 16 years after it
first emerged in England. Throughout the 1800s, virtually thousands of Masonic Lodges mushroomed throughout the United
States.[16]

Understandably, Freemasonry grew to become a powerful
influence in terms of American religion, politics, and the social

---

* Further details on the emergence and historical development of Masonry are
provided in chapter 3, "Understanding Freemasonry."

scene. Today about half the Grand Lodges and two-thirds of the Freemasons in the world are in the United States.

An Important Qualification

At the outset of this book, I must note that no single definition of Freemasonry will be acceptable to all Masons. There are so many degrees in Freemasonry, with escalating levels of revealed mysteries to initiates, that what constitutes Freemasonry to one person may be quite different from how another Mason sees it. Some low-level Masons may view Freemasonry as little more than a social club or fraternal fellowship that is beneficial for business contacts and an enjoyable time. For others, particularly those in more advanced degrees, Freemasonry takes on much more significance—often *religious* significance—and can even become a way of life.[17]

Some Masons believe that one cannot understand true Masonry outside of the higher degrees. The lower degrees are viewed merely as the "cover of the book," so to speak, and to understand what Masonry really is requires opening that book and diving into some of the higher degrees.[18] Indeed, as will be demonstrated later in this book, members of the low-level Blue Lodge are purposely kept in ignorance of the true meaning of Masonry—an ignorance that will persist *unless* and *until* they participate in the higher degrees of Freemasonry. Aside from this, it is a fact that within Masonry, no one Mason speaks for another. "Freemasonry has no 'official voice' and that freedom of thought and expression is one of the fundamental principles of the Order."[19]

Yet, Freemasonry *is* a historical movement that has produced a large body of literature and acknowledges certain leaders within the movement whose writings are viewed as representative. This book will focus on the "core" beliefs that are at the heart of respected and representative Masonic literature, especially that produced by such respected Masonic leaders as Henry Wilson Coil, Joseph Fort Newton, Albert G. Mackey, and Albert Pike.

Masonic Grand Masters across the United States consider these leaders authoritative spokesmen for their beliefs.

Challenging Masonic Beliefs

Masonic leader Albert Mackey has written that "there is no country of the civilized world where Freemasonry has existed, in which opposition to it has not, from time to time, exhibited itself; although it has always been overcome by the purity and innocence of the institution."[20] John Robinson, in his book *Born in Blood: The Lost Secrets of Freemasonry*, commented that "Freemasonry probably has aroused more enmity than any secular organization in the history of the world."[21] Indeed, he says, Freemasonry is "outlawed in a number of countries" and has even been branded by some as the Antichrist.[22]

Masons certainly do not like it when "fundamentalist" Christians criticize their movement. They feel they are misrepresented and misunderstood. Sometimes Christians who criticize Freemasonry are portrayed as holding to a narrow and bigoted interpretation of Christianity.[23] For this reason, Masons set forth some rather unflattering caricatures of evangelical apologists, such as my friend John Ankerberg, who have taken a stand against Freemasonry.[24] Mason Richard Thorn, in his book *The Boy Who Cried Wolf: The Book that Breaks Masonic Silence*, seeks to unmask "some of those who pretend to be Christians, but who evidently lack the love and tolerance stressed by the Man from Galilee."[25]

Of course, Jesus was and is a person of love, compassion, and meekness—but He is also the divine judge of humankind (see Romans 2:16; 2 Timothy 4:1; Revelation 19:11). This man of "tolerance," as Thorn describes Jesus, took an unbending stand against false prophets and false Christs (see Matthew 7:22,23; 24:4,5,23,24). He spoke harshly against false religious leaders (Matthew 23). And Scripture assures us that Jesus will one day come again and separate the sheep from the goats, inviting the sheep (true Christians) into His kingdom but dooming the goats (unbelievers) to suffer eternally in hell (Matthew 25:31-46). Thorn has quite clearly portrayed Jesus in a way favorable to Freemasonry, but completely foreign to the pages of Scripture.

In this book, Scripture will be the measuring stick—our *"barometer of truth"*—for testing the claims of Freemasonry. Further, this book will set forth scriptural arguments Christians can use in reasoning with a Mason, whether he is a non-Christian Mason or a Mason who claims to be a Christian. Of course, in the case of the "Christian" Mason, the goal is first to make sure the person *is* a Christian according to the biblical definition, then provide substantive reasons why the "Christian" Mason should no longer be affiliated with the Masonic Lodge. In the case of the non-Christian Mason, the goal is first evangelism (leading him to faith in Christ for salvation), and then "exit counseling"—helping the person see why he should leave the Lodge and become active in a good, Bible-believing church.

The next chapter lays a foundation by providing some basic tips on witnessing to Masons. Following this, I will deal with the primary issues that will likely arise in a witnessing encounter.

1

Dialoguing with Masons

Masons do not engage in door-to-door visitations like Mormons and Jehovah's Witnesses. They do not proselytize. Therefore, your encounters with Masons will not be like that of other cultic groups. You will more likely come into contact with Masons at the workplace, in your neighborhood, or at a public gathering. It could even be that you come into contact with a Mason at your church. Whatever the case, it is important that you be ready to discuss Masonry whenever the opportunity arises.

Dialoguing with Masons can be a trying experience. Your chances of success in reaching a Mason for Christ, or in convincing a "Christian Mason" to leave the Masonic Lodge, can be greatly enhanced by *deciding in advance* to handle your interactions in a certain way. Here are some helpful tips.

Prepare by Prayer

Pray regularly in regard to your witnessing opportunities. Only God in His mighty power can lift the veil of cultic and occultic darkness from the human heart (2 Corinthians 4:4; compare with 3:17; John 8:32). Pray fervently and often for those to whom you are witnessing (Matthew 7:7-12; James 5:16). Prayer is especially important if you have a prearranged appointment with a Mason. In such cases you can pray for the person by name and ask for God's intervention in his life. Pray especially that God would bring conviction to the Mason's heart in regard to the truth you share (see John 16:8).

Get to Know Masons on a Personal Level

It is important that you develop a personal relationship with the Mason to whom you want to witness. Make every effort to be hospitable by inviting him to dinner or refreshments.

People like to know that you genuinely care for them. So be interested and be a good listener. As the saying goes, "People don't care how much you know until they know how much you care." Do not be phony about your concern; sooner or later the Mason will perceive your true motivation and become disillusioned. Encourage your friend to tell you about himself. If he has a need and there is a way you can reach out in a helpful way, by all means make that a priority. This is important because many Masons feel that only other Masons will reach out to help them during times of need. Let the love of Christ shine through you.

Acknowledge that Masons Do Many Good Things

L. James Rongstad, author of *The Lodge: How to Respond*, says, "We would be remiss if we were to ignore the Lodge's many positive aspects."[1] It is important to let the Mason know that you are aware of the helpful deeds of the Masonic Lodge, for whenever Masons are theologically criticized, one of their first responses is typically, "Aren't you aware of all the good things we do?"[2]

Positive aspects of the Lodge include the fact that most Masons are highly patriotic and interested in the well-being of our country. They also place a high premium on morality. It is true that many Masons incorrectly think they can earn salvation by high morality, but the fact that they are moral is praiseworthy in the immoral culture in which we live. Further, Masonic members are often humanitarian and very generous in their charitable giving. Acknowledging such positive aspects of the Masonic Lodge often helps prevent barriers being erected when you point out the serious theological problems in Freemasonry.

Find Common Ground

Scripture tells us that the apostle Paul was quite angry when he entered Athens and discovered that the city was full of idols (Acts 17:16). If he had acted upon his emotions, he probably would have vented his anger by dealing with the Athenians in a hostile way. But Paul did not do this. Instead, he sought a *common ground* from which he could communicate the good news of the gospel.

Paul began his message: "Men of Athens! I see that in every way you are very religious. For as I walked around and looked carefully at your objects of worship, I even found an altar with this inscription: TO AN UNKNOWN GOD. Now what you worship as something unknown I am going to proclaim to you" (Acts 17:22,23).

Applying what we learn from Paul's encounter with the Athenians to present-day encounters with Masons, the *wrong* approach would be to deal with them in a hostile way. The better approach is to speak to them kindly and respectfully (like Paul did to the Athenians), and begin on the common ground of their commitment to the "Great Architect of the Universe." Starting off in this way, you can then move on to discuss how their "God" differs from what the Bible says about Jesus Christ, sin, salvation, and the afterlife.

Be Kind and Gentle—and Firm

We, as Christians, are called to share the good news of the gospel with people so they might be saved from sure destruction

(Matthew 28:19,20). We are to do this with gentleness and respect (1 Peter 3:15). Yet, even as we are gentle and respectful, we are to be firm in telling the truth. Remember: Eternal souls are at stake. Just as the first-century Christians were bold in their witness for Christ, so must we be bold witnesses (Acts 2:32; 3:15; 4:33; 13:30,31). Giving a bold testimony to truth is, in fact, the most loving thing we can do.

Look at it this way. If you came to find out that some pills in a local store had been laced with cyanide, you would do everything you could to warn individuals about the danger so they would not be poisoned and killed. That would be the most caring action you could do. What we must realize is that there is also *spiritual* cyanide being disseminated on a massive level by Freemasonry. The most loving thing we can do when speaking with Masons is to warn them of the dangers of Freemasonry and share the truth with them. To hold back telling the truth would be withholding vital information that can lead them to salvation.

Take Your Time

The tendency of many Christians is to lambaste Masons (and other cultists) with all the false doctrines in their belief system. This is what I call the "flame-thrower" approach to evangelism. The flame-thrower approach rarely yields positive results in terms of leading someone to faith in Christ.

A much better approach is to take your time and not force the Mason to digest more than he can take during one sitting. Many cult experts have noted that it is better to focus on *one* or *two* issues during each meeting and thoroughly deal with them than to "get it all out on the table" in a single sitting. Remember, even Jesus told the disciples: "I have many more things to say to you, but you cannot bear them now" (John 16:12 NASB). Jesus was sensitive to how much His listeners could digest at a time.

If you engage in a thoughtful discussion of one or two subjects during your initial encounter with a Mason—and you remain kind and respectful in the process—he will not only be impressed with your manner but will likely be open and willing to have other discussions in the future. *This is what you want to happen!*

Not All Masons Believe Alike

It is important to not assume that all Masons believe the same thing or that all Masons know exactly what Freemasonry teaches about all matters. If you witness to Masons long enough, you will soon discover the wisdom of this policy. Many low-level Masons* are unaware of what is taught in the advanced degrees in Freemasonry. In fact, many Masons in the Blue Lodge are purposely kept in ignorance; certain teachings are reserved only for the more advanced degrees.

Instead of telling a Mason what he believes, it is better to simply ask him what he believes on a particular matter, then deal with that issue. Ask, "Do you believe...?" If they say no to a particular question about their doctrine, you might say, "I'm glad *you* don't believe that, but do you know whether Freemasonry teaches it?" If they answer that Freemasonry does not teach such a doctrine, you can ask, "What would you do if you found out Freemasonry really does teach that?" This can open the door to some lively discussions.

Define Your Terms

Masons use many Christian words such as "God," "Jesus Christ," "salvation," and "the afterlife," but their organization redefines them. The Christian must ever be on guard regarding this semantic subterfuge. As my late colleague Walter Martin once put it in reference to Mormons but applicable to Masons:

> The importance of destroying the "terminology block" cannot be overemphasized. No matter how good your presentation is, and no matter how much you have researched and studied, so that you can present the gospel in an orthodox

---

* Masons who participate in only the lower degrees in Freemasonry, such as the Entered Apprentice degree in the Blue Lodge.

> manner, if you cannot communicate, you are
> wasting your time.[3]

It is especially important to not push for a decision for Christ until you have shown the Mason the differences between the Masonic god and the biblical God, between the Masonic Jesus and the biblical Jesus, between the Masonic gospel and the biblical gospel. Remember, it is *only* the true God and the true Jesus and the true gospel of the Bible that can bring *true* salvation.

Disarm the "Ignorance" Accusation

Christian apologist Walton Hannah argues "how utterly without foundation is the Masonic parrot-cry that no one who is not a Mason can possibly form any opinion of Masonic teachings or come to any understanding of what it all means."[4] He goes on to point out that it is not necessary, after all, to become a member of the Roman Catholic Church in order to understand its teachings. Nor is it necessary to become a member of a particular cultic group in order to understand its teachings.

The reality is that there is a huge volume of literature produced by highly respected Masonic leaders such as Henry Wilson Coil, Joseph Fort Newton, Albert G. Mackey, and Albert Pike. Masonic Grand Masters across the United States consider such leaders authoritative spokesmen for Masonry's beliefs. The accusation that critics of Freemasonry are ignorant of Masonic beliefs is without foundation. Christians need to be ready to firmly make this point.

Ask Leading Questions

If you can help a Mason discover problems in Freemasonry for himself, then you have accomplished a good thing. This method is much more productive than trying to force your opinion on him.

One great way of helping your friend discover problems in Freemasonry is by asking strategic questions based on key Bible verses, all the while remaining tactful and kind. Remember, Jesus often asked questions to make a point (see, for example, Luke 7:42; 10:26; 12:56). A person can close his ears to facts he does not want to hear, but if a pointed question causes him to form the answer in his own mind, he cannot escape the conclusion because it is reached by himself. Use this same type of methodology with Masons.

The right question asked in a nondefensive, nonchallenging, unemotional way may cause the Mason to find himself face-to-face with a doctrine, such as Jesus being the only way of salvation, that is completely contrary to what Freemasonry teaches. By considering such a question, the Mason is forced to come to a conclusion in his own mind. L. James Rongstad writes, "You can ask penetrating and thought-provoking questions in a humble, contrite spirit that will be nonthreatening to the lodge member.... It is not too difficult to help a lodge member see his own contradictions if the right questions are asked."[5]

In most chapters of this book, there are sample questions on a variety of subjects you can ask the Mason in order to initiate dialogue and make important points. Keep in mind that many Masons believe they are Christians, while others affiliate with Hinduism, Islam, or other religious groups. Use your judgment regarding the most appropriate questions to ask the particular Mason to whom you are speaking.

Avoid the mindset that simply because you ask one or more of these crucial questions, the Mason will promptly repent of his faulty view and immediately become a Bible-based Christian or leave the Masonic Lodge. The questions offered in this book *are not* presented as "scripts" that if precisely followed guarantee the Mason will "see the light." The Mason may or may not respond on any given occasion. If used consistently, questions such as these can help you effectively demonstrate to the Mason that his view is unbiblical. If all goes well, the Lord may bless you with the wonderful privilege of leading a Mason to faith in Christ or leading a "Christian Mason" out of the Masonic Lodge.

How to Use this Book

As you peruse the Table of Contents of this book, you will notice that most of the chapters deal with a specific doctrinal issue. Each chapter begins with a summary of what Freemasonry teaches on a particular subject. Following this, you will find doctrinal responses to their viewpoints, as well as discussions of some of the major Bible verses they cite in their various rituals. You should note, however, that Masons are unlike cultic groups like the Jehovah's Witnesses and Mormons who cite specific scriptural prooftexts to support their doctrines. More often than not, Masons loosely relate certain biblical passages to their rituals, without providing theological support regarding how the verse relates to the Masonic ritual or belief. Still, as this book will demonstrate, the verses that are cited by Masons can be used as a launchpad to make important doctrinal points that the Mason desperately needs to hear.

Quotations from Masonic literature are *liberally* sprinkled throughout our discussion. The reason for this is that Masons often claim their viewpoints are misrepresented by Christians. The numerous quotes from Masonic literature are intended to provide the needed proof that they are not, in fact, being misinterpreted. The "leading questions" included in each chapter are boxed for your convenience, making it easy for you to quickly find them to make your point and initiate discussion.

This book may be read straight through, giving you a good grasp of Masonic beliefs and how to refute them. Or, you may consult individual chapters as needed. Each chapter is self-contained and deals with a distinct doctrinal area with some of the major biblical passages cited by Masons. *Reasoning from the Scriptures with Masons* is an easy-to-use reference tool that you can pull off the bookshelf to "bone up" in a matter of minutes on key Masonic ideas.

2

Masonic Families

There is not just one kind of Mason. There are *families* of Masons, each with distinctive characteristics. This chapter briefly summarizes these families, but the actual rituals and teachings of these families are reserved for later, more in-depth chapters.

When a person first becomes a Mason, he undergoes an initiation into the "Blue lodge." This is the starting point for anyone wishing to become a Mason. Some Masons explain the significance of the word "blue" in "Blue Lodge" in terms of being a symbol of the purity of God, thus serving to remind Masons to work hard to keep their lives pure. (As we will see later, Masons believe it is by personal purity and morality that one earns a place in heaven, the "Celestial Lodge Above.") Other Masons say that blue was simply the official color for the first Grand Lodge of England.[1]

Entrance into the Blue Lodge

Membership in the Blue Lodge has been, in years past, restricted to white males 21 years of age or older.* The applicant must be recommended by a lodge member. Following such a recommendation, a vote is taken using white and black balls. "White balls elect; black balls reject. In casting the ballot all members are required to base their vote on personal knowledge, information of the committee on investigation, and reputed character of the candidate."[2] Should the member receive a blackball, a "foul" is announced and a second vote is taken.[3] Barring any further blackballs, the candidate is accepted and takes some rather solemn oaths (I'll discuss these later in the book). If he receives a second blackball, he is rejected.[4]

Once accepted, the candidate begins to earn the degree of Entered Apprentice. This is a preliminary degree, intended to prepare the candidate for the higher and fuller instructions of the succeeding degrees.[5]

One is initially required to bow before "The Worshipful Master" and say something to this effect, "I am lost in darkness, and I am seeking the light of Freemasonry."[6] He then proceeds on a path through progressive degrees whereby he increasingly receives the "light" of Masonry.

Besides Entered Apprentice, there are two additional degrees within Blue Lodge Freemasonry—Fellow Craft and Master Mason. Like the Entered Apprentice degree, the Fellow Craft degree is preparatory for the higher Master Mason degree (the third degree of the Blue Lodge), and yet it differs essentially from it in its symbolism. We are told that "as the First Degree was typical of youth, the Second is supposed to represent the stage of manhood."[7] Indeed, "the Apprentice Degree is devoted to a

---

* Although most Masonic Lodges and organizations now embrace an official nondiscrimination policy, a defacto segregation seems to be promoted in some lodges through the "white ball/black ball" acceptance vote. Although "Prince Hall Freemasonry" was founded to allow African Americans to participate in Masonry, the fact remains that the vast majority of Masons are Caucasians.

beginner; the Fellow-Craft to a more advanced searcher for light."[8] The word *fellow* etymologically signifies "bound in mutual trust," "a follower," "a companion," "an associate."[9] Masonic brotherhood is a heavy emphasis in this degree. Masonic leaders also tell us that the Fellow Craft degree involves "the cultivation of the reasoning faculties and the improvement of the intellectual powers."[10] This progresses throughout adulthood.

The Master Mason degree represents full maturity in the Mason, and prepares one for entrance into eternal life in the Celestial Lodge Above (heaven). This degree is symbolic of the period of mature adult life—a time for increased learning, ripened experiences, heavier responsibilities, and preparing for the inevitable termination in death.[11] "Foremost in the conceptions of this period of life is that it is a time of waiting by the wearied workman for the word of the Grand Master of the universe which will summon the Master Mason from the labors of earth to the eternal refreshments of heaven."[12] The Master Mason believes, "Having been faithful to all his trusts, he is at last to die, and to receive the reward of his fidelity."[13]

One must participate in required rituals for each of these degrees. And in each, the initiate receives further Masonic "light" to guide him throughout life.

The York Rite

Once a man completes the three degrees in the Blue Lodge, he is then free to pursue higher degrees in either the York Rite or the Scottish Rite. The York Rite is named after York, England, the seat of the Ancient York Grand Lodge.[14] York Rite Masonry comprises three separate bodies called Grand Chapters: Royal Arch Chapter, The Council of Royal and Select Masters, and The Commandery of Knights Templar. A person may earn degrees in each of these.

According to Masonic literature, a Mason can attain four "Chapter" degrees that are awarded by the General Grand Chapter of the York Rite, each rooted in Solomonic legend:

- 4th Degree—Mark Master (the ritual of which relates to the legend of finding the missing keystone for Solomon's temple in a pile of rubble in ancient Tyre[15])
- 5th Degree—Past Master (which involves training in leadership[16])
- 6th Degree—Most Excellent Master (the ritual of which involves the completion of Solomon's temple[17])
- 7th Degree—Royal Arch Mason (the ritual of which relates to three Most Excellent Masters being carried into captivity by Nebuchadnezzar who later return from exile to rebuild Solomon's temple[18])

The Mason can then opt to pursue "Council" degrees, the rituals of which involve additional legends surrounding the building of Solomon's temple:

- 8th Degree—Royal Master
- 9th Degree—Select Master
- Super Excellent Master (unnumbered degree)[19]

Finally, one can pursue "Commandery Degrees," which include the Knights of Malta and the Knights Templar.

The Scottish Rite

The Scottish Rite branch of Freemasonry—perhaps the most popular form of Freemasonry—may also be pursued after one has completed the Master Mason degree in the Blue Lodge. As to where the Rite obtained its name "Scottish," Masonic enthusiast Harold Voorhis explains that one of the degrees founded in France was called Scottish Master: "The chapter no doubt had Scots Masters in its membership and when a Supreme Council was organized in Charleston, the name 'Scottish Rite' was adopted for these degrees."[20]

The Scottish Rite confers an additional 29 degrees, the highest of these being the 33rd-degree Mason.[21] An example of a well-known 33rd-degree Mason is "positive thinking" author Norman Vincent Peale. The degrees of the Scottish Rite are:

- 4th   Degree—Secret Master
- 5th   Degree—Perfect Master
- 6th   Degree—Intimate Secretary
- 7th   Degree—Provost and Judge
- 8th   Degree—Intendant of the Building
- 9th   Degree—Master Elect of Nine
- 10th   Degree—Master Elect of Fifteen
- 11th   Degree—Sublime Master Elected
- 12th   Degree—Grand Master Architect
- 13th   Degree—Master of the Ninth Arch
- 14th   Degree—Grand, Elect, Perfect and Sublime Mason
- 15th   Degree—Knight of the East or Sword
- 16th   Degree—Prince of Jerusalem
- 17th   Degree—Knight of the East and West
- 18th   Degree—Knight of the Rose Croix
- 19th   Degree—Grand Pontiff
- 20th   Degree—Master Ad Vitam
- 21st   Degree—Noachite or Prussian Knight
- 22nd   Degree—Prince of Libanus
- 23rd   Degree—Chief of the Tabernacle
- 24th   Degree—Prince of the Tabernacle
- 25th   Degree—Knight of the Brazen Serpent
- 26th   Degree—Prince of Mercy

- 27th Degree—Knight Commander of the Temple
- 28th Degree—Knight of the Sun
- 29th Degree—Knight of St. Andrew
- 30th Degree—Knight Kadosh
- 31st Degree—Grand Inspector Inquisitor Commander
- 32nd Degree—Sublime Prince of the Royal Secret
- 33rd Degree—Sovereign Grand Inspector General.[22]

Without going into great detail, these various degrees emphasize such things as fidelity, respect, zealousness, faithfulness, justice, equity, impartiality, charity, compassion, honesty, sincerity, virtue, humility, generosity, temperance, and honor. Degree by degree, the Mason allegedly becomes a better person and more worthy of the Celestial Lodge Above.

Special Interest Masonic Orders

Aside from the Blue Lodge, the York Rite, and the Scottish Rite, there are a number of minor orders that cater to what one might call "special interest groups" within Freemasonry.* Following is a brief summary of some of the more notable of these.[23]

Ancient Arabic Order of the Nobles of the Mystic Shrine

This Order was founded in 1872 for the primary purpose of "extracurricular fraternization." Shriners, as they are called, are high-level York Rite and Scottish Rite Masons (one must have obtained at least the 32nd degree of the Scottish Rite or the Knights Templar degree of the York Rite) who gather for fun and socializing apart from the normal meetings in Masonic Lodges. They are the most highly visible among Masons and are sometimes seen participating in parades of various sorts.

Please refer to the note on page 22.

Today, Shriners are heavily involved with children's hospitals and burn centers. They are well known for their charitable work in these areas. Indeed, Arthur Edward Waite writes that "the Shriners have built and they maintain the largest chain of crippled children's hospitals in the world. They are open free of charge to children of all creeds and all races."[24]

The Order of the Eastern Star

This Order was founded in 1850 by Dr. Robert Morris. It is open to women who are related to Masons, including wives, daughters, mothers, sisters, granddaughters, and female relatives. The Order supports both the causes and the doctrines of Masonry. It is a means by which women related to Masons "might be brought into closer relationship with the Order of Freemasonry, might share in the benefits of Masonry to a fuller extent, especially in obtaining assistance and protection when needed, and might be given the privileges of closer cooperation with Masonic Lodges in their labors of charity, and in their endeavors for human progress."[25]

The five degrees attainable within this order are named after women in the Bible:

- *Adah*, the first degree (the daughter's degree), stresses obedience
- *Ruth*, the second degree (the widow's degree), stresses devotion
- *Esther*, the third degree (the wife's degree), stresses fidelity
- *Martha*, the fourth degree (the sister's degree), stresses faith
- *Electa*, the fifth degree (the Christian martyr's degree), stresses charity.[26]

It is not surprising, in view of the male exclusivity of Freemasonry, that some Masons reacted less than charitably when this order was formed. One well-known Mason, Albert Mackey, thought the whole idea was reprehensible and was aghast that women could be permitted to learn the sacred secrets of Freemasonry. Others have viewed it more beneficially in view of the fact that Masonic education of wives and others in the family can help them be better supports to the man of the house.

Daughters of the Eastern Star

This Order is for females, ages 14 to 20, whose fathers are Masons or whose mothers are members of the Eastern Star. The order was founded in 1925, and confers three degrees—Initiatory, Honorary Majority, and Public.

The Order of DeMolay

This Order is named after Jacques DeMolay, leader of the Knights Templar, who was burned at the stake in the fourteenth century. It was founded by Frank Land, and is an order for males, ages 14 to 21, that focuses on such noble things as citizenship, patriotism, morality, cleanliness, and faith in God.[27]

The International Order of Job's Daughters

This Order was founded in 1920 by Ethel T. W. Mick and is obviously named from the book of Job: "Nowhere in all the land were there found women as beautiful as Job's daughters, and their father granted them an inheritance along with their brothers" (Job 42:15). This Order is for females between the ages of 11 and 20. It focuses heavily on moral and spiritual development and actively promotes charitable work in the community.

The International Order of Rainbow for Girls

This Order was founded in 1922 by Reverend Mark Sexson. The goal of this Order is to prepare girls for eventual membership in the Eastern Star. Membership is limited to females, ages 12 to 20, and requires a recommendation by a Mason or a member of the Eastern Star. The "Rainbow" ritual is built on the foundation of faith, hope, and charity (love).

Masonic College Fraternities

There are a number of fraternal organizations on college campuses that are directly affiliated with Freemasonry—including Acacia, The Square and Compass, Sigma Mu Sigma, The Order of the Golden Key, and Tau Kappa Epsilon. Most of these emerged in the late 1800s or early 1900s. Many college campuses across the country sponsor these and other fraternal organizations.

Prince Hall Freemasonry

It is not surprising that an all-black lodge was eventually formed since blacks had been consistently denied membership in Freemasonry. Prince Hall Freemasonry emerged due to the efforts of Prince Hall, in the late 1700s. His petition for a charter was granted by the Grand Lodge of England in 1784.[28]

No Single Kind of Mason

As you can see, there are *families* in Masonry. Truly there is no single kind of Masonry. This is one of the things that makes evaluating the Masonic Lodge somewhat complex. Yet I am convinced it *can* be evaluated by looking at some of the specific beliefs that are common to the majority of Masons today.

Perhaps the best place to begin would be to address fundamental questions such as: Where did Freemasonry come from? How do most Masons understand Freemasonry? What are we to make of some of the symbols of Freemasonry taken from the Bible? Let us now explore these issues.

3

Understanding Freemasonry

Freemasonry is not easy to define—something that even Masons recognize. Though I disagree with much of what popular Masonic writer Henry Wilson Coil believes, he is certainly right in his affirmation that no one fully agrees with others as to what Freemasonry is. In his book *A Comprehensive View of Freemasonry*, Coil noted that "what one asserts, another of apparently equal ability doubts or denies. Though different persons may agree upon some phases or points of the subject, few will be able to agree upon all."[1]

Why is this? The answer is quite simple. According to Coil, the Masonic fraternity has no central authority to declare its creed and no censor of books to check aberrations. *Anyone,* inside or outside the Lodge, can speak or write about it what he wills.[2]

Still, it is possible to come to a basic understanding as to what Freemasonry is all about based upon Masonry's most popular (and representative) writers and leaders across the country. Coil himself defined Freemasonry this way:

> Freemasonry is an oath-bound, fraternal order of men; deriving from the medieval fraternity of operative Freemasons; adhering to many of their Ancient Charges, laws, customs, and legends; loyal to the civil government under which it exists; inculcating moral and social virtues of symbolic application of the working tools of the stonemasons and by allegories, lectures, and charges; the members of which are obligated to observe principles of brotherly love, equality, mutual aid and assistance, secrecy, and confidence; have secret modes of recognizing each other as Masons when abroad in the world; and meet in lodges, each governed somewhat autocratically by a Master, assisted by Wardens, where applicants, after particular inquiry into their mental, moral, and physical qualifications, are formally admitted into the Society in secret ceremonies based in part on old legends of the Craft.[3]

While at this early juncture certain aspects of this detailed definition may not seem clear to the reader (they *will* become clear later in the book), a primary point is that Freemasonry is a fraternal organization—and, in fact, it is claimed elsewhere to be the largest fraternal organization in the world.[4] More important, Freemasonry is a fraternal organization that places heavy emphasis on morality.

Albert Mackey, another of Masonry's most respected leaders, gives us a much more basic definition when he says, "Freemasonry is a system of morality veiled in allegory and illustrated by symbols."[5] What he meant by this is that Freemasonry, as an organization, places a very high premium upon—and seeks to produce in its members—an elevated level of morality, and the various rituals and teachings in the respective degrees are couched in allegory and illustrated by symbols derived from the Bible and other sources (including other religions).[6]

These allegories and symbols are not necessarily interpreted in a uniform fashion. Masons of different religious persuasions may understand them differently. It is in view of this that a Mason using the name Vindex wrote that "Freemasonry, having no background of credal dogmas, is a system of allegory and symbolism...into which the brethren can read any aspect of the universal religious truths which they represent. This gives to Masonic symbolism a richness and depth."[7]

Mason Harold Voorhis affirmed that "Masonry is universal and men of every creed are eligible for membership so long as they accept the fatherhood of God and the brotherhood of man."[8] Men of differing religious persuasions can become Masons and interpret the allegories and symbols in Masonry according to their own distinctive beliefs. They can also base their morality on whatever holy book their religion espouses (for example, Hindus can use the Vedas, Muslims can use the Koran, and Christians can use the Bible).

For the purposes of this chapter, I will focus on how Masons appeal to the Bible in support of their early beginnings and their emphasis on brotherhood. You will discover that Masons are very selective in their approach to the Bible.

The Beginnings of Freemasonry

Some Masons have made the claim that, ultimately, Masonry finds its beginnings in the ancient pagan religions that existed in biblical times. John Robinson, author of *Born in Blood: The Lost Secrets of Freemasonry*, notes that claims have been made "to establish the origins of Masonry in ancient Egypt, and some traced Masonic sources to the Essenes, Zoroastrians, Chaldeans, and especially the Phoenicians."[9]

While it is true that some of the rituals of Masonry have strong parallels to some of the ancient mystery religions, Masons have done a bit of "creative borrowing." It is *not* true that there is a direct, unbroken historic line of development between these ancient religions and modern Masonry. Those who suggest such a thing are dishing out a revisionist version of Masonic history. Freemasonry may have *borrowed* some of its ritual from the ancient mystery religions, but it did not emerge from them.

More fanciful yet are suggestions that Masonry goes back to the time of Adam and Eve...or at least back to the time of Solomon. Masons believe the Bible provides support for such claims.

GENESIS 3:7: *Masonry in Adam and Eve's Time?*

Masonic View: I noted in the Introduction that some Masons have claimed Freemasonry goes back to the time of Adam and Eve. They point to Genesis 3:7, where we read that following Adam and Eve's sin, "the eyes of both of them were opened, and they realized they were naked; so they sewed fig leaves together and made coverings for themselves." Some Masons argue that the fig-leaf coverings were actually the first Masonic "aprons."[10] (In Freemasonry special aprons are used in various initiatory rituals.)

Biblical View: Masons are practicing *eisogesis* (reading a meaning *into* the text) instead of *exegesis* (drawing the meaning *out of* the text). Masonic rituals are nowhere to be found in the context of Genesis 3, or the rest of the Bible. The fig leaves in Genesis 3 had the sole purpose of covering Adam and Eve's nakedness; they were not utilized in any rituals or initiatory ceremonies. It is highly telling that a number of recent Masonic leaders have acknowledged their utter embarrassment that some earlier Masons ever suggested this Adam and Eve theory.

____ *Ask...* _____

- Would you please read Genesis 3:7 aloud?

- Doesn't this verse make it clear that the fig leaves had the sole purpose of covering Adam and Eve's nakedness?

- Do you see any indication of Masonic rituals in this verse?
- Are you familiar with the term *eisogesis*? Be ready to define this term, then contrast it with *exegesis*.

GENESIS 1:1-3: *Masonry Founded by God?*

Masonic View: In Genesis 1:1-3 we read, "In the beginning God created the heavens and the earth. Now the earth was formless and empty, darkness was over the surface of the deep, and the Spirit of God was hovering over the waters. And God said, 'Let there be light,' and there was light." Some Masons have argued, based on this passage, that *God* was responsible for the emergence of Masonry. In his book *Scottish Rite Masonry Illustrated,* J. Blanchard writes:

> When the spirit of God moved upon the face of the waters; when the great Jehovah ordained the creation of the world; when the first Sun rose to greet with its beams, the new morning and the august command was uttered: "Let there be light." The lips of deity breathed Masonry into existence and it must live forever; for truth is eternal, and the principles of truth are the foundation of Masonry.[11]

Biblical View: This is nothing more than sheer eisogesis. We will see throughout the rest of this book that Masonry contradicts Bible doctrine at numerous points (including the doctrines of God, Jesus Christ, sin, and salvation), and hence it is impossible that the God of the Bible could be the source of Freemasonry. The reality is that "biblical light" radically contradicts "Masonic light" in many ways; they cannot have the same source.

_____ *Ask...* _____

- Please read aloud from Genesis 1:1-3.

- Isn't it clear from the context that the reference to "light" in this passage is literal, physical light—not the light of Masonry?

- Is there even the slightest clue in this passage that Masonic light is being referred to?

- Since Masonry contradicts the Bible on major doctrines (teaching, for example, that Jesus is just one of many ways to salvation), is it not clear that "biblical light" contradicts "Masonic light"? This being the case, is it not impossible to say that "biblical light" and "Masonic light" come from the same source?

---

1 KINGS 5: *Origin in Solomon's Temple?*
(See also 2 Chronicles 2:3-16)

Masonic View: Without question, the most popular theory for the origin of Freemasonry relates to Solomon's temple. Masons often teach that Hiram, the King of Tyre, aided Solomon in the building of the Jerusalem Temple.[12] He supplied trees, carpenters, and masons for this project and had close relations with King Solomon concerning problems of mutual interest. Arthur Edward Waite, author of *A New Encyclopedia of Freemasonry*, tells us that "the ritual of the Blue Lodge, the foundation of all Masonic bodies, is structured around the story of the building of King Solomon's Temple and the murder by ruffians of Hiram Abif of Tyre, the chief architect and master of all the stonemasons in the construction of the Temple"[13] (see 1 Kings 7:13,14; 2 Chronicles 2:14; 4:16).

Biblical View: It is true that Scripture speaks of a King Hiram providing materials to Solomon for the building of the temple. It is also true that Hiram provided Solomon with expert workmen, skilled in the craft of building. But there is no mention of Freemasonry in the scriptural account of Solomon. There is no mention in Scripture of any fraternal organization made up of Masons. Further, there is no mention of Hiram and Solomon being bound by any kind of Masonic ties.[14]

Consider the biblical data on Hiram and his relationship with Solomon. Read through 1 Kings 5. (I realize it's long, but bear with me.) As you do so, contemplate whether *you* think this account depicts 1) one king merely assisting another king in a building project or 2) an account depicting the beginnings of the Masonic Lodge:

> When Hiram king of Tyre heard that Solomon had been anointed king to succeed his father David, he sent his envoys to Solomon, because he had always been on friendly terms with David. Solomon sent back this message to Hiram:
>
>> You know that because of the wars waged against my father David from all sides, he could not build a temple for the Name of the LORD his God until the LORD put his enemies under his feet. But now the LORD my God has given me rest on every side, and there is no adversary or disaster. I intend, therefore, to build a temple for the Name of the LORD my God, as the LORD told my father David, when he said, "Your son whom I will put on the throne in your place will build the temple for my Name."
>>
>> So give orders that cedars of Lebanon be cut for me. My men will work with yours, and I will pay you for your men whatever wages you set. You know that we have no one so skilled in felling timber as the Sidonians.
>
> When Hiram heard Solomon's message, he was greatly pleased and said, "Praise be to the LORD today, for he has given David a wise son to rule over this great nation."

So Hiram sent word to Solomon:

> I have received the message you sent me and will do all you want in providing the cedar and pine logs. My men will haul them down from Lebanon to the sea, and I will float them in rafts by sea to the place you specify. There I will separate them and you can take them away. And you are to grant my wish by providing food for my royal household.

In this way Hiram kept Solomon supplied with all the cedar and pine logs he wanted, and Solomon gave Hiram twenty thousand cors of wheat as food for his household, in addition to twenty thousand baths of pressed olive oil. Solomon continued to do this for Hiram year after year. The LORD gave Solomon wisdom, just as he had promised him. There were peaceful relations between Hiram and Solomon, and the two of them made a treaty.

King Solomon conscripted laborers from all Israel— thirty thousand men. He sent them off to Lebanon in shifts of ten thousand a month, so that they spent one month in Lebanon and two months at home. Adoniram was in charge of the forced labor. Solomon had seventy thousand carriers and eighty thousand stonecutters in the hills, as well as thirty-three hundred foremen who supervised the project and directed the workmen. At the king's command they removed from the quarry large blocks of quality stone to provide a foundation of dressed stone for the temple. The craftsmen of Solomon and Hiram and the men of Gebal cut and prepared the timber and stone for the building of the temple.

What is your assessment? Is this passage referring to one king helping another king on a building project? Or does it portray the beginnings of the Masonic Lodge? I think the answer is clear. There is not a hint of any kind of fraternal organization in these scriptures. Yes, the context mentions skilled craftsmen and stone-cutters, but it is a quantum leap in logic from these words to the existence of a Masonic fraternity in ancient times.

_____ *Ask...* _____

- Where is there evidence for the existence of a Masonic fraternity in 1 Kings 5? Please be specific.

- Doesn't a plain reading of the text indicate that one king is helping another king in a building project?

- Do you recall what the term *eisogesis* means? How does it relate to this situation?

Of course, one reason the narrative regarding Solomon's temple is so important to Masons is that much of their modern ritual is based upon it. "The Ritual and symbols are replete with the days of King Solomon of Israel and the building of the Temple."[15] Modern Masons often refer back to Solomon's temple as the most perfect edifice ever erected by man. It has come to symbolize, in an allegorical fashion, the perfect development of mind in character and virtue.[16] Just as the ancient stonemasons sought perfection in the building of the physical temple of Solomon, so Masons today seek perfection in the building of character and virtue in their own lives. Despite this worthy goal, it must nevertheless be emphasized that when *exegesis* is prac-ticed instead of *eisogesis*, support for the beginnings of the Masonic Lodge in Solomon's time evaporates.

A Preponderance of Fanciful Legend

In view of the previous discussion, it is clear that many of the claims for the origin of Freemasonry are nothing more than fanciful legend. According to John Robinson, "All of the various the-ories of the origins of Freemasonry are legendary. Not one of them is supported by any universally accepted evidence."[17] Michael Baigent and Richard Leigh, in their book *The Temple and the Lodge*, make the point a bit more strongly:

> Freemasonry is itself profoundly uncertain of its own origins. In the four centuries or so of its formal existence, it has endeavored, sometimes desperately, to establish a pedigree. Masonic writers have filled numerous books with efforts to chronicle the history of their craft. Some of these efforts have been not just spurious, but, on occasion, positively comical in their extravagance, naiveté and wishful thinking.[18]

In the Introduction of this book, I noted that despite some of the claims for an early origin of Freemasonry, documented history reveals that Freemasonry *formally* began in London, England, in A.D. 1717, due to the efforts of Anglican clergymen James Anderson, George Payne, and Theopholis Desaguliers.[19] This was when the Grand Lodge of London was first organized. Prior to this time, there was no Grand Lodge and no Grand Masters.

It should be noted, theologian Robert Morey tells us, that what was founded in 1717 involved "Speculative Masonry," which is distinct from "Operative Masonry." Here is the backdrop. During the Middle Ages and after, there were "operative Masons," so called because they worked at the specific trades—builders, stonemasons, and architects engaged in construction work.[20] They were *working* Masons. "Operative Masons were actually stone-masons engaged in actual construction work up through the 17th century."[21] They were building the great churches and cathedrals in Europe.

It was not long before they joined forces and formed a guild. Critic James Rongstad tells us that "because they usually worked closely together and because they frequently were away from home, they formed a tight-knit group in which they shared discussions on philosophies, politics, religion, and all other interests of their society."[22] Forming a guild not only served to protect them but also served to enhance their professional credibility.[23]

As to why these operative Masons were called "*Free*masons," a number of possibilities have been suggested by researchers. Some believe that because these men worked with "free stone," which could be easily carved, they became known as "free stone masons"—later shortened to "Freemasons."[24] Others believe they were called Freemasons because they were free to move around from city to city or country to country.[25] Still others say that perhaps these were just free men as opposed to serfs. Another possibility is that as traveling workmen they were given freedom in the towns in which they worked.[26] My personal feeling is that the second option above is correct—they were "Freemasons" because they were free to move around from city to city or country to country to engage in their profession.

There is certainly no evidence that at this early juncture, this guild of "Freemasons" had secret rituals and ceremonies, degrees, or a vast array of symbols derived from the Bible and other religions.[27] It was more or less a professional union of sorts.[28]

The Grand Lodge that was founded in London in 1717 was not "Operative Masonry" (involving professional builders), which had existed for quite some time. Rather, it involved "Speculative Masonry" (nonbuilding masons). Membership in Masonic Lodges today is *totally* speculative.[29] Speculative Masonry is "another name for Freemasonry in its modern acceptance."[30]

While the old operative Masons were engaged in building cathedrals and temples dedicated to the service and worship of God, Albert Mackey tells us that "the Speculative Mason is engaged in the construction of a spiritual temple in his heart, pure and spotless, fit for the dwelling place of Him who is the author of purity; where God is to be worshiped in spirit and in truth, and whence every evil thought and unruly passion are to be banished."[31]

The *old* work of the stonemasons is allegorically applied today to the building of a pure and undefiled heart. Many of the symbols that are used in Masonic Lodges are actually tools that stonemasons would use in construction, but now they are allegorically interpreted to refer to the development of some particular virtue in the life of the modern Mason. "Freemasonry is a society of men concerned with moral and spiritual values. Its members are taught its precepts by a series of ritual dramas, which follow ancient form and use stonemasons' customs and tools as allegorical guides."[32] The Compass and Square, for example, are allegorically interpreted in terms of building virtue in the human heart.

The Emphasis on Brotherly Love

Mason Harold Voorhis claims that the primary purposes of Freemasonry are "to enlighten the mind, arouse the conscience, and stimulate the noble and generous impulses of the human heart. It seeks to promote the best type of manhood based upon the practice of Brotherly Love and the Golden Rule. In short, to make good men better."[33]

No matter what religion one subscribes to, these purposes can be fulfilled in every Mason. Masons believe that by the exercise of brotherly love, they learn to regard the whole human race as a single family created by one Almighty Parent and inhabiting the same planet. They are thus compelled to aid, support, and protect each other. Toward this end, "Masonry unites men of every country, sect, and opinion."[34] Masons believe there is biblical support for this practice.

EXODUS 23:4: *Masonry's "Biblical" Support for Their Fraternity*

Masonic View: In Exodus 23:4 we read, "If you come across your enemy's ox or donkey wandering off, be sure to take it back to him." Masons sometimes cite this verse in support of their emphasis on brotherly love. "Emphatic throughout the ritual of the Masonic Fraternity are the teachings of the great Light of Masonry that Brotherly Love is to be more than an abstract principle; it is to be in deed and in truth."[35]

Biblical View: Treating others kindly is a good thing. Christians do not criticize Masons for this, but rather applaud them. And Christians can agree that Exodus 23:4 communicates brotherly love in action. What Masons often forget, and what evangelical Christians stress, is that this injunction is found in the context of the Law of Moses, which not only speaks of brotherly love, but also speaks of the requirements of *worshiping the only true God of Israel* and not worshiping the false gods of paganism.

Indeed, in the Ten Commandments, recorded earlier in the book of Exodus, we read: "You shall have no other gods before me. You shall not make for yourself an idol in the form of anything in heaven above or on the earth beneath or in the waters below. You shall not bow down to them or worship them; for I, the LORD your God, am a jealous God, punishing the children for the sin of the fathers to the third and fourth generation of those who hate me" (Exodus 20:3-5). This passage clearly portrays the God of Israel as the *sole* object of worship for the people of God (see also Exodus 15:11; Deuteronomy 5:7). Deuteronomy 6:14 flatly commands, "Do not follow other gods, the gods of the peoples around you."

Masonic Lodges admit not just Christians, but Muslims, Hindus, and others who claim to believe in God. Inasmuch as the god of Islam and the god of Hinduism are entirely different than the one true God of Israel, *their* gods are *false* gods. (For proof of this assertion, see chapter 7—"God: The Great Architect of the Universe.") There can be no *true* spiritual brotherhood among Christians, Hindus, and Muslims within the confines of a Masonic Lodge. In fact, Scripture calls believers in the one true God to "come out from them and be separate" (2 Corinthians 6:17).

___ Ask... _____

• Did you know that the gods of Hinduism and Islam are false gods, inasmuch as they are portrayed in terms contradictory to the God of the Bible? (Point out that the god of Islam is nontriune, and that Islam involves a concept of a god named Allah that cannot have a son. In Hinduism, there are virtually millions of gods who are considered extensions of an all-pervasive deity known as Brahman. Such ideas are entirely at odds with the Christian triune view of God.)

- Do you see any inconsistency in choosing to follow the command in Exodus 23:4 regarding brotherly love, but choosing to ignore God's command not to worship false gods in Exodus 20:3-5?

DEUTERONOMY 10:19

Masonic View: In Deuteronomy 10:19 we read, "And you are to love those who are aliens, for you yourselves were aliens in Egypt." Masons sometimes cite this verse in support of their emphasis on brotherly love.[36]

Biblical View: Christians agree that this verse points to the need for brotherly love in dealing with people we don't know. Yet, it is important not to divorce this verse from its context. Just two verses earlier, we read: "For the LORD your God is God of gods and Lord of lords, the great God, mighty and awesome..." (Deuteronomy 10:17). The "gods" the Israelites encountered in Egypt were local deities who, in fact, were not deities at all. They were false gods. The true God of Israel is "God of gods and Lord of lords" in the sense that He is the *only true* God.

Indeed, as I will demonstrate in chapter 8—"Masonry's Connection to Paganism and the Mystery Religions," God's infliction of the ten plagues on the Egyptians constituted a judgment against their false gods. These plagues are alluded to in Deuteronomy 10:21: "He is your God, who performed for you those great and awesome wonders you saw with your own eyes."

While it is good and right to recognize the importance of following brotherly love, let us not forget that God also calls us to worship and follow Him alone and avoid false pagan deities (such as those affiliated with Hinduism and Islam). *We cannot be selective in our obedience to God.*

___ *Ask...* ___

- I commend the Masonic Lodge for its brotherly love, a quality reflected in Deuteronomy 10:19.

- But what about the rest of Deuteronomy 10 (especially verse 17), which speaks of worshiping *only* the God of the Bible, and not pagan deities such as those affiliated with Hinduism and Islam? (If the Mason argues that the gods of the various religions involve different names for the same deity, see chapter 7—"God: The Great Architect of the Universe" for how to respond.)

---

1 PETER 2:17

Masonic View: Albert Mackey holds that the apostle Peter illustrated the type of brotherhood that Masonry stands for in 1 Peter 2:17, when he commanded, "Love the brotherhood." Mackey writes:

> When our Savior designated his disciples as his brethren, he implied that there was a close bond of union existing between them, which idea was subsequently carried out by St. Peter in his direction to "love the brotherhood." Hence the early Christians designated themselves as a brotherhood, a relationship unknown to the Gentile religions....The association or Fraternity of Freemasons is, in this sense, called a brotherhood.[37]

Biblical View: The brotherhood of which Scripture speaks is one that results from a group of people who have personally trusted in Jesus as Savior. Unlike the Masonic view, Jesus taught that *He alone* was humankind's means of coming into a right relationship with God. He flatly asserted, "I am the way and the truth and the life. No one comes to the Father except through me" (John 14:6). Peter made a similar point in Acts 4:12 when he said, "Salvation is found in no one else, for there is no other name under heaven given to men by which we must be saved." (See also 1 Timothy 2:5.) Those who have trusted in Jesus for salvation are now adopted into the family of God (Ephesians 1:5). They are *spiritual* brothers and sisters *in Christ*. This is completely unlike the brotherhood of Masonry, for there is no true spiritual unity among them (for Christians, Muslims, Hindus, and those of other religions participate in Masonry together).

___ *Ask...* ___

- Please read aloud Jesus' words in John 14:6.

- Please read aloud Peter's words in Acts 4:12.

- Is it clear from these verses that Jesus and Peter viewed faith in Christ as the *only* means of salvation?

- Doesn't Peter's reference to "brotherhood" in 1 Peter 2:17 refer not to the world of humanity at large, or to those in the Masonic Lodge, but to spiritual brothers and sisters who trust in Christ for salvation?

- Since faith in Christ is the only means by which one is adopted into God's forever family (Ephesians 1:5), can Christians be in a *true* "brotherhood" with Hindus and Muslims, who do not trust in Christ?

HEBREWS 13:1

Masonic view: In Hebrews 13:1 we read, "Keep on loving each other as brothers." Masons sometimes cite this verse in support of their emphasis on brotherly love.[38]

Biblical view: What "brothers" are being referred to in Hebrews 13:1? Is it Masonic Christians, Muslims, and Hindus worshiping together under the same roof? Or is it Hebrew Christians who enjoy spiritual unity as a result of their mutual, personal faith in Jesus Christ? Contextually, it is clear that these are Hebrew Christians who have trusted in Christ for salvation. Earlier in Hebrews we read that "the one who makes men holy and those who are made holy are of the same family. So Jesus is not ashamed to call them brothers" (Hebrews 2:11). The author of Hebrews urges, "Therefore, holy brothers, who share in the heavenly calling, fix your thoughts on Jesus, the apostle and high priest whom we confess" (3:1). He pleads, "See to it, brothers, that none of you has a sinful, unbelieving heart that turns away from the living God" (3:12). The writer also exhorts, "Therefore, brothers, since we have confidence to enter the Most Holy Place by the blood of Jesus, by a new and living way opened for us through the curtain, that is, his body, and since we have a great priest over the house of God, let us draw near to God with a sincere heart in full assurance of faith, having our hearts sprinkled to cleanse us from a guilty conscience and having our bodies washed with pure water" (10:19-22).

In Hebrews 13:1, the author is simply exhorting his *spiritual* brethren to maintain love for each other. As one scholar put it, "These who are linked in the common bond of having been saved by the death of Jesus cannot but have warm feelings toward one another (cf. Romans 12:10; 1 Thessalonians 4:9; 1 Peter 1:22; 2 Peter 1:7; see also Psalm 133:1)."[39]

Scholars have noted that many of the recipients of this letter were Jewish Christians in the church of Jerusalem, and certainly these Christians were well known for the love they showed to their fellow Christians (brothers). "Selling their possessions and goods, they gave to anyone as he had need" (Acts 2:45). "There were no needy persons among them. For from time to time those who owned lands or houses sold them, brought the money from the sales and put it at the apostles' feet, and it was distributed to anyone as he had need" (Acts 4:34,35). "The disciples, each according to his ability, decided to provide help for the brothers living in Judea. This they did, sending their gift to the elders by Barnabas and Saul" (Acts 11:29,30). And in the book of Hebrews, the writer notes: "God is not unjust; he will not forget your work and the love you have shown him as you have helped his people and continue to help them" (Hebrews 6:10). Again, contextually, the benevolent brothers in Hebrews 13:1 are *Christian* brothers, not Christian/Muslim/Hindu brothers in Masonic Lodges.

_____ *Ask...* _____

- Did you know that in the context of the book of Hebrews, the word *"brothers"* refers to *Christian* brothers, not Christian/Muslim/Hindu brothers? (Be ready to review Hebrews 2:11; 3:1,12; 10:19-22.)

- Did you know that according to the book of Hebrews, a person becomes a "Christian brother" by faith in Christ alone (Hebrews 4:14; 10:19-23; 12:2)?

- Would you like to become a Christian brother? (Be ready to share the gospel. See appendix A: "An Invitation to Believe.")

ROMANS 12:9–13:2

Masonic View: Mason Richard Thorn cites Romans 12:9–13:2 and argues that this passage reflects key principles of Freemasonry. In Romans 12:9–13:2 we read:

Love must be sincere. Hate what is evil; cling to what is good. Be devoted to one another in brotherly love. Honor one another above yourselves. Never be lacking in zeal, but keep your spiritual fervor, serving the Lord. Be joyful in hope, patient in affliction, faithful in prayer. Share with God's people who are in need. Practice hospitality. Bless those who persecute you; bless and do not curse. Rejoice with those who rejoice; mourn with those who mourn. Live in harmony with one another. Do not be proud, but be willing to associate with people of low position. Do not be conceited. Do not repay anyone evil for evil. Be careful to do what is right in the eyes of everybody. If it is possible, as far as it depends on you, live at peace with everyone. Do not take revenge, my friends, but leave room for God's wrath, for it is written: "It is mine to avenge; I will repay," says the Lord. On the contrary: "If your enemy is hungry, feed him; if he is thirsty, give him something to drink. In doing this, you will heap burning coals on his head." Do not be overcome by evil, but overcome evil with good. Everyone must submit himself to the governing authorities, for there is no authority except that which God has established. The authorities that exist have been established by God. Consequently, he who rebels against the authority is rebelling against what God has instituted, and those who do so will bring judgment on themselves.

Based on this passage, Thorn derives 17 principles the Bible has in common with Masonry:

1. Be devoted to one another in brotherly love.
2. Honor one another above yourselves.

3. Keep your spiritual fervor, serving the Lord.

4. Be joyful in hope, faithful in prayer.

5. Share with God's people who are in need.

6. Practice hospitality.

7. Bless and do not curse.

8. Rejoice with those who rejoice; mourn with those who mourn.

9. Live in harmony with one another.

10. Do not be proud, but be willing to associate with people of low position. Do not be conceited.

11. Do not repay anyone evil for evil.

12. Be careful to do what is right in the eyes of everybody.

13. If it is possible, as far as it depends on you, live in peace with everyone.

14. Do not take revenge.

15. If your enemy is hungry, feed him; if he is thirsty, give him something to drink.

16. Do not be overcome by evil, but overcome evil with good.

17. Everyone must submit himself to the governing authorities.[40]

Biblical View: Though Thorn cites the apostle Paul's words in Romans 12:9–13:2 to show parallels with Freemasonry, other words spoken by Paul clearly refute key Masonic doctrines. Thorn does not seem to recognize that the apostle Paul firmly believed in the *inspiration and inerrancy of the Bible alone*, believed in the Trinity (which Masonry denies), believed that Jesus is absolute deity (which Masonry typically denies), believed that good works have nothing to do with salvation (contrary to

Masonry's philosophy), and believed that *only* by trusting in Jesus as Savior can a person be saved and live forever with the one true God (see 2 Timothy 3:16; 2 Corinthians 13:14; Ephesians 4:4-6; Philippians 2:6; Colossians 1:15, 2:9; Romans 3:28; Acts 16:31).

The brotherly love of which Paul spoke relates to a brotherhood among those who *trust in Christ alone* and who have been adopted into God's forever family (see Romans 8:14; Ephesians 1:5). Paul certainly did not believe that proponents of other religions were "spiritual brothers" with Christians (see Romans 1:18-25; 1 Corinthians 8:4-6; 10:14; Galatians 5:19–21). He even asserted, "Do not be yoked together with unbelievers. For what do righteousness and wickedness have in common? Or what fellowship can light have with darkness?" (2 Corinthians 6:14). This verse alone shows that in Paul's mind, Christians, Hindus, and Muslims are *not* spiritual brothers.

___ *Ask...* ___

- Would you please read aloud the apostle Paul's words in 2 Corinthians 6:14?

- Since Muslims and Hindus hold an entirely different view on God, Jesus, sin, and salvation than Christianity, wouldn't "yoking together" with Muslims and Hindus violate Paul's injunction? (If the Mason denies that Hindus, Muslims, and Christians hold to different views on these issues, see chapters 7, 9, 10, and 11 for information on how to respond.)

In the next chapter I will further illustrate that the Masonic "brotherhood" is based not on spiritual unity but on extravagant rituals and bizarre oaths.

4

Becoming a Mason

Freemasons often make much of the fact that men regularly take the initiative to apply for Masonic Lodge membership, despite the fact that the Lodge does not seek converts, does not engage in any kind of publicity, does not distribute literature in public, and does not engage in popular demonstrations or public meetings. One Mason went so far as to claim that men are attracted to the Lodge "by some magnetism that seems almost the supernatural workings of the Holy Spirit."[1]

What follows describes what it is like when a candidate first seeks to join a Masonic Lodge. I should note at the outset, however, that not every Masonic ritual in every state in the United States is identical. The Grand Lodge of each respective state has the power to regulate the ritual as practiced in that state. However, the ritual is, for all practical purposes, essentially the same in the various Lodges.[2]

Immediately after the opening of a typical Lodge session, Psalm 133:1-3 is quoted: "How good and pleasant it is when brothers live together in unity! It is like precious oil poured on the head, running down on the beard, running down on Aaron's beard, down upon the collar of his robes. It is as if the dew of Hermon were falling on Mount Zion. For there the LORD bestows his blessing, even life forevermore." Following this reading, all the brethren present in the Lodge respond, "Amen! So mote it be!"[3]

Following the opening of the Lodge, the formal business commences. Part of that business relates to new candidates seeking to join. Such a candidate is not even considered unless he is a "worthy individual" who has been vouched for by another Mason in good standing. Bernard Jones, author of *Freemasons' Guide and Compendium*, tells us:

> A candidate for Freemasonry must be a man of good reputation and integrity and well fitted to become a member of the lodge in which he seeks initiation. He must be a free man, of the full age of twenty-one years, and the tongue of good report must have been heard in his favor. He must be well and worthily recommended and have been regularly proposed and approved in open lodge. He must come of his own free will and accord, humbly soliciting to be admitted to the mysteries and privileges of Freemasonry. He will be asked to make a solemn affirmation that he puts his trust in God, and he must, at the right time and in the right way, be presented to the lodge to show that he is a fit and proper person to be made a Mason.[4]

The highly respected *Duncan's Masonic Ritual and Monitor* informs us that an example of a Mason vouching for a candidate might go something like this: "I would say to the Lodge that I have examined into his character and find it good, and, consequently, report on it favorably. I think he will make a good Mason.

In his younger days, he was rather wild; but now he is considered very steady, and a good member of society."[5]

The candidate's petition is then reviewed, as are his character and reputation, and a vote is taken in the lodge. A single negative vote, as evidenced by a "black ball," is enough to bar the candidate's petition.[6] "If no black ball appears, the candidate is declared duly elected; but if one black ball or more appear, he is declared rejected."[7]

Assuming no black ball appears, the candidate promptly goes through the ritual for the Entered Apprentice degree, which is the first degree of the Blue Lodge. The ritual is quite bizarre. One researcher summarizes it this way:

> The typical ceremony begins with the initiate being first divested of his jacket and his tie and any money or metal articles he has. His left trouser leg is then rolled up over the knee, his shirt is opened to expose his left breast, and his right shoe is removed and replaced by a slipper. Then the person who is to be initiated will have a blindfold put on him and a noose put around his neck. This is called a "Cable Tow." The blindfolded initiate (*they call this being "hoodwinked"*) is brought, with the noose around his neck, to the outer door of the Lodge.
>
> The candidate thus attired is said to be in darkness, an allegory of Masonry that signifies that everyone outside of Masonry is in darkness and that only Masons have the true knowledge that will bring light to the world.
>
> The new Mason is brought to the outer door seeking the light of the Lodge, and there the Doorkeeper, or Tiler, will put a sword or a sharp point to his breast and lead him into the lodge room, where an altar sits in its center. The lodge

members await the candidate in the darkness that surrounds the altar, which is lit from a single light above. Behind the altar stands a man called "The Worshipful Master." He is the master of the Lodge and presides over the initiation.

When the initiate is brought before him, he bows before "The Worshipful Master" and says something like this: "I am lost in darkness, and I am seeking the light of Freemasonry." He is then told he is entering into a secret organization and that he must keep the secrets he is going to be taught.

At this time he is required to take a blood initiation oath. Every Mason who joins the Lodge takes his thumb or his hand to his throat and repeats an oath that has been repeated by every Mason who has joined the Lodge.[8]

Swearing a blood oath is required not just for the Entered Apprentice degree, but for the other degrees of Freemasonry as well. Before taking such oaths, however, the Master assures the candidate that the oath will not interfere with any duty that is owed to God, country, family, or friends.[9]

After expressing his willingness to take the oath, the candidate, still blindfolded, is led into the proper position for an Entered Apprentice. He kneels on his bare left knee, with his right leg in front of him in the angle of a square. Before him on the altar is the *opened* holy book of his faith (the Bible for Christians, the Koran for Muslims, and the Vedas for Hindus), with the compass and square on the open book.[10] The candidate then places his left hand under the book, palm up, while his right hand is on top of the compass and square, palm downward.[11] He then utters the following words:

I...do hereby and hereon most sincerely promise
and swear that I will always hail, ever conceal

and never reveal, any of the arts, parts, or points of the hidden mysteries of ancient Free Masonry which may have been, or hereafter shall be, at this time, or any future period, communicated to me as such, to any person or persons whomever, except it be to a true and lawful brother Mason, or in a regularly constituted lodge of Masons....I furthermore promise and swear that I will not print, paint, stamp, stain, cut, carve, mark, or engrave them, to cause the same to be done on anything movable or immovable, capable of receiving the least impression of a word, syllable, letter, or character, whereby the same may become legible or intelligible to any person under the canopy of heaven, and the secrets of Masonry thereby unlawfully obtained through my unworthiness.

All this I most solemnly, sincerely promise and swear, with a firm and steadfast resolution to perform the same, without any mental reservation or secret evasion of mind whatever, binding myself under no less penalty than that of having my throat cut across, my tongue torn out by its roots, and my body buried in the rough sands of the sea, at low-water mark, where the tide ebbs and flows twice in twenty-four hours, should I ever knowingly violate this my Entered Apprentice obligation. So help me God, and keep me steadfast in the due performance of the same.[12]

When seeking entrance into the Fellow Craft degree (the second degree in Blue Lodge Freemasonry), the oath includes additional words: "Binding myself under no less a penalty than that of having my left breast torn open, my heart plucked out and given as prey to the wild beasts of the fields and the fowls of the air."[13]

When seeking entrance into the third degree—the Master Mason degree of the Blue Lodge—the oath adds:

> Binding myself under no less penalty than to have
> my body severed in twain and divided to the north
> and south, my bowels burnt to ashes in the center,
> and the ashes scattered before the four winds of
> heaven, that there might not the least track or trace
> of remembrance remain among men, or Masons,
> of so vile and perjured a wretch as I should be,
> were I ever to prove willfully guilty of violating
> any part of this my solemn oath and obligation of
> a Master Mason. So help me God, and keep me
> steadfast in the due performance of the same.[14]

If one should decide to go beyond Blue Lodge Masonry, and, say, become a Royal Arch Mason, the oath would include the following words:

> To all which I do most solemnly and sincerely
> promise and swear, with a firm and steadfast res-
> olution to keep and perform the same, without
> any equivocation, mental reservation, or self-eva-
> sion of mind in me whatever; bind myself under
> no less a penalty than to have my skull smote off,
> and my brains exposed to the scorching rays of
> the meridian sun, should I unknowingly or will-
> fully violate or transgress any part of this my
> solemn oath or obligation of a Royal Arch
> Mason. So help me God and keep me steadfast in
> the due performance of the same.[15]

Enough said!
The Entered Apprentice candidate, following the taking of his oath, is instructed to kiss the holy book as a token of his sincerity.

He is then asked what he desires most, to which the proper answer is "Light." At this response, the blindfold is promptly removed and the secrets of the Entered Apprentice are revealed to him. These include the secret handgrip and two hand signs.[16]

Following this, a lambskin is presented to the candidate. He is told that the white apron is an emblem of innocence "more ancient than the Golden Fleece or the Roman Eagle," more honorable a badge than any that could ever be bestowed by any prince or potentate.[17] This emblem of innocence is said to point to the purity of life necessary for one who seeks entrance into the Celestial Lodge Above (heaven). (The works-oriented system of salvation in Masonry is addressed later in this book.)

Now we come to a very peculiar part of the ceremony that is loaded with significance for the Mason. According to *Duncan's Masonic Ritual and Monitor*, the Master says to the candidate:

> Agreeably to an ancient custom, adopted among the Masons, it is necessary that you should be requested to deposit something of a metallic kind or nature, not for its intrinsic valuation, but that it may be laid up among the relics in the archives of this Lodge, as a memento that you were herein made a Mason. Anything, brother, that you may have about you, of a metallic nature, will be thankfully received—a button, pin, five or ten cent piece—anything, my brother.[18]

At this point, the candidate feels around in his pockets and becomes confused, realizing that all his money and metallic objects have been previously stripped from him. He finds that he has virtually nothing of value in his pockets; he is destitute. He says to the Master that if he would be permitted to go to the anteroom where his clothes are, he would be most happy to contribute something. The Master refuses this request, and the candidate becomes even more confused.[19] After letting the candidate ponder things for a few moments, the Master says to him:

> You are indeed an object of charity—almost naked, not one cent, no, not even a button or pin to bestow on this Lodge. Let this ever have, my brother, a lasting effect on your mind and conscience; and remember, should you ever see a friend, but more especially a brother, in a like destitute condition, you will contribute as liberally to his support and relief as his necessities may seem to demand and your ability permit, without any material injury to yourself or family.[20]

There are some further elements to the Entered Apprentice ritual, but the above represents the gist of it. To recap the highlights, Freemasonry claims the candidate is in darkness and that the Lodge alone can impart spiritual light to him. (The blindfold typifies his state of darkness.) The candidate is stripped of money to symbolize his poverty without the Lodge. The cable-tow around his neck symbolizes his humility in coming to the Lodge for help. He is asked what the desire of his heart is, to which he responds, "Light." He takes a blood oath, promising to never reveal to others the secrets of Freemasonry. He is then given a lambskin to symbolize the purity necessary to enter heaven.

Masons believe there is biblical support for the key elements of this ritual.

REASONING FROM THE SCRIPTURES

GENESIS 1:1-3: *The Need for Masonic Light?*

Masonic View: Masons often try to find support for the need for Masonic light in the pages of the Bible. Indeed, as noted in the previous chapter, Genesis 1:1-3 is often cited in this regard:[21] "In the beginning God created the heavens and the earth. Now the earth was formless and empty, darkness was over the surface of the deep, and the Spirit of God was hovering over the waters. And God said, 'Let there be light,' and there was light."

Masons believe that darkness is a symbol of ignorance, while light is a symbol of enlightenment. True enlightenment is said to come through Freemasonry.[22]

Biblical View: I noted in the previous chapter that the light mentioned in Genesis 1 is *literal, physical light*, not Masonic light. Masons are reading their own meaning into this Scripture text.

The main point to emphasize here, however, is how inconceivable it is that a Christian could, in good conscience, bow before "The Worshipful Master" and say, "I am in darkness and I am in need of the light of Freemasonry." After all, through Christ, Christians have been delivered from the kingdom of darkness and brought into the kingdom of God's Son—which is the kingdom of light (see Colossians 1:12-14). As God's children, we walk in the light, not in darkness (see 1 John 1:5-7). In John 12:46 Jesus said, "I have come into the world as a light, so that no one who believes in me should stay in darkness." He also said, "I am the light of the world. Whoever follows me will never walk in darkness, but will have the light of life" (John 8:12). The apostle Paul affirmed, "You were once darkness, but now you are light in the Lord. Live as children of light" (Ephesians 5:8). Christians have already escaped the defilement of the dark world system, and are enlightened by the Word of God (2 Peter 1:3,4; Psalm 119:105).

Ask...

If the Mason to whom you are speaking claims to be a Christian, as is likely, ask the following questions.

- Would you please read aloud from John 8:12? John 12:46? Colossians 1:12-14? Ephesians 5:8?

- In view of these statements from Scripture, how can an Entered Apprentice candidate who is a Christian affirm in the Masonic ritual, "I am lost in darkness, and I am seeking the light of Freemasonry"?

- Doesn't this statement represent a denial of your Christian faith?

Interestingly, Masons also sometimes cite 2 Corinthians 4:6 in support of the need for Masonic light.[23] This verse makes reference to "God, who said, 'Let light shine out of darkness.'" However, the verse quoted in its entirety shows that true light comes through Jesus Christ: "For God, who said, 'Let light shine out of darkness,' made his light shine in our hearts to give us the light of the knowledge of the glory of God in the face of Christ." This verse tells us that the same God that illuminated the creation with physical light illuminates our hearts spiritually through Jesus Christ. As commentator Adam Clarke put it, "It is in and through Jesus that we can receive the divine light, and it is in and by him that we can be made partakers of the divine glory."[24]

DEUTERONOMY 6:13: *Support for Masonic Oaths?*

Masonic View: In Deuteronomy 6:13 we read, "Fear the LORD your God, serve him only and take your oaths in his name." Masons sometimes cite this verse in support of the oaths they take upon initiation. Such an oath "cannot be regarded as the slightest perversion of Holy Scripture or in any sense objectionable or sinful."[25] They also cite Joshua 14:6-9, where we find Moses swearing an oath,[26] and Genesis 14:21-24, where Abram swears an oath.[27]

Biblical View: It is true that Moses and Abram swore oaths, and it is true that the Old Testament makes reference to taking oaths in the name of God alone. But does this substantiate the Masonic blood oaths?

Let me be perfectly frank: The Masonic oaths spoken within the confines of Masonic Lodges are nothing less than barbaric, even though many Masons claim that the oaths are not to be taken literally. One pro-Mason historian claims, "No Mason believes that the penalties of his oath will be visited upon him, and every candidate would hurry out of the room if ever told that he must help to inflict those penalties on someone else."[28] Still, the very spirit of such oaths should be exceedingly offensive to the consciences of civilized people, especially Christians.

In arguing against such barbaric oaths, some well-meaning Christians have taken a stand against oaths altogether by appealing to Jesus' words in Matthew 5:33-37:

> Again, you have heard that it was said to the people long ago, "Do not break your oath, but keep the oaths you have made to the Lord." But I tell you, Do not swear at all: either by heaven, for it is God's throne; or by the earth, for it is his footstool; or by Jerusalem, for it is the city of the Great King. And do not swear by your head, for you cannot make even one hair white or black. Simply let your "Yes" be "Yes," and your "No," "No"; anything beyond this comes from the evil one.

The problem with citing this particular passage against the Masonic use of oaths is that there are other verses in Scripture which do, in fact, indicate that certain kinds of oaths are okay. Aside from the legitimate oaths mentioned in the Old Testament (Leviticus 5:1; 19:12; Numbers 30:2-15; Deuteronomy 23:21-23; Exodus 20:7), there are some mentioned in the New Testament as well (Acts 2:30; Hebrews 6:16-18; 7:20-22). Even the apostle Paul said, "I call God as my witness..." (2 Corinthians 1:23), just as he also said, "I assure you before God that what I am writing you is no lie" (Galatians 1:20). On another occasion Paul said, "God can testify how I long for all of you with the affection of Christ Jesus" (Philippians 1:8). From a biblical standpoint, there are at least *some* cases in which oaths or oathlike statements can be made.

What, then, are we to make of Jesus' words in Matthew 5:33-37? The problem Jesus was dealing with in this passage is rooted in Pharisaism. The Pharisees promoted the use of oaths to affirm that someone was telling the truth, and the oath always involved some type of curse that the person placed on himself if his word was not true or the promise was not fulfilled. It got to the point that one assumed someone was not telling the truth if an oath was not attached to his statement.

Jesus was against this use of oaths. He was telling His followers that their character, their reputation for honesty, and the words they speak should be so consistently true, undefiled, and without duplicity that no one would ever think it necessary to put them under an oath. By constantly adding oaths to our verbal statements, we are implying to others that our usual speech is untrustworthy. It should not be that way. As F.F. Bruce put it, "The followers of Jesus should be known as men and women of their word. If they are known to have a scrupulous regard for truth, then what they say will be accepted without the support of any oath."[29]

Having said all this, the problem Christians have with Masonic oaths is not the fact that oaths are taken, but the *content* and *purpose* of those oaths. No Christian has any business taking oaths that speak of cutting the throat or tearing out his tongue if he gives away the secrets of the Lodge. If a Christian joins a Masonic Lodge and participates in this bloody oath, then realizes the terrible mistake he has made, he is best off breaking this oath and leaving the Masonic Lodge. Better to break an "earthly" oath than to remain committed to one that is clearly wrong and against God's will (see Leviticus 5:4-6).

It is worth noting that many Christians who have taken the Masonic oaths have likely taken them under false pretenses. After all, before taking the oath, the candidate is assured by the Master that the oath will not interfere with any duty that is owed to God, country, family, or friends. This is flatly false, since the oath most certainly does interfere with the Christian's duty to the one true God of the Bible. Regarding this, Walton Hannah, author of *Darkness Visible: A Christian Appraisal of Freemasonry*, makes a forceful point:

> An oath taken on false pretenses is null and void. Suppose, to take an extreme and unlikely example, a man interested in social work swore an oath of loyalty and secrecy to an organization on the express understanding that its aims were to provide holiday homes for tired mothers. After he has taken this oath it is revealed to him that the real aim of the society is to drop an atom bomb on Buckingham Palace. His oath of loyalty to that organization is obviously not binding in conscience, because it was taken on false grounds, and he could not fulfill it without sin....Now the Masonic oaths are taken on the express understanding that they can in no way conflict with a man's social, moral, or religious duties....But should a Christian initiate come to realize that Masonry in regarding all gods as equal, or in offering prayers which deliberately exclude our Lord, or in proclaiming the name of God in terms of heathen deities as in the Royal Arch (things which were not disclosed to him on initiation) does violate his Christian principles, his oath ceases to be binding in conscience.[30]

___ Ask... ___

If the Mason to whom you are speaking claims to be a Christian, ask the following questions.

- Am I correct in saying that before taking the oath, the candidate is assured that the oath *will not conflict* with any duty that is owed to God, country, family, or friends?

- Since you are a Christian, this means that the Masonic oath cannot conflict with duty owed to God as defined in the Bible, right?

- According to the Bible, prayers are to be offered to God in the name of Jesus Christ. (See John 14:13,14; 15:16; and 16:23,24 if there is any question about this.) The Masonic ritual *excludes* the name of Jesus Christ in its prayers, doesn't it?

- Did you know that in the Royal Arch degree, God is given a name (*Jabulon*) that relates the God of the Bible to pagan deities Baal and Osiris? Did you know that the God of the Bible absolutely condemns anyone participating in Baal worship and any other false religious system? (Share Exodus 20:4-6; Leviticus 19:4; 26:1; Deuteronomy 4:15-19; 2 Samuel 7:22.)

- In view of these factors, isn't it clear that the Masonic oath conflicts with duty owed to God as defined in the Bible?

Many Masons argue that the words in the Masonic oaths are only to be understood *symbolically*. Jim Tresner, for example, writes: "Some anti-Masonic writers have complained about the so-called 'penalties' in the Masonic obligations. Those penalties are purely symbolic and refer to the pain, despair, and horror which any honest man should feel at the thought that he had violated his sworn word."[31]

However, as Christian apologists John Ankerberg and John Weldon have noted, "No candidate entering into Masonry is told during the ritual that the penalties of the oaths he is swearing to are merely symbolic. In his mind, there is no reason for him not to believe that every Masonic obligation deals with vows of literal life and death."[32] Either the oaths mean what they say or they do not. If the oaths *do* mean what they say, then the person is entering into a bloody pact consenting to his own murder by torture and mutilation as a penalty for violation. If the oaths *do not* mean what they say, then the person is swearing with his hands on a Bible something that is not taken seriously. This is a serious abuse of the holy Bible.[33]

Still further, the oaths are taken "without any mental reservation or secret evasion of mind whatever." How can a Mason explain this in any other way than meaning that the oaths are to be taken quite literally?

___ *Ask...* ___

- Though I understand that some Masons claim the oaths are merely symbolic, isn't it fair to say that no candidate entering into Masonry is *told* that the oaths are symbolic?

- When the candidate is swearing the oath, is there any indication given that the penalties are not literal?

- Is it fair to say that either the oaths mean what they say or they do not?

- If the oaths *do* mean what they say, does this mean you are entering into a pact consenting to your own murder as a penalty for violation?

- If the oaths *do not* mean what they say, are you swearing with your hands on a Bible something that is not true and is, in fact, a lie?

- How do you interpret the Masonic stipulation that the oaths are to be taken "without any mental reservation or secret evasion of mind whatever"?

Some Masons try to lighten the barbarism of the oaths by saying that it is never Masons who are responsible for inflicting the penalties of the oaths, but rather only God: "No Mason swears to inflict the penalties, but only invites them down on his own head. There has never been any indication whatsoever of just what person or power is supposed to carry out the penalty, and since the oath is taken on the Holy Bible it is highly likely that God was being asked to take on that responsibility."[34]

A plain reading of the Masonic ritual, however, indicates that the oath was taken on the holy Bible to ensure that the truth was being told, *not* to imply that God would inflict the judgments. And let us be clear on this: The cutting of throats is a *human* technique of execution, not a *divine* technique. Surely Masons do not expect us to believe that God would reach down from heaven with a physical hand and knife and slit someone's throat!

_____ *Ask...* _____

- Do you agree that the cutting of throats is a *human* technique of execution, not a *divine* technique? After all, God doesn't reach down from heaven with physical hands and a knife to slit throats, right?

- How, then, do you reconcile this with the oft-heard Masonic claim that God is the one who carries out the judgments in the oaths?

It is revealing to note that there may be at least one case on record where the penalty of the Masonic oaths may indeed have been carried out in an all-too-literal fashion. I am referring to the well-known case of the murder of William Morgan in the state of New York in 1826. Apparently Morgan had signed a contract for a book revealing all the secret grips, signs, and rituals of Freemasonry. The local Masons did not like this, and, according to some, he was seized and dashed off in a car.

He was taken to the abandoned Fort Niagara and held there as a captive. This was confirmed by five Masons who confessed to the abduction and confinement. Masons claim he was released or perhaps escaped, after which he allegedly fled to Canada. Masonic critics, by contrast, claim his captors took him out on the river in a boat, tied him to heavy stones, and rolled him overboard. No body was ever recovered. Many believe Morgan was murdered in an attempt to protect Masonic secrets.[35]

This case led to mass resignations from Lodges, a denial of liability, and the general eclipse of Freemasonry in the United States for a significant time. Even Congressman John Quincy Adams expressed his indignation by writing a letter to Edward Ingersoll on September 22, 1831, in which he said that "ever since the disclosure of the Morgan-murder crimes, and of the Masonic oaths and penalties by which they were instigated, the indispensable duty of the Masonic Order in the United States is either to dissolve itself or to discard forever from its constitution and laws all *oaths*, all *penalties*, all *secrets*, and as ridiculous appendages to them, all *mysteries* and *pageants*."[36]

EXODUS 12:3-5; ISAIAH 53:7; JOHN 1:29; 1 PETER 1:18-19; REVELATION 5:8-13: *The Purity of the Lambskin*

Masonic View: Masons cite a number of biblical passages in support of their view that the lambskin is an emblem of the purity necessary to gain entrance into the Celestial Lodge Above. For example, in Exodus 12:3-5 the Israelites are instructed to use a lamb that is "without defect" in their sacrifices.[37] In Isaiah 53:7-9 we find a prophecy of the Lamb of God who is blameless and spotless. [38] In John 1:29, John the Baptist makes reference to Jesus as the Lamb of God who is without sin.[39] In 1 Peter 1:18,19, we find reference to a "lamb without blemish or defect." Then in Revelation 5:8-13, we find reference to the Lamb of God in heaven who is portrayed as holy.[40] In view of such verses, Masons say "the lamb has in all ages been deemed an emblem of innocence."[41]

Biblical View: It is true that the Lamb of God (Jesus) is sinless, spotless, and without defect of any kind. It is also true that God's people in Old Testament times were called to use lambs that were without defect in their sacrifices. But the Masonic adaptation of these verses to argue for a lambskin that is an emblem of the personal purity necessary for entrance into heaven is completely at odds with the Bible. Let us consider Revelation 5:8-13 as an example:

> ...The four living creatures and the twenty-four elders fell down before the Lamb. Each one had a harp and they were holding golden bowls full of incense, which are the prayers of the saints. And they sang a new song: "You are worthy to take the scroll and to open its seals, because you were slain, and with your blood you purchased men for God from every tribe and language and people and nation. You have made them to be a kingdom and priests to serve our God, and they will reign on the earth." Then I looked and heard the voice of many angels, numbering thousands upon thousands, and ten thousand times ten thousand. They encircled the throne and the living creatures and the elders. In a loud voice they sang: "Worthy is the Lamb, who was slain, to receive power and wealth and wisdom and strength and honor and glory and praise!" Then I heard every creature in heaven and on earth and under the earth and on the sea, and all that is in them, singing: "To him who sits on the throne and to the Lamb be praise and honor and glory and power, for ever and ever!"

Consider this passage in terms of the broader teachings of the book of Revelation. Notice that the "Lamb" (Christ) in the book of Revelation is the one slain for our salvation (Revelation 5:6). He *alone* is found "worthy" (5:12) and is worshiped (5:8). Believers are washed in the blood of the Lamb (7:14). Any victory the saints have is *through His merits* (12:11), not because of our works. And the saved are the fruit of *His* work, not ours (14:4). Thus we are *His* followers and sing *His* praises. We do not earn salvation by personal purity as represented by the Masonic lambskin. Rather, the salvation of believers hinges *entirely* on the fact that Christ, as the Lamb of God, *purchased* our *salvation* at Calvary.

_____ Ask... _____

These questions can be asked after sharing the above facts from the book of Revelation.

- Is it not clear from the book of Revelation that our salvation is not based on our good works but rather through what Christ accomplished on our behalf by dying on the cross as the Lamb of God? (See 12:11.)

- Do you agree that Revelation makes it clear that we become pure *not* by our own efforts but by being washed in the blood of the Lamb of God? (See 7:14.)

- Doesn't the entire tone of the book of Revelation communicate praise for Jesus Christ for what He has accomplished in our salvation?

- Where is there praise for human beings "earning" their salvation by attaining personal purity?

The Bible is emphatic that "it is by grace you have been saved, through faith—and this not from yourselves, it is the gift of God—not by works, so that no one can boast" (Ephesians 2:8,9). For "he saved us, not because of righteous things we had done, but because of his mercy" (Titus 3:6). And "to the man who does not work but trusts God who justifies the wicked, his faith is credited as righteousness" (Romans 4:5). In view of such verses, the Masonic teaching about salvation by human effort, as represented by the lambskin, is unbiblical.

This is further illustrated in 1 Peter 1:18,19. Masons often limit their attention to the part of this passage that speaks of "a lamb without blemish or defect." But the *entire* passage reads this way: "For you know that it was not with perishable things such as silver or gold that you were redeemed from the empty way of life handed down to you from your forefathers, but with the precious blood of Christ, a lamb without blemish or defect." This verse centers on salvation *in Jesus alone*. If Masons take this verse seriously, they should accept it for what it really says in terms of Christ being the *only* means of salvation by virtue of His being the Lamb of God who laid down His life on behalf of sinners.

Ask...

- How do you interpret Ephesians 2:8,9? Titus 3:3-6? Romans 4:5?

- Can these verses be reconciled with the Masonic claim that a man can merit the Celestial Lodge Above by living a pure life?

- How does someone become "perfect" according to Hebrews 10:14?

As the Lamb of God, Jesus affirmed that it was for the very purpose of dying that He came into the world (John 12:27). Moreover, He perceived His death as being a sacrificial offering for the sins of humanity. (He said His blood "is poured out for many for the forgiveness of sins"—Matthew 26:28.) Jesus took His sacrificial mission with utmost seriousness, for He knew that without Him, humanity would certainly perish (Matthew 16:25) and spend eternity apart from God in a place of great suffering (Luke 16:22-26).

Jesus described His mission this way: "The Son of Man did not come to be served, but to serve, and to give his life as a ransom for many" (Matthew 20:28). "The Son of Man came to seek and to save what was lost" (Luke 19:10).

In John 10, Jesus compared Himself to a good shepherd who not only gives His life to save the sheep but lays His life down of His own accord (see verses 11,18). This is precisely what He did at the cross. He laid His life down as a sacrificial offering for the sins of humanity (Matthew 26:53,54). He is the Lamb of God. And the personal purity that yields entrance into heaven comes only by being washed in His blood (Revelation 7:14).

LUKE 2:35: *Sword Pointing to the Naked Heart?*

Masonic View: Masons believe that in the Masonic ritual, the "sword pointing to the naked heart" signifies that "justice is one of the most rigorous laws and if we are unjust in our hearts, the center of our being, the inevitable result of injustice will find us out."[42] Therefore, people had better be sincere in taking Masonic oaths. Masons on occasion appeal to Luke 2:35 in support of this sword. In this verse we read that the Holy Spirit was upon Simeon and he spoke to Mary saying, "This child is destined to…be a sign that will be spoken against.…And "a sword will pierce your own soul too."

Biblical View: Even a casual reading of this verse indicates that it provides no support for the Masonic view of the sword, but is rather referring to the grief Mary would suffer as she watched her son be killed for the sins of humankind (John 1:29,36; 1 Peter 3:18; Romans 6:23). Scholars have noted that the sword "is a metaphor used by the most respectable Greek writers to express the most pungent sorrow" and "it may here refer to the anguish Mary must have felt when standing beside the cross of her tortured son" (see John 19:25).[43] There is no connection between this verse and Masonic ritual.

As we continue to consider Masonic ritual in this book, one of the hottest issues of debate that has emerged between Masons and non-Masons is whether Freemasonry is a religion. It is to this controversial issue that we next turn our attention.

5

Is Masonry a Religion?

One of the more controversial aspects of Freemasonry relates to the question of whether or not it is a religion. Even Masons disagree among themselves on this issue.

Well-known Masonic authors, such as Albert Pike and Henry Wilson Coil, say Freemasonry *is* a religion. These men refer to the fact that Freemasonry requires a belief in a Supreme Being and involves temples, doctrines, altars, worship, and even chaplains. Such factors point to the reality that Freemasonry is a religious organization.[1]

Coil asserted that "Freemasonry is undoubtedly a religion,"[2] and compared the Masonic Lodge to a church.[3] Masonry "is a religion without a creed, being of no sect but finding truth in all."[4] "The fact that Freemasonry is a mild religion does not mean that it is no religion."[5] He argued that "Freemasonry certainly requires a belief in the existence of, and man's dependence upon, a Supreme Being to which he is responsible. What can a church add to that, except to bring into fellowship those who have like feelings? That is exactly what the Lodge does."[6] Further, Coil pointed out, "it is said that Freemasonry is not sectarian, by which is meant that it has not identified itself with any well-known sect. But, if it has a religious *credo*, may it not, itself, constitute a sect to be added to the others?"[7] He suggested that "only by judging from external appearances and applying arbitrary gauges can we say that Freemasonry is not religion."[8]

Albert Pike likewise said that "every Masonic Lodge is a temple of religion, and its teachings are instruction in religion."[9] He argued that "the ministers of this religion are all Masons who comprehend it and are devoted to it; its sacrifices to God are good works, the sacrifices of the base and disorderly passions, the offering up of self-interest on the altar of humanity, and perpetual efforts to attain to all the moral perfection of which man is capable."[10] He believed Masonry "is the universal, eternal, immutable religion, such as God planted it in the heart of universal humanity."[11] He further believed this view of religion is supported by James 1:27: "Religion that God our Father accepts as pure and faultless is this: to look after orphans and widows in their distress and to keep oneself from being polluted by the world."

There are a number of other Masons who, while not explicitly calling Masonry a religion, nevertheless make statements that imply Masonry is "religious" or is a "religious institution." Albert Mackey, for example, said: "Look at its ancient landmarks, its sublime ceremonies, its profound symbols and allegories—all inculcating religious observance, and teaching religious truth, and who can deny that it is eminently a religious institution."[12] Mackey's discussion of the altar in the Masonic Lodge is highly telling of the Lodge's religious nature:

> The most important article of furniture in a Lodge room is undoubtedly the altar....It is an altar of sacrifice, for on it the candidate is directed to lay his passions and vices as an oblation to the Deity,

> while he offers up the thoughts of a pure heart as a fitting incense to the Grand Architect of the Universe. The altar is, therefore, the most holy place in a Lodge....It is a sacred utensil of religion, intended, like the altars of the ancient temples, for religious uses, and thus identifying Masonry, by its necessary existence in our Lodges, as a religious institution. Its presence should also lead the contemplative Mason to view the ceremonies in which it is employed with solemn reverence, as being part of a really religious worship.[13]

Certainly the Masonic Lodge teaches its members a specific doctrine of God, which would thus qualify it as a religious institution. Joseph Fort Newton asserted that "everything in Masonry has reference to God, implies God, speaks of God, points and leads to God. Not a degree, not a symbol, not an obligation, not a lecture, not a charge but finds its meaning and derives its beauty from God the Great Architect, in whose temple all Masons are workmen."[14] Martin Wagner similarly notes, "It is to him [God] that Masonic altars are built, priests consecrated, sacrifices made, temples erected and solemnly dedicated. This Great Architect of the Universe is the 'one God' in Freemasonry and besides him there is no other in that institution. Freemasonry as such knows no deity save the Great Architect of the Universe."[15]

Moreover, this God is *worshiped*, which is something that clearly points to the religious nature of the Masonic Lodge. Mason Carl Claudy tells us that "Freemasonry's Lodges are erected to God....Symbolically, to 'erect to God' means to construct something in honor, in worship, in reverence to and for him. Hardly is the initiate within the West Gate before he is impressed that Freemasonry worships God."[16]

Some Masons have taken the position that Freemasonry is essentially a religion or religious institution that encompasses *all* religions. For example, one Mason writes: "What is the religion of Freemasonry? It is the oldest of all religious systems, dating from time immemorial. It is not in itself a separate religion, and has never claimed to be one, but it embodies in itself the fundamental truths and ancient mysteries of which every religion is based."[17] Another Mason writes: "The true Mason...realizes with the divine illumination of his lodge that as a Mason his religion must be universal: Christ, Buddha, or Mohammed, the name means little, for he recognizes only the light and not the bearer. He worships at every shrine, bows before every altar, whether in temple, mosque or cathedral, realizing with his truer understanding the oneness of all spiritual truth."[18]

Other Masonic authors—in fact, the majority of Freemasons—deny altogether that Freemasonry is a religion. It is acknowledged that Freemasonry does require belief in a Supreme Deity and the immortality of the soul. But the differences between Freemasonry and religion are said to be far greater than any similarities that may exist. These Masons argue that the term "religion" implies new revelation, a plan of salvation, a theology, dogmas, sacraments, clergy, and ways of communicating with God. Freemasonry does none of these things, *it is claimed*.[19] Mason Alphonse Cerza writes, "Freemasonry cannot be a religion because it has no creed; it has no confession of faith; it has no theology, no ritual of worship."[20] We are told: "There is nothing better understood among Masons than that [Masonry] is not a religion."[21] Indeed, "Freemasonry is not a religion, it is a philosophy."[22] Freemasonry is viewed by these Masons as a philosophy or system of morals and ethics based on the commonly held beliefs of all monotheistic religions. "It therefore cannot, and does not, tell any man how to find the will of God, because it is not religion. But it can, and does, encourage and reinforce a man's search for truth, as he understands truth."[23]

Moreover, the fact that each Mason is free to interpret religious ideas as he chooses is believed to dictate against the claim that Freemasonry is a religion. How the individual Mason perceives and worships the Supreme Being in which he believes is said to be his own business, as is the means by which he hopes to attain immortality. No brother Mason is permitted to attempt to dissuade him from those beliefs.

In Freemasonry, then, a man is free to follow his own personal religious beliefs—whether he is a Christian, a Jew, a Muslim, or a Hindu. "He may believe the teachings of any organized religion, or he may even have religious convictions that are his alone—as did Thomas Jefferson and John Locke—so long as he believes in a Supreme Being. On that basis, Masonry has welcomed Jews, Moslems, Sikhs, and others, all of whom take the oaths on their own Holy Books."[24] Masonry brings together people of different persuasions to enjoy a "common fellowship," despite different personal religious beliefs.[25]

Some Masons argue that if Freemasonry were a religion it would specifically define the Supreme Being, but it does not do this. Dr. Norman Vincent Peale, a high-level Mason, wrote: "Freemasonry is not a religion, though, in my experience, Masons have predominantly been religious men and for the most part, of the Christian faith....All Masons believe in the deity without reservation. However, Masonry makes no demands as to how a member thinks of the Great Architect of the Universe."[26]

Freemasonry is said by these Masons to be more about following the ethical standards *espoused* by their particular religion.[27] One Mason asserts: "An honest interpretation of the teachings of Freemasonry will show that instead of teaching men *what* to believe, men are simply asked to put the religion they already have, when they become a Mason, into everyday practice."[28] Another Mason says Freemasonry "teaches Masons that their daily life should reflect the principles of their own religion, whatever *their religion* might be."[29] Indeed, "Masonry seeks only to reinforce my own faith, so that it becomes faith in action."[30]

Interestingly, not all Masons are perfectly consistent in their statements regarding this issue. One of the highest, most respected Masons of times past, Albert Pike, has made contradictory statements on the issue. Whereas Pike in one place said (as noted previously) that "every Masonic Lodge is a temple of religion, and its teachings are instruction in religion,"[31] in another place he said, "Masonry is not a religion. He who makes of it a religious belief, falsifies and denaturalizes it."[32]

It is fair to say that despite the controversy over this issue, most Masons today believe Freemasonry is not a religion. One likely reason for this is that it would be exceedingly hard for Masonry to draw people into its ranks from a variety of religious persuasions if it positioned itself as a new religion. It makes good "business sense" to position Masonry as outside the realm of religion so that people of varying religious persuasions will feel more inclined to join.

Freemasonry Is a Religion

I believe a strong case can be made that Freemasonry *is* a religion by virtue of the fact that belief in a deity is required and that atheists are barred from membership. Further, the fact that one finds such things as altars and pulpits and "Worshipful Masters" in Masonic Lodges, *and* the fact that rituals, prayers, pledges, sacred vows, reading from sacred literature, singing hymns, and funeral services take place within Masonic Lodges, constitute a strong argument that Freemasonry is a religion.[33] In fact, if someone were to argue that despite these things Freemasonry is not a religion, he could by that same virtue argue that Christianity is not a religion.

____ *Ask...* ____

- Do you think Masonry is a religion?

- In view of the fact that participation in a Masonic Lodge involves altars, pulpits, Worshipful Masters, rituals, prayers, pledges, sacred vows, reading from sacred literature, singing hymns, and funeral services, can you see why many people classify Masonry as a religion?

- If these things don't constitute Freemasonry as a religion, couldn't it then be argued that Christianity is also not a religion? Will you please explain the difference to me?

Many Masons argue that because Freemasonry is open to *all* religions, it in itself is not a religion. However, such thinking is fallacious. As George Mather and Larry Nichols point out, Hinduism also believes that all religious paths lead to God, yet this tolerance on the part of Hinduism does not in any way negate the fact that it is a religion.[34] Baha'i, too, essentially embraces all religions within its folds, but that does not in any way mitigate the fact that it is a religion. As noted earlier, one Mason conceded that Freemasonry "is a religion without a creed, being of no sect but finding truth in all."[35] In other words, it is a *religion* finding truth in *numerous religions*.

___ *Ask...* ___

- Did you know that Hinduism is classified as an individual religion, even though it believes that all religious paths lead to God?

- Did you know that the Baha'i Faith is a religion, even though it embraces all religions within its folds?

- In view of these facts, can you see why it could be argued that Freemasonry is a religion, even though it sees truth in many religions?

When a person first becomes a Mason, the first ritual he must agree to go through describes him as being "in darkness, helplessness, and ignorance," and being "covered with the pollution of the profane world."[36] The initiate is required to bow before "The

Worshipful Master" and say, "I am in darkness and I am in need of the light of Freemasonry."[37] Doesn't this sound like a religious ceremony?

Understandably, many Christian denominations in both Europe and America have forbidden its members to join with Freemasonry. These include the Roman Catholic Church, the Eastern Orthodox Church of Greece, the Lutheran Church Missouri Synod, the Reformed Presbyterian Church, the Church of God, the Orthodox Presbyterian Church, the Pentecostal Church, the Church of the Nazarene, the Wesleyan Methodist Church, the Mennonite Church, Seventh-day Adventists, and the Quakers.[38] Such churches take exception to the ideas that all religions are true, that Christ is not truly God, that the God of Christianity is the same as the God of Islam and Hinduism, that Christ is not the only way of salvation, and that the Bible is merely one among many "symbols" of religious truth. They further take exception to the Masonic teaching that all people of all religions are part of a single brotherhood. Scripturally, one does not become a part of the family of God without believing in the one true Savior, Jesus Christ (John 3:16; Acts 16:31; Titus 2:13,14).

As an exercise, it is interesting to consult how the most respected dictionaries and encyclopedias describe "religion"— and how well Freemasonry fits such definitions. For example, Webster's *Third New International Dictionary* defines religion this way: "A personal awareness or conviction of the existence of a supreme being or of supernatural powers or influences controlling one's own, common humanity's, or all nature's destiny."[39] The *Encyclopedia Britannica* defines religion as "consisting of a person's relation to God or to gods or spirits. Worship is probably the most basic element of religion, but moral conduct, right belief, and participation in religious institutions are generally also constituent elements of the religious life as practiced by believers and worshipers."[40]

Ask...

After reviewing the previous definitions of religion with the Mason, ask the following questions.

- Will you agree that Freemasonry advocates a personal awareness or conviction of the existence of a supreme being?

- Does Freemasonry focus attention on a person's relation to God?

- Does worship take place within Masonic Lodges?

- Is moral conduct emphasized in the Masonic Lodge?

- Is the Masonic Lodge a religious institution?

- According to the *Encyclopedia Britannica's* definition, is Masonry a religion?

What about the common Masonic claim that Freemasonry is not a religion but is just "religious"? This claim has yielded considerable discussion among both Masons and critics of Masonry. Masonic authority Henry Wilson Coil pointed out that "to call Masonry not *religion* but *religious* merely substitutes an adjective for a noun, both meaning the same thing. It is as absurd as saying that a certain individual has no intellect but is intellectual or that he has no wealth but is wealthy."[41] John Ankerberg and John Weldon add that "it would be just as sensible to say that a man has no power but is powerful; or he has no courage, but is courageous...or he has no patience, but is patient...or that he has no honor, but is honorable."[42] Walton Hannah likewise notes that "it is equivalent to saying that a thing is not an abomination, but it is abominable."[43]

Ask...

- Can an individual have no intellect but be intellectual?

- Does it make sense to say that a certain individual has no wealth but is wealthy?

- Realistically, can someone have no power but be powerful?

- Is it possible for a man to have no courage, yet be courageous?

- Likewise, does it really make sense to say that the Masonic Lodge is not a religion but is religious? Please explain.

Whether or not Masons want to accept it, the reality is that the Masonic Lodge claims to be an institution that:

- draws men closer to God
- gives men a clearer picture of their responsibility to God
- teaches the immortality of the soul
- asserts that entrance into the Celestial Lodge Above depends on following its moral dictates
- engages in worship
- utilizes rituals, prayers, and altars (with Bibles on them)
- calls the Lodge leader "Worshipful Master."

Critic Walton Hannah adds:

> The [Masonic] ritual is worked in the spirit of a solemn religious ceremony; it is a frequent

custom to sing hymns at the opening and closing of the Lodge, candles are lighted before the three pedestals, and the Bible is always open before the Worshipful Master. The Lodge must be opened and closed with prayer....The places where Lodges meet are customarily known as temples, a word strongly associated with worship and religion. Most Lodges have chaplains and organists who have their regular part to play in the ceremonies.[44]

An honest and unbiased look at the facts reveals that Freemasonry is a religion. If Freemasonry is not a religion then it is certainly the most religious nonreligion I have encountered in my 25 years of religious studies!

6

The Bible: A "Great Light"

M asons believe that even though the Bible is a significant book, it is not the sole Word of God. They refuse to confine divine revelation "exclusively to the tenets or writings of any one particular faith, realizing that all contain elements of vital truth."[1] For this reason, each Mason swears his oath on whatever holy book seems to him the most satisfactory and the most complete. Each Mason "respects the convictions of the others who may prefer a different Volume of the Sacred Law containing a different interpretation of that same revealed will."[2]

The Bible is not viewed as God's *only* revelation to humankind, but is viewed as one of many holy books that contain religious and moral truth. Masons often refer to the Bible as a *symbol* of God's will.[3] "The prevailing Masonic opinion is that the Bible is only a symbol of Divine Will, Law, or Revelation, and not that its contents are Divine Law, inspired, or revealed. So far, no responsible authority has held that a Freemason must believe the Bible or any part of it."[4] Indeed, Albert Mackey notes, "Although in

Christendom very few Masons deny the divine authority of the Scriptures of the Old and New Testaments, yet to require, as a preliminary to initiation, the declaration of such a belief is directly in opposition to the expressed regulations of the Order."[5]

Other "symbols" of God's will include the Koran (used by Muslims), the Vedas (used by Hindus), and the Pentateuch (used by Jews). Albert Pike writes, "The Bible is an indispensable part of the furniture of a Christian Lodge, only because it is the sacred book of the Christian religion. The Hebrew Pentateuch in a Hebrew Lodge, and Koran in the Mohammedan one, belong on the Altar....We have no other concern with your religious creed."[6] Mackey likewise writes, "Whether it be the Gospels to the Christian, the Pentateuch to the Israelites, the Koran to the Muslim, or the Vedas to the Brahman, it everywhere Masonically conveys the same idea—that of the symbolism of the divine will revealed to man."[7]

All holy books are thus acceptable within the confines of any Masonic Lodge. All these books provide not just *religious* truth but *moral* truth and, hence, constitute ethical guides by which to govern one's life. This is ultimately the most important thing for the Mason. The Bible is viewed as a "light which enlightens the path of our duty to God."[8] Indeed, the Bible is "a trustworthy guide to conduct" that "contains sufficient self-evident truths to provide direction and guidance for those who will regulate their lives by the light of its teaching."[9] The Bible "remains unique in literature as a compendium of moral instructions and a source of ethical inspiration."[10]

Many Masons utilize an *esoteric* approach in interpreting the Bible, seeking symbolic meanings to individual Bible verses. Pike believed that the biblical books "were written in symbols unintelligible to the profane" (that is, to the ignorant).[11] Masonry views the Bible "as the repository of symbolic truth, itself a symbol of the truth of God."[12] Martin Wagner noted that "the eminent Masons all contend that there is a veil upon the Scriptures, which when removed, leaves them clearly in accord with Masonic teachings and in essential harmony with other sacred books."[13] Richard Thorn said that "Jesus taught in parables...to impart hidden knowledge to a select few; not for capricious reasons, but because the larger group was not yet prepared to hear and understand."[14] This is a clear allusion to a discussion Jesus had with His disciples in Matthew 13. After teaching a parable, "the disciples came to him and asked, 'Why do you speak to the people in parables?' [Jesus] replied, 'The knowledge of the secrets of the kingdom of heaven has been given to you, but not to them'" (Matthew 13:10,11). Pike holds that Masonry reveals its esoteric secrets *only* to those who are worthy:

> Masonry, like all Religions, all the Mysteries... conceals its secrets from all except the Adepts and Sages, or the Elect, and uses false explanations and misinterpretations of its symbols to mislead those who deserve only to be misled; to conceal the Truth, which it calls Light, from them, and to draw them away from it. Truth is not for those who are unworthy or unable to receive it, or would pervert it.[15]

_____REASONING FROM THE SCRIPTURES_____

The Bible Contradicts Other "Holy Books"

The Bible is not merely "one among many symbols" of religious truth, in a league with the Muslim Koran and the Hindu Vedas. In fact, it is fair to say that if one of these books (or any other "holy" book) is correct, then the others are necessarily wrong, since they set forth diametrically opposing ideas on basic religious concepts.

Consider the doctrine of God, which is the most fundamental doctrine of any religious system. According to the Christian Bible,

Jesus taught there is one personal God who is triune in nature (Mark 12:29; John 4:24; 5:18,19; Matthew 28:19). *Muhammad,* the prophet of Islam, taught that there is only one God, but that God cannot have a son and there is no Trinity. In fact, the Koran teaches that the very idea that God can have a son is blasphemous. *Hinduism* espouses virtually millions of gods who are viewed as extensions of the all-permeating deity, Brahman. *Krishna* espoused a combination of polytheism (many gods) and pantheism (all is god). *Zoroaster,* in his writings, set forth religious dualism—there is both a good god and a bad god. *Buddha* taught that the concept of God was essentially irrelevant. Clearly, the leaders of the world's major religions held completely contradictory views regarding the nature of God. And since the doctrine of God is the most fundamental doctrine of any religious system, it cannot legitimately be said that all these "holy" books are true.

There are other significant differences. The Koran and the Vedas, for example, set forth a works-oriented view of salvation, whereas the Bible says salvation is a free gift for those who trust in Christ alone (Ephesians 2:8,9). While religions such as Hinduism and Buddhism teach reincarnation, Christianity denies this doctrine and teaches that we live once and die once and then face the judgment (Hebrews 9:27). While Christianity teaches that Jesus is absolute deity, Islam teaches that He is just a prophet of God (lesser than Muhammad). Muslims view the Bible as being corrupted, containing not the actual words of Jesus, but rather other peoples' words *about* Jesus (Surahs 2:75; 2:78,79). Christians, by contrast, view the Bible as inspired by God (see 2 Timothy 3:16,17; 2 Peter 1:21). Muslims say Jesus did not die on the cross, for it would have been unthinkable that Allah would have allowed one of his prophets to be crucified. According to Christianity, however, Jesus most certainly died on the cross for our sins (Matthew 20:28; 2 Corinthians 5:21); He "gave himself as a ransom for all men" (1 Timothy 2:6).

The bottom line is that there are many radical and irreconcilable points of difference between the Bible, the Vedas, the Koran, and other "holy" books. If the Bible *is* God's Word, then the others *cannot* be God's Word.

____ *Ask...* ____

- Did you know that while Jesus taught a triune concept of God (Matthew 28:19), the Muslim Koran denies the Trinity and argues that God cannot have a son?

- Did you know that the Hindu Vedas espouse millions of gods who are viewed as extensions of the all-permeating deity of Brahman? How does this compare with Jesus' assertion that there is one God only?

- Did you know that both the Muslim Koran and the Hindu Vedas set forth a works-oriented view of salvation? How does this reconcile with the Bible's teaching that salvation is a free gift based entirely on God's grace and received through faith in Christ?

- Did you know that Hinduism teaches reincarnation? Can this belief coexist with Christianity's teaching that we live once and die once and then face judgment (Hebrews 9:27)?

- In view of such irreconcilable differences, the Bible, the Koran, and the Vedas cannot *all* be right, can they? Based on their differences, wouldn't you agree that if one is truly right, the others must be wrong?

- If one of these books truly came from God, isn't it realistic to say that the others cannot have come from God since God does not contradict Himself?

It is important to understand at this juncture that Jesus was unbendingly exclusivistic in His truth claims—indicating that what He said took precedence over all others. Jesus said He is exclusively *man's only means* of coming into a relationship with God: "I am the way and the truth and the life. No one comes to the Father, except through me" (John 14:6). Jesus' exclusivity caused Him to warn: "Watch out that no one deceives you. For many will come in my name, claiming, 'I am the Christ,' and will deceive many" (Matthew 24:4,5; see also verse 23). These words alone are enough to close the door on other so-called revelations from God.

The Inspiration of the Bible

When you engage in discussions with Masons, be prepared to affirm *and* defend the inspiration, inerrancy, and authority of the Bible. This is important because, as noted earlier, Masonry denies the uniqueness of the Bible and considers it one of many symbols of God's will. In what follows, you will find a brief defense of the Bible's inspiration, inerrancy, and authority. I recommend that you memorize some of the Bible references so that when you encounter a Mason—particularly a "Christian Mason"—you will be ready to prove the Bible as God's Word to humankind.

In a capsule, the Christian Bible is utterly unique because it is *inspired.* Inspiration does not mean the biblical writer felt enthusiastic, like the composer of the "Star Spangled Banner." Nor does it mean the writings are necessarily inspiring to read, like an uplifting poem. The Greek word used in the Bible for *inspiration* literally means "God-breathed." Because Scripture is breathed out by God—because it *originates* from Him—it is true and inerrant.

Biblical inspiration may be defined as God's superintending of the human authors so that, using their own individual personalities (and even their own writing styles) they composed and recorded *without error* His revelation to humankind in the words of the original autographs. In other words, the original documents of the Bible were written by men, who, though permitted to exercise their own personalities and literary talents, wrote under the control and guidance of the Holy Spirit. The result is a perfect and errorless recording of the exact message God desired to give to man.

Second Peter 1:21 provides a key insight regarding the human-divine interchange in the process of inspiration. This verse informs us that "prophecy [Scripture] never had its origin in the will of man, but men spoke from God as they were carried along by the Holy Spirit." The phrase *carried along* in this verse literally means "forcefully borne along."

Even though human beings were used in the process of writing down God's Word, they were literally "borne along" by the Holy Spirit. The human wills of the authors were not the originators of God's message. God did not permit the will of sinful human beings to misdirect or erroneously record His message. Rather, "God *moved* and the prophet *mouthed* these truths; God *revealed* and man *recorded* His word."[16]

Interestingly, the Greek word for "carried along" in 2 Peter 1:21 is the same as that found in Acts 27:15-17. In this passage the experienced sailors could not navigate the ship because the wind was so strong. The ship was being *driven, directed,* and *carried along* by the wind. This is similar to the Spirit's driving, directing, and carrying the human authors of the Bible as He wished. The Greek word is a strong one, indicating the Spirit's complete superintendence of the human authors. Yet, just as the sailors were active on the ship (though the wind, not the sailors, ultimately controlled the ship's movement), so the human authors were active in writing as the Spirit directed.

It is fascinating to observe that many Old Testament passages quoted in the New Testament are said to have the Holy Spirit or God as their author, even though a human prophet actually uttered the words in the Old Testament. The words spoken by the human prophets carried divine authority.

Acts 1:16 is highly significant in this regard, for we read: "Brothers, the Scripture had to be fulfilled which *the Holy Spirit spoke long ago through the mouth of David* concerning Judas, who served as guide for those who arrested Jesus" (emphasis added). Though David was used in the process of communicating God's words, it is clear that the Holy Spirit was in charge of the process so that no human error or opinion entered into the picture. We see this same pattern repeated throughout the Bible. What the psalmist said in Psalm 95:7 is attributed to the Holy Spirit in Hebrews 3:7,8. What the psalmist said in Psalm 45:6 is attributed to God in Hebrews 1:8. What Isaiah said in Isaiah 7:14 is attributed to the Lord in Matthew 1:22,23.

In 2 Timothy 3:16 we read, "All Scripture is God-breathed and is useful for teaching, rebuking, correcting and training in righteousness." The Greek form of "God-breathed" (or "inspired") in this verse is passive. This means the Bible is the *result* of the "breath of God." If the form were active, the verse would be saying that all the Bible breathes or exudes God. But here we are told that God *breathed out* the Scriptures. The origin of the Bible—both Old and New Testaments—is thus seen to be God.

The apostle Paul certainly understood that his own writings were inspired by God and therefore authoritative. In 1 Corinthians 2:13, Paul said he spoke "not in words taught us by human wisdom but in words taught by the Spirit, expressing spiritual truths in spiritual words." In this passage, Paul (who wrote more than half the New Testament) affirmed that his words were authoritative because they were rooted not in fallible men but infallible God (the Holy Spirit). The Holy Spirit is the *Spirit of truth* who was promised to the apostles to teach and guide them into all the truth (see John 16:13).

Later, in 1 Corinthians 14:37, Paul said, "If anybody thinks he is a prophet or spiritually gifted, let him acknowledge that what I am writing to you is the Lord's command." In 1 Thessalonians 2:13, Paul likewise said, "And we also thank God continually because, when you received the word of God, which you heard from us, you accepted it not as the word of men, but as it actually is, the word of God, which is at work in you who believe." Again, the reason why Paul's words were authoritative is that they were rooted in God, not in man. God used Paul as His *instrument* to communicate *His* word to man.

In view of such facts, it is obvious that the Bible is not just one among many other so-called holy books or symbols of God's will, as Masons try to claim. The Bible is *truly inspired* and is derived from God. And because the Bible is inspired (unlike the Muslim Koran and Hindu Vedas), *it alone speaks with the authority of God.*

The Absolute Authority of the Bible

The Bible alone is the supreme and infallible authority for the individual believer (2 Peter 1:21; 2 Timothy 3:16,17; 1 Corinthians 2:13; 1 Thessalonians 2:13). Certainly Jesus and the apostles often gave testimony to the absolute authority of the Bible as the Word of God. Jesus affirmed the Bible's divine inspiration (Matthew 22:43), its indestructibility (Matthew 5:17,18), its infallibility (John 10:35), its final authority (Matthew 4:4,7,10), its historicity (Matthew 12:40; 24:37), its scientific accuracy (Matthew 19:2-5), and its factual inerrancy (John 17:17; Matthew 22:29).

The Bible has final authority because it is a direct revelation from God and carries the authority of God Himself (Galatians 1:12). What the *Bible* says, *God* says. The Scriptures are the final court of appeal on all doctrinal and moral matters. The *Bible alone is sufficient* as our sole guide for matters of faith and practice. Jesus said, "Scripture cannot be broken" (John 10:35). He also said, "I tell you the truth, until heaven and earth disappear, not the smallest letter, not the least stroke of a pen, will by any means disappear from the Law until everything is accomplished" (Matthew 5:18). He said, "It is easier for heaven and earth to disappear than for the least stroke of a pen to drop out of the Law" (Luke 16:17). To the Sadducees Jesus said, "You are in error because you do not know the Scriptures or the power of God" (Matthew 22:29). To the devil, Jesus consistently responded, "It is written…" (Matthew 4:4-10). Following Jesus' lead, we must conclude that the Bible alone is our supreme and final authority.

Archeological Support for the Bible's Reliability

Unlike other books that claim to be Scripture (including the Koran and the Vedas), the Bible's accuracy and reliability has been proven over and over again by archeological finds discovered by believing *and* nonbelieving scholars and scientists. This includes verification for numerous customs, places, names, and events mentioned in the Bible.

One among many examples is the fact that for many years the existence of the Hittites (a powerful people who lived during the time of Abraham) was questioned because no archeological digs had uncovered anything about them. Critics claimed the Hittites were pure myth. Today the critics are silenced. Abundant archeological evidence for the existence of the Hittites during the time of Abraham has been uncovered.

Another example has to do with the claim that Moses could not have written the first five books of the Bible (Genesis, Exodus, Leviticus, Numbers, and Deuteronomy) because handwriting had not yet been invented. But archeological finds now conclusively prove that there indeed was handwriting back during the time of Moses. The claims of critics have been silenced.

Still another example relates to the ancient cities of Sodom and Gomorrah. Critics used to say this part of the Bible (Genesis 10, 13, 14, 18, 19) is mere myth because of a lack of evidence that these cities ever even existed. These critics have been silenced in view of the abundant archeological evidence for the existence of these towns.

Addressing how archeology has continually verified the reliability of the Bible, scholar Donald J. Wiseman notes, "The geography of Bible lands and visible remains of antiquity were gradually recorded until today more than 25,000 sites within this region and dating to Old Testament times, in their broadest sense, have been located."[17] Nelson Glueck, a specialist in ancient literature, did an exhaustive study and concluded: "It can be stated categorically that no archaeological discovery has ever controverted a biblical reference."[18] Well-known scholar William F. Albright, following a comprehensive study, wrote: "Discovery after discovery has established the accuracy of innumerable details, and has brought increased recognition of the value of the Bible as a source of history."[19]

The Bible Should Not Be Added To

Solomon once warned that "every word of God is tested....Do not add to his words, or he will rebuke you and prove you a liar" (Proverbs 30:5,6). In like manner, the apostle John closed the last words of the book of Revelation with essentially the same exhortation, declaring, "I warn everyone who hears the words of the prophecy of this book: If anyone adds anything to them, God will add to him the plagues described in this book. And if anyone takes words away from this book of prophecy, God will take away from him his share in the tree of life..." (Revelation 22:18,19). It is clear that God does not wish anything that falsely claims divine authority to be added to His inspired words. Those who set forth other holy books that are in reality man-made fall under God's condemnation.

Even if one hypothetically granted that God did wish to reveal additional truths through other holy books, that revelation would have to be consistent with previous divine revelation. God does not contradict Himself. The apostle Paul said that "even if we or an angel from heaven should preach a gospel other than the one we preached to you, let him be eternally condemned!" (Galatians 1:8). Paul spoke of the importance of making sure that new claims to truth be measured against what we *know* to be true from Scripture (see Acts 17:11; 2 Timothy 3:16). Since the "revelations" in the Hindu Vedas and the Muslim Koran, and other such books, directly contradict the revelation found in the pages of the Christian Bible on so many different doctrines, we can rightly ascertain that they did not come from the same source.

If the Bible came from God, then these other books did not. For these books to be put on an equal level of authority in the Masonic Lodge is an outrage against the one true God and His Word. At the future day of judgment, Masons will have to face God and give an account for their actions.

Ask... _____

- Would you agree that God would never contradict Himself?

- Since the "revelations" in the Hindu Vedas and the Muslim Koran directly contradict the revelation found in the Bible in regard to numerous doctrines, doesn't it seem logical to assume that these "revelations" did not come from the same source? (Be ready to give some proof of some contradictions.)

- If the Bible _truly did_ come from God, and if God does not contradict Himself, then, in view of the numerous contradictions, can we not assume that the Hindu Vedas and Muslim Koran _did not_ come from God?

An Esoteric Approach to the Bible Is Unreliable

As noted at the beginning of this chapter, the Masonic allusion to Matthew 13:10,11 (Jesus using parables) in support of an esoteric (symbolic) approach to the Bible is untenable. In Matthew 13, Jesus is speaking in front of a mixed multitude. He did not attempt to separate the believers from the unbelievers and then instruct only the believers. Rather, He constructed His teaching so that believers would understand what He said but unbelievers would not.

After teaching one such parable, the disciples asked Jesus: "Why do you speak to the people in parables?" (Matthew 13:10). Jesus answered, "The knowledge of the secrets of the kingdom of heaven has been given to you [believers], but not to them [unbelievers]" (verse 11). Masons conclude that in view of this verse, there must be secrets in the words of Jesus that only true "believers" (or initiates) can discern.

While it is true that Jesus said the "knowledge of the secrets" has been given to believers, the Greek word for _secret_ in this passage simply means "mystery." A mystery in the biblical sense is a truth that cannot be discerned simply by human investigation, but it requires special revelation from God. Generally, this word refers to a truth that was unknown to people living in Old Testament times, but is now revealed to humankind by God (see Colossians 1:26). In Matthew 13, Jesus provides information to believers about the kingdom of heaven that has never been revealed before.

One might legitimately ask why Jesus engineered His parabolic teaching so that *believers* could understand His teaching but *unbelievers* could not. The backdrop to this is that the disciples, having responded favorably to Jesus' teaching and having placed their faith in Him, already knew much truth about the Messiah. Careful reflection on Jesus' parables would enlighten them even further.

However, hardened unbelievers who had willfully and persistently refused Jesus' previous teachings were prevented from understanding. Jesus was apparently following an injunction He provided earlier in the Sermon on the Mount: "Do not give dogs what is sacred; do not throw your pearls to pigs" (Matthew 7:6). Yet there is grace even here. For it is possible that Jesus may have prevented unbelievers from understanding the parables because He did not want to add more responsibility to them by imparting new truth for which they would be held responsible.

We should not miss the fact that the parables of the Sower (Matthew 13:3-9) and the Tares (weeds) (13:24-30) show that Jesus wanted His parables to be clear to those who were receptive. Jesus Himself provided the interpretation of these parables for His disciples. He did this not only so there would be no uncertainty as to their meaning, but to guide believers in the proper method to use in interpreting the other parables. The fact that Christ did not interpret His subsequent parables shows that He fully expected believers to understand what He taught by following the methodology He illustrated for them. Clearly Matthew 13 does not support but rather argues against an esoteric method of interpreting Scripture.

There are other factors that also argue against a symbolic approach to Scripture. Foundationally, right from the first book in the Bible, there is virtually no indication that Scripture was intended to be taken esoterically. Rather, a plain reading of the text seems to be assumed throughout. A nonesoteric reading of Genesis indicates that when God created Adam in His own rational image, He gave Adam the gift of intelligible speech, thus enabling him to communicate objectively with his creator (and with other human beings) via language (Genesis 1:26; 2:19,20). Indeed, God sovereignly chose to use human language as a medium of revelational communication.

If God's primary purpose for originating language was to make it possible for Him to communicate with human beings, as well as to enable human beings to communicate with each other, then it must follow that He would generally use language and expect people to use it in its literal, normal, and plain sense. This view is a prerequisite to understanding not only God's spoken word but His written Word (Scripture) as well.

It is important to help Masons see that the Bible, as a body of literature, exists because human beings need to know certain spiritual truths they cannot attain by themselves. These truths must come to them from without—that is, via objective, special revelation from God (Deuteronomy 29:29). This revelation can only be understood if one interprets the words of Scripture according to God's original design for language—according to the ordinary, straightforward sense of each word.

In keeping with a literal approach to Scripture, each biblical text has only *one legitimate meaning* and therefore only *one legitimate interpretation*. In 1983, the International Council on Biblical Inerrancy (ICBI) published a commentary on "The Chicago Statement on Biblical Hermeneutics," in which Article VII states: "We affirm that the meaning in each biblical text is single, definite, and fixed."[20] The commentary explains that "the affirmation here is directed at those who claim a 'double' or 'deeper' meaning of Scripture than that expressed by the authors. It stresses the unity and fixity of meaning as opposed to those who find multiple and pliable meanings."[21]

Masons may respond to this statement by saying that their symbolical interpretation of Scripture is just as legitimate as anyone else's. Certainly everyone is entitled to his or her own interpretation of the Bible. At the same time, however, we must insist that not all interpretations are equally correct. Bible scholar Douglas Groothuis comments:

> You may, in fact, "interpret" the bright, large orb that irradiates the solar system as being a remarkably durable and powerful satellite constructed by Peruvian peasants in A.D. 300. You have a "right," so to speak, to interpret things that way; but that in no way makes your view correct. Your interpretation is either true or false; you are either right or wrong. Having "your own interpretation" about the Bible does not, in itself, legitimate that interpretation as truth any more than "your interpretation" of your IRS return legitimates itself before the penetrating eyes of an income-tax auditor. He goes by "the book," not your book. The it's-my-interpretation cop-out may land you a big fine or even time behind bars (which no amount of creative interpretation will dissolve).[22]

Unlike objective methodology, in which interpretations (of both the major and minor details in Scripture) can be rationally evaluated and tested by comparing Scripture with Scripture and by objectively weighing historical and grammatical considerations, there is no objective way to test esoteric interpretations of Scripture. By nature, esotericism is subjective and nonverifiable. There is no way to prove that a given interpretation is right or wrong since "proof" presupposes rationality and objectivity.

The objective interpreter of Scripture seeks to discover the author's intended meaning (the only true meaning). We must recognize that what a passage means is fixed by the author and is not subject to alteration by readers. Meaning is *determined* by the author; it is *discovered* by readers.[23]

Our goal must be *exegesis* (drawing the meaning out of the text) and not *eisogesis* (superimposing a meaning onto the text). By using eisogesis instead of exegesis, a Marxist interpreter could, for example, so skew the meaning of the U.S. Constitution that it comes out sounding like it supported socialism.[24] Masonic esotericists have done the same type of thing with the Bible. They approach Scripture with a Masonic preunderstanding and so skew the meaning of the biblical text that it comes out saying something entirely different than what was intended by the author. (For example, some Masons have argued that the fig leaves God used to cover Adam and Eve's nakedness were in reality the first Masonic aprons. Other Masons have argued that when God said "let there be light" in Genesis 1:3, He was referring to Masonic light.)

Context

In seeking the biblical author's (and God's) intended meaning, it is critical to interpret Bible statements in context. Every word in the Bible is part of a sentence; every sentence is part of a paragraph; every paragraph is part of a book; and every book is part of the whole of Scripture. There is both an immediate and a broader context of a given verse. The immediate context of a statement is the paragraph (or paragraphs) of the biblical book in question. No text of Scripture is independent from the statements around it. Interpreting a text apart from its immediate context is like trying to make sense of a Rembrandt painting by looking at only a single square inch of the painting or like trying to analyze Handel's "Messiah" by listening to a few short notes. The surrounding Scriptures are absolutely critical to a proper understanding of individual verses.

The broader context of any given text is the whole of Scripture. We must ever bear in mind that the interpretation of a specific passage must not contradict the total teaching of Scripture on a point. Individual texts do not exist as isolated fragments, but as parts of a whole. The exposition of these texts must involve exhibiting them in right relation both to the whole and to each other. This principle is grounded in the fact that each of the biblical writers wrote within the larger context of previous biblical teachings. And they assumed that *all* of Scripture—though communicated through human instruments—had one author (God) who didn't contradict Himself (2 Peter 1:21).

History

Historical considerations are especially important as a backdrop in ascertaining the author's intended meaning. Christianity is based on historical fact. More specifically, Christianity rests on the foundation of the historical Jesus of Nazareth, whose very life represents God's full and objective self-communication to humankind (John 1:18). In the empirical (experiential) world of ordinary sense perceptions, Jesus was seen and heard by human beings as God's ultimate revelation (1 John 1:1-3). This is why He could claim, "If you really knew me, you would know my Father as well" (John 14:7).

The apostle Paul warned the religious men of Athens of the objective reality of the future judgment of all humanity on the basis of the objective, historical evidence for the resurrection of Jesus (Acts 17:16ff.). This evidence is recorded for us in propositional statements (affirmations of specific truths) in the New Testament Gospels, documents that are based on eyewitness testimony and written very close in time to the events on which they report. Just as in Paul's day, how we respond to God's objective, historical revelation contained in Scripture will determine where we spend eternity—in a real heaven or a real hell. Esoteric manipulation of truth will not be possible on the day of judgment.

Masonic esotericists would do well to consider the example set by Jesus Christ in how to properly interpret Scripture. Jesus never sought an esoteric or symbolic meaning when interpreting the Old Testament Scriptures. On the contrary, He consistently interpreted the Old Testament quite literally, including the Creation account of Adam and Eve (Matthew 13:35; 25:34; Mark 10:6), Noah's Ark and the Flood (Matthew 24:38,39; Luke 17:26,27), Jonah and the whale (Matthew 12:39-41), Sodom and Gomorrah (Matthew 10:15), and the account of Lot and his wife (Luke 17:28,29). In his book *The Savior and the Scriptures*, theologian Robert P. Lightner notes—following an exhaustive study—that Jesus' interpretation of Scripture "was always in accord with the grammatical and historical meaning. He understood and appreciated the meaning intended by the writers according to the laws of grammar and rhetoric."[25]

In contradiction to Masonic esotericists who say there is a hidden, spiritual meaning in Bible verses discernible only by esoteric "initiates," Jesus taught openly and with clarity. Recall that following His arrest, Jesus was questioned by the High Priest about His disciples and His teachings. Jesus responded: "*I have spoken openly* to the world...I always taught in synagogues or at the temple, where all the Jews come together. *I said nothing in secret*. Why question me? Ask those who heard me. Surely they know what I said" (John 18:20, emphases added). Since Jesus had said nothing in secret, those who heard Him would be able to clearly enunciate what He had openly communicated. There were no hidden meanings beneath His words.

Why It Matters

Jesus said His words lead to eternal life (John 6:63). But for us to receive eternal life through His words, they must be taken *as He intended them to be taken*. A Masonic, esoteric reinterpretation of Scripture that yields another god and another Jesus and another gospel will yield only eternal death (see 2 Corinthians 11:3,4; Galatians 1:6-9). Jesus' life-giving invitation is plainly open to all: "Whoever hears my word and believes him who sent me has eternal life and will not be condemned; he has crossed over from death to life" (John 5:24).

7

God: The Great Architect of the Universe

A key requirement of joining a Masonic Lodge is that one must subscribe to belief in a Supreme Being. It does not matter what one *calls* that deity, but one must believe *in* a deity. No atheist can be a Mason.[1]

God is often described by Masons as the "Great Architect of the Universe," "Supreme Being," "Grand Geometrician of the Universe," "Grand Artificer of the Universe," and "God, the Creator, Author, and Architect of the Universe, Omnipotent, Omniscient, and Omnipresent."[2] Masonic literature gives the distinct impression that the Supreme Being of the Masonic Lodge is essentially *unknowable* and, consequently, *inoffensive*. If God is infinitely beyond our ability to comprehend, then that means it is inappropriate for mere humans to have fights about how to define Him. Carl Claudy says that the individual Mason "may name him as he will, think of him as he pleases; make him an impersonal law or personal and anthropomorphic."[3] Vindex asserts that "it is

quite contrary to the spirit of Masonry to claim that any one interpretation of God is exclusively the right one."[4]

In keeping with this, Masons generally speak of God in general without speaking of His individual attributes when in the
Lodge. William Hammond comments that Masonry "makes no
attempt to explain how such a being came to be, nor to enumerate
and define His divine attributes. It leaves its members free to their
private views."[5] H.L. Haywood likewise writes:

> Freemasonry nowhere offers a definition of the
> nature and attributes of God, but leaves such
> matters to each individual to fashion as best he
> can. It asks of a man only that he believe that
> God is. It does not even try to prove the existence
> of God, after the fashion of the dogmatic theolo-
> gians, but assumes that its candidates already
> have that belief in their hearts.[6]

Perhaps the one key exception to the Masonic avoidance of
discussing God's attributes is their view of God as the "all-seeing
eye." According to Albert Mackey, the all-seeing eye "is a symbol
of the omnipresent deity."[7] He says it is "an important symbol of
the Supreme being, borrowed by the Freemasons from the nations
of antiquity."[8] Indeed, "the Egyptians represented Osiris, their
chief deity, by the symbol of an open eye, and placed this hiero-
glyphic of him in all their temples....The all-seeing eye may then
be considered as a symbol of God manifested in his omnipres-
ence—to which Solomon alludes in the book of Proverbs."[9]
Mackey is speaking of Proverbs 15:3, which tells us "the eyes of
the LORD are everywhere, keeping watch on the wicked and the
good." Some psalms are also cited in this regard: "The eyes of the
LORD are on the righteous and his ears are attentive to their cry"
(Psalm 34:15); "indeed, he who watches over Israel will neither
slumber nor sleep" (Psalm 121:4).

Masons believe that Jews, Christians, Hindus, Muslims, and those of other faiths are all worshiping the same "all-seeing" God using different names. God is known as "the nameless one of a hundred names."[10] As Albert Mackey put it, "God is equally present with the pious Hindoo [sic] in the temple, the Jew in the synagogue, the Mohammedan in the mosque, and the Christian in the church."[11]

Freemasonry teaches that people worship God under different names only because they do not know any better—*people are in spiritual darkness*. Masonry claims it can remove this darkness by revealing that all men are actually worshiping the same God. Martin Wagner explains: "While it tacitly admits the existence of other gods in allowing its disciples to hold their private views, it does so on the theory that these god-ideas are perversions and corruptions of its own theistic conceptions and which it aims to correct."[12] Apologists John Ankerberg and John Weldon are correct in saying that "Masonry actually believes she alone possesses the truth about God, and that every other concept of God must be false and therefore rejected....That is why Masonry teaches that everyone must be reeducated to learn that their ideas of God are incorrect—that they are merely inferior reflections concerning the true Great Architect of the Universe."[13]

Though different Masons refer to God using different names, and though different Masons may view God differently, Freemasonry *as an institution* does not affirm the Christian belief in the doctrine of the Trinity. Masons believe that if Freemasonry affirmed belief in the Trinity, that would amount to sponsoring the Christian religion, since Christianity is the only religion that holds to this doctrine. The Masonic policy is that "no phrase or terms should be used in a Masonic service that would arouse sectarian feelings or wound the religious sensibilities of any Freemason."[14] Because the doctrine of the Trinity "would arouse sectarian feelings" and would "wound the religious sensibilities" of such groups as Jews, Hindus, and Muslims, this doctrine is avoided in the Masonic Lodge.

One cannot help but observe that even though Freemasonry teaches that individuals are free to hold to their own view of God,

Masonry does in fact teach a concept of God—that is, that *all religions believe in the same God*. So, despite the fact that Masonry denies teaching a doctrine of God, it is in fact doing so. This is nowhere more evident than in the Royal Arch degree of the York Rite where the Mason is told that the real name of God is *Jabulon*. This is said to be a compound word derived from "Ja" (for Jehovah), joined with "Bel" or "Bul" (for Baal, the ancient Canaanite God), and "On" (for Osiris, the ancient Egyptian mystery god). According to *Coil's Masonic Encyclopedia*, "Jah, Bel, and On appear in the American ritual of the Royal Arch degree on the supposition that Jah was the Syriac name of God, Bel (Baal), the Chaldean, and On, the Egyptian."[15] We are told that "in this compound name an attempt is made to show by a coordination of divine names...the unity, identity and harmony of the Hebrew, Assyrian and Egyptian god-ideas, and the harmony of the Royal Arch religion with these ancient religions."[16]

REASONING FROM THE SCRIPTURES

Different Gods

As noted previously, Masons believe that God is equally present with the Hindu in the temple, the Jew in the synagogue, the Muslim in the mosque, and the Christian in the church.[17] "If Masonry were simply a Christian institution, the Jew and the Moslem, the Brahman and the Buddhist, could not conscientiously partake of its illumination. But its universality is its boast. In its language citizens of every nation may converse; at its altar men of all religions may kneel; to its creed disciples of every faith may subscribe."[18] We are also told, "If the Christian and a Hindu be together in a Lodge, and pray together to God, it is surely axiomatic in this atmosphere of broad charity that the Christian must acknowledge that the Hindu's God is ultimately the same as his own."[19]

But is this true? A hard look at what these religions individually teach about God proves the folly of such a notion. Indeed, in view of the fact that 1) the Bible teaches the Trinity, 2) the Koran denies the Trinity and exalts Allah, and 3) the Vedas espouse millions of gods, the teaching of Freemasonry that the different religions are worshiping the same God using different names shows astonishing ignorance. If one of these concepts of God is correct, the others must necessarily be incorrect. If Yahweh is the one true God, as the Bible teaches (Exodus 3:14,15), then the god of Islam and the god of Hinduism cannot be the true God. For illustration purposes, let us consider the Hindu view of God.

While Christianity espouses a God that is *eternally distinct* from His creation, Hinduism is polytheistic, espousing millions of gods who are considered extensions of the all-permeating deity of Brahman, and, in fact, views all of reality as Brahman. In Hinduism there has long been a heavy emphasis on ritual offerings to various deities. Some of these gods were viewed as personifications of natural forces, such as the storm, the sun, the moon, and the fertility of the soil.[20] Eventually, certain of these gods became preeminent. These include Brahma, Vishnu, and Siva.

The Upanishads (sacred Scriptures in India) fundamentally teach that behind the many gods of Hinduism stands the one monistic ("all is one") reality of Brahman.[21] "Every aspect of the universe, both animate and inanimate, shares the same essentially divine nature. There is actually only one Self in the universe."[22] All these lesser gods are viewed as extensions of this "all-is-one" god, Brahman.

According to this school of thought, every person possesses an individual soul known as *atman* that is related to the universal soul (Brahman).[23] Brahman is viewed as an impersonal, monistic ("all is one") force. The universe is viewed as extended from the being of Brahman. Through seemingly endless deaths and rebirths (reincarnation), an individual finally comes to realize that *atman is Brahman*. "Most adherents of Hinduism believe that they are in their true selves (*atman*) extended from and one with *Brahman*....Our essence is identical to that of the essence of Brahman."[24] "The living beings that inhabit our world are really only expressions of the Brahman. They are souls (*atman*) that are a part of the great ocean of souls that make up the Brahman."[25]

Because Vedanta Hinduism is monistic, distinctions are considered unreal. When we perceive distinctions, it is nothing more than a mental illusion (*maya*).[26] "A person's individuality apart from the Brahman—the world in which one lives, that which one sees, hears, touches, and feels—is all an illusion, a dream."[27] As world religion specialist Mark Albrecht put it, "Hinduism holds that the world is really 'Brahman in disguise'—all matter, especially biological and human life, is merely a temporary, illusory manifestation of this universal spirit."[28]

The big problem for human beings, according to Hinduism, is that they are ignorant of their divine nature. People have forgotten that they are extended from Brahman. "Humans have a false knowledge (*maya*) when they believe that this life and our separation from Brahman are real."[29] They have mistakenly attached themselves to the desires of their separate selves (or *egos*).

The Upanishads teach that the basic problem of human beings is ignorance (*avidya*) of their plight, and only when people realize this ignorance through enlightenment and come to true knowledge will they find release.[30] When true knowledge of the illusion of life is realized through many lifetimes (via reincarnation), a person can be freed from the bondage of life and achieve unity with the Brahman. "The Upanishads teach that all men can achieve the divine state if they strive for it. The individual personality is denied, being considered part of the world of illusion, or *maya*, and deification involves the shedding of *maya*, the merging and obliteration of the self in the sea of the One Reality, God."[31] As my late colleague Walter Martin put it, "As long as the individual appears to exist within *maya*, he is subject to such laws [of karma and reincarnation]. When he awakens [after many lifetimes] to the fact that all is one, he is no longer bound to them and they cease to have any relative reality."[32]

In view of the above, it seems patently obvious that Christians and Hindus are not worshiping the same God, and cannot—indeed, *must not*—worship together in unity under one roof with each other. If the Christian view of God is correct—a view that involves a personal deity who created the entire universe out of nothing and is *eternally distinct* from the universe (Psalm 89:11; Isaiah 44:24; Ephesians 3:9; Revelation 4:11)—then the Hindu view of God (that *all is Brahman*) is necessarily *incorrect* since it flatly contradicts the Christian view.

This same point may be made in regard to the god of Islam. According to the Koran, Allah is the one true God. The term "Allah" is probably derived from *al illah*, which means "the god." Allah is an absolute unity; he can have no son and no partner. To say God could have a son, Muslims believe, is blasphemous, implying some kind of sexual generation. Allah is *not* viewed as "the Father" (Surahs 19:88-92; 112:3). He is viewed as a transcendent being and seems more characterized by judgment, not grace; by power, not mercy (Surahs 6:142; 7:31).[33] By contrast, the Christian view is that God is a *Trinity*, that the first person of this Trinity is a "Father," that this Father has an eternal Son named Jesus (the second person of the Trinity), that God is both transcendent *and* immanent, and that while God is characterized by judgment and power, he is also characterized by grace and mercy. The Christian view of God is incompatible with the Muslim view.

___ *Ask...* ___

- Are you aware that Hinduism espouses millions of gods who are viewed as extensions of an all-permeating deity known as Brahman?

- Did you know that in Hindu thought, every part of the universe shares the divine nature and is viewed as a manifestation of Brahman?·

- If human beings are viewed as "one" with Brahman, doesn't that imply that we are divine?

- Does this sound like a biblical description of God? Doesn't the Bible portray God as separate from His creation? (Be ready to share such verses as Genesis 1:1; Numbers 23:19; Psalm 33:9; 148:5; Ecclesiastes 5:2; Isaiah 45:18; Nehemiah 9:6; and Hebrews 11:3.)

- Did you know that according to Islam, there is one god named Allah, and Allah cannot have a son?

- Since both Hinduism and Islam portray radically different ideas about God than does Christianity, isn't it clear that these religions are not talking about the same God at all?

- Is it fair to say, then, that if the Christian view of God is right, then the Hindu and Islamic views are not? Please explain.

Let this be clear: Scripture emphatically declares that there is *only one true God*. In Isaiah 44:8, God asks, "Is there any God besides me? No, there is no other Rock; I know not one." In Isaiah 43:10, God affirms: "Before me no god was formed, nor will there be one after me." That there is only one God is the consistent testimony of Scripture (John 5:44; 17:3; Romans 3:29,30; 16:27; 1 Corinthians 8:4; Galatians 3:20; Ephesians 4:6; 1 Thessalonians 1:9; 1 Timothy 1:17; 2:5; James 2:19; 1 John 5:20; Jude 25). This God is *Yahweh* (Exodus 3:14,15), which translates as LORD, *not* Allah and *not* Brahman.

1 CORINTHIANS 13:12: *Are Different Views of God Due to Limited Understanding?*

Masonic View: Some Masons argue that we simply do not know everything about God, and this accounts for the *seemingly* different ideas that the various religions have about God. After all, 1 Corinthians 13:12 tells us: "Now we see but a poor reflection as in a mirror; then we shall see face to face. Now I know in part; then I shall know fully, even as I am fully known."

Building on this biblical passage, Mason Christopher Haffner wrote in his book *Workman Unashamed: The Testimony of a Christian Freemason*:

> Now imagine me standing in a lodge with my head bowed in prayer between Brother Mohammed Bokhary and Brother Arjun Melwani. To neither of them is the Great Architect of the Universe perceived as the Holy Trinity. To Brother Bokhary He has been revealed as Allah; to Brother Melwani He is probably perceived as Vishnu. Since I believe that there is only one God, I am confronted with three possibilities: They are praying to the Devil whilst I am praying to God; They are praying to nothing, as their gods do not exist; They are praying to the same God as I, yet their understanding of His nature is partly incomplete (as indeed is mine—1 Corinthians 13:12). It is without hesitation that I accept the third possibility.[34]

Biblical View: The fallacy of this viewpoint is more than evident in the fact that even though finite human beings have limited knowledge, we have been given *enough* understanding from God (through Scripture) to know the difference between the true God and false gods and idols. If this were not true, then the Bible would not go to such great lengths to warn us about false gods and the false prophets that speak about them. In the New Testament, Jesus warned His disciples to beware of false prophets who "come...in sheep's clothing, but inwardly they are ferocious wolves" (Matthew 7:15). When speaking of the signs of the times and the end of the age, He also said, "Many false prophets will appear and deceive many people....For false Christs and false prophets will appear and perform great signs and miracles, to deceive even the elect"—if that were possible (Matthew 24:11,24). A false prophet is characterized in Deuteronomy 13:2 as one who comes to the people and says, "'Let us follow other gods' (gods you have not known) 'and let us worship them.'"

While it is true that human beings are finite and are limited in understanding, we have nevertheless been given more than enough special revelation from God in the pages of the Bible to discern the true from the false (see Acts 17:11; 1 Thessalonians 5:21). If this were not true, then God's command not to worship other gods or idols would not make sense (see Exodus 20:3-6).

___ Ask... ___

- One of the Ten Commandments warns us not to worship false gods or idols, right? (Be ready to share Exodus 20:3-6.)

- And didn't Jesus warn us about false prophets who speak of false gods? (Be ready to share Matthew 24:11,24.)

- Would these verses make sense if we were not given sufficient information to distinguish the true God from false gods?

- Even though human beings are limited in their knowledge, doesn't the Bible assume that even our finite understanding of God is enough to make us responsible for avoiding false deities?

God Is Knowable

Contrary to the implication in Masonry that God is somewhat distant and unknowable, the Bible reveals that God is a personal being with whom intimate, loving, personal relationships can be established and enjoyed. A person is a conscious being—one who thinks, feels, purposes, and carries these purposes into action. A person engages in *active* relationships with others. We can talk to a person and get a response. We can share feelings and ideas. We can argue with him, love him, and even hate him if we so choose. Surely by this definition God must be understood as a person who can be known. After all, God is a conscious being who thinks, feels, purposes, and carries these purposes into action. He engages in relationships with others. We can talk to God and get a response from Him.

The biblical picture of God is that of a loving, personal Father to whom believers cry, "Abba" (Romans 8:15). ("Abba" is an Aramaic term of great intimacy, loosely meaning "daddy.")

Jesus often spoke of God as a loving Father. Indeed, God is the "Father of compassion" of all believers (2 Corinthians 1:3). He is often portrayed in Scripture as lovingly responding to the personal requests of His people. (See, for example, Exodus 3:7,8; Job 34:28; Psalm 81:10; 91:14,15; 2 Corinthians 1:3,4; and Philippians 4:6,7.)

___ *Ask...* ___

- Since God can be addressed by believers as "Abba" (*daddy*), and is the "Father of compassion," do you think the Masonic portrayal of God accurately reflects the biblical reality that we can enjoy an intimate, loving, personal relationship with Him?

- Does the more intimate God of the Bible seem more appealing to you than the distant Masonic deity? (Be ready to share verses such as Job 34:28; Psalm 81:10; 91:14,15; 2 Corinthians 1:3,4; and Philippians 4:6,7.)

GENESIS 1:26-28: *Support for the Fatherhood of God*

Masonic View: In Genesis 1:26-28 we read:

> Then God said, "Let us make man in our image, in our likeness, and let them rule over the fish of

the sea and the birds of the air, over the livestock, over all the earth, and over all the creatures that move along the ground." So God created man in his own image, in the image of God he created him; male and female he created them. God blessed them and said to them, "Be fruitful and increase in number; fill the earth and subdue it. Rule over the fish of the sea and the birds of the air and over every living creature that moves on the ground."

Masons sometimes point to this passage in support of their teaching on the universal fatherhood of God. "Masonry teaches that man is the offspring of God by creation, that God made mankind of one blood, and that God's fatherly love for man finds its greatest expression in his redemptive plan for fallen humanity."[35]

Biblical View: It is true in one sense that God is the father of all human beings by virtue of the fact that He is our creator. This is illustrated for us in Acts 17:24-28:

The God who made the world and everything in it is the Lord of heaven and earth and does not live in temples built by hands. And he is not served by human hands, as if he needed any-thing, because he himself gives all men life and breath and everything else. From one man he made every nation of men, that they should inhabit the whole earth; and he determined the times set for them and the exact places where they should live. God did this so that men would seek him and perhaps reach out for him and find him, though he is not far from each one of us. "For in him we live and move and have our being." As some of your own poets have said, "We are his offspring."

God in this sense is the divine "parent" of all creation.

Yet, it is critical to understand that from a biblical perspective there is a much more *specific* aspect of the fatherhood of God that relates *only* to those who become a part of His "forever family" by trusting in Christ for salvation. John 1:12,13 tells us, "To all who received him [*Jesus*], to those who believed in his name, he gave the right to become children of God—children born not of natural descent, nor of human decision or a husband's will, but born of God." Galatians 3:26 tells us, "You are all sons of God through faith in Christ Jesus." In view of such verses, one scholar commented that "in this relation of nearness and privilege to the Father in the kingdom of His Son (Colossians 1:13), believers are 'sons of God' in a sense true of no others."[36] Clearly, there is no universal Fatherhood of God in the sense of everyone being in God's eternal family, for entrance into *this* family is restricted—it comes *only* by faith in Christ (see John 3:16; Acts 16:31).

Not only is God *not* everyone's spiritual "Father," some people actually have the devil as their spiritual "father." Jesus said to some Jews who wanted to kill Him: "You belong to your father, the devil, and you want to carry out your father's desire. He was a murderer from the beginning, not holding to the truth, for there is no truth in him. When he lies, he speaks his native language, for he is a liar and the father of lies" (John 8:44). John 8:47 indicates that if we do not do as God commands, we are not God's children. On a practical level, this means that if Masons do not do as God commands, such as trusting in Christ alone for salvation (John 3:16,17), they are not truly God's spiritual children and God is not truly their spiritual Father. *There is only one way into God's eternal family—and His name is Jesus Christ* (see John 14:16; Acts 4:12; 1 Timothy 2:15)!

All this relates to the New Testament teaching that believers are *adopted* into God's forever family. By faith in Christ, believers literally become "sons of God" (Romans 8:14). The believers have received the "spirit of sonship" (verse 15). The word *sonship* literally means "placing as a son." This is significant, for in New

Testament times an adopted son enjoyed all the rights and privileges of a natural-born son. Because of this new relationship with God, believers are called "heirs of God" and "co-heirs with Christ" (verse 17). In a typical family, each child receives a share in their parents' estate. This makes each child an "heir"; the children as a group are "co-heirs." As God's children we are "heirs," and collectively we are "co-heirs" with Christ (see Galatians 4:7).

Believers inherit "every spiritual blessing in Christ" (Ephesians 1:3). And upon entering glory, believers will inherit all the riches of God's glorious kingdom (1 Corinthians 3:21-23).

_____ *Ask...* _____

- Will you please read aloud from John 1:12,13? Galatians 3:26?

- Can you see from these verses that there is a *specific* aspect of the fatherhood of God that relates *only* to those who become a part of His "forever family" by trusting in Christ for salvation?

- Are you a member of God's forever family, as defined in these verses?

God Is Not Jabulon

The Masonic claim that God's true name is *Jabulon* is atrocious and highly offensive. As noted earlier, this word is said to be derived from "Ja" (for Jehovah), joined with "Bel" or "Bul" (for Baal), and "On" (for Osiris). The attempt to relate the God of the Bible with Baal is nothing less than blasphemy. Baal worship is perhaps the epitome of evil idol worship in the ancient world, and involved such things as ritual prostitution (Judges 2:17; Hosea 4:12-14), self-mutilation (1 Kings 18:28), and the sacrificing (ritual murder) of little children (Jeremiah 19:4,5). In

Judges 3:7, we read, "The Israelites did evil in the eyes of the LORD; they forgot the LORD their God and served the Baals and the Asherahs." From this, we can easily surmise that the Masonic view that God is Jabulon is detestable to the Lord.

It is interesting to note that the one sin for which God judged the people of Israel more severely than any other was that of participating in heathen religions (see, for example, Exodus 20:4-6; Leviticus 19:4; 26:1; Deuteronomy 4:15-19). Again and again the Bible implies and states that God hates, despises, and utterly rejects anything associated with heathen religions and practices. Those who follow such idolatry are not regarded as groping their way to God but rather as following the ways of darkness. This means that people today who make reference to God as Jabulon, thus indicating their view that Jehovah and Baal are the same deity, have turned their backs on the true God.

It is highly revealing that not all Masons go along with the idea of calling God *Jabulon*. Masonic leader Albert Pike wrote; "No man or body of men can make me accept as a sacred word, as a symbol of the infinite and eternal Godhead, a mongrel word, in part composed of the name of an accursed and beastly heathen God, whose name has been for more than 2000 years an appellation of the devil."[37] Though I disagree with most of what Pike believed as a Mason, he is certainly right in this comment.

___ *Ask...* ___

- Did you know that in the Royal Arch degree, it is taught that God's true name is *Jabulon*, which is a compound word derived from "Ja" (for Jehovah), joined with "Bel" or "Bul" (for Baal, the ancient Canaanite God), and "On" (for Osiris, the ancient Egyptian mystery god)?

- Were you aware that according to the Bible, Baal worship was the epitome of evil idol worship in the ancient world—and involved such things as ritual prostitution

(Judges 2:17; Hosea 4:12-14), self-mutilation (1 Kings 18:28), and the sacrificing and ritual murder of little children (Jeremiah 19:4,5)?

- Should Christians be part of an organization that relates the God of the Bible with Baal?

The Biblical Names of God

Even though the names the different religions use for God actually point to false gods, it is important to note that the Christian Bible does in fact use a variety of names for the one true God. In the ancient world, a name was not a mere label as it is today. Names revealed certain characteristics about people. Knowing a person's name amounted to knowing his essence. We learn much about God from the names ascribed to Him in the Bible. These names are not man-made; God used these names to describe Himself. They are *characteristic* names, each one making known something new about Him. Here are just a few of the Hebrew names used of God in Scripture.

God Is Yahweh

In the original Hebrew, the name *Yahweh* occurs over 5,300 times in the Old Testament. It is connected with the Hebrew verb "to be." We first learn of this name in Exodus 3, where Moses asked God by what name He should be called. God replied to him, "I AM WHO I AM....Thus you shall say to the sons of Israel, 'I AM has sent me to you'" (verse 14 NASB).

"I AM" may seem like an odd name to the modern ear, but Moses understood in some measure what God was saying to him. The name clearly conveys the idea of eternal self-existence. Yahweh never came into being at a point in time, for He has always existed. He was never born; He will never die. He does not grow older, for He is beyond the realm of time. To know Yahweh is to know the Eternal One. The word *Yahweh* is usually translated as LORD throughout the Old Testament.

God Is Yahweh-Nissi

Yahweh-Nissi means "the Lord Our Banner" (*Yahweh* = "Lord," *Nissi* = "our banner"). Israel could not defeat her enemies in her own strength. She was weak in the face of her mighty foes. But the battles were to be the Lord's because He was Israel's banner, Israel's source of victory (Exodus 17:15). This name associates God with warfare on behalf of His people. God wants us to know that He is the one who fights our battles.

Elohim

Elohim is a common name for God in the Old Testament (used about 2,570 times), and it literally means "strong one." Its plural ending (*im* in Hebrew) indicates fullness of power. Elohim is portrayed as the powerful and sovereign governor of the universe, ruling over the affairs of humankind. As related to God's sovereignty, the word Elohim is used to describe Him as the "God of all the earth" (Isaiah 54:5), the "God of all flesh" (Jeremiah 32:27 NASB), the "God of heaven" (Nehemiah 2:4), and the "God of gods and Lord of lords" (Deuteronomy 10:17).

God Is El Shaddai

While "El" in Hebrew refers to "Mighty God," "Shaddai" qualifies this meaning and adds something to it (Genesis 17:1-20). Many scholars believe "Shaddai" is derived from a root word that refers to a mother's breast. This name, then, indicates not only that God is a Mighty God, but that He is full of compassion, grace, and mercy, just like a mother. This is a tender name of God. Our Mighty God and Creator is to His children what a loving mother is to her dependent infant. He sustains us and nurtures us.

God Is Lord of Hosts

This title reveals God as the sovereign commander of a great heavenly army of angels (Psalm 89:6,8). These heavenly angels—headed by God, the Lord of hosts—is commanded by God to watch over us (Psalm 91:11,12).

There are many other names used of God in Scripture. For example, God is our *rock* (Deuteronomy 32:4-31), a name that points to God's strength and power. God is our *fortress* (Psalm 18:2), a name that speaks of the protection God provides us. God is our *shield* (Genesis 15:1), a name that points to God as our daily defense. God is also our *strength* (1 Samuel 15:29 KJV), a name that points to how God infuses us with His power so we can face any circumstance.

While Masonry wrongly believes that the various names used of God in different religions (like Hinduism and Islam) refer to the same God as that of Christianity, the truth is that the deities of Hinduism and Islam are false deities. Yet the one true God of the Bible is known by a variety of names, which are revealed *by God Himself* in the Bible, and these names reveal key characteristics of God.

The Perfections of God

Critic Walton Hannah notes that in Freemasonry, "God is presented and titled in such terms that people of all reputable faiths may agree in a lowest-common-denominator deity shorn of all attributes distinctive of any single system of belief."[38] Contrary to the Masonic view, Scripture reveals that we can know a great deal about God—including some very specific attributes, or perfections, of God. It is important to have a good grasp of these characteristics so that in your discussions with Masons you can share what God is really like. Further, an understanding of what the Bible says about these attributes will help you distinguish the true God from the false deities Masons sometimes make reference to.

God Is Eternal

God, as an eternal being, has always existed. He never came into being at a point in time. He is beyond time altogether. God is the King eternal (1 Timothy 1:17), who alone is immortal (6:16). God is the "Alpha and Omega" (Revelation 1:8) and is the "first and the last" (see Isaiah 44:6; 48:12). God exists "from eternity" (Isaiah 43:13 NASB), and "from everlasting to everlasting"

(Psalm 90:2). He lives forever from eternal ages past (Psalm 41:13; 102:12,27; Isaiah 57:15).

God Is Love

God is not just characterized by love. He is the very personification of love (1 John 4:8). Love virtually permeates His being. And God's love is not dependent upon the lovability of the object (human beings). God loves us despite the fact that we are fallen in sin (John 3:16). (God loves the *sinner*, though He hates the *sin*.) God abounds in love (Psalm 86:5). The Earth is said to be full of His love (Psalm 33:5). His love endures forever (1 Chronicles 16:34; Psalm 106:1) and is unfailing (Psalm 130:7; Isaiah 54:10).

God Is Everywhere-Present

The Scriptures tell us that God is everywhere-present. In Psalm 139:7,8 the psalmist muses: "Where can I go from your Spirit? Where can I flee from your presence? If I go up to the heavens, you are there; if I make my bed in the depths, you are there." There is nowhere one can go where God is not. Even the highest heaven cannot contain God (1 Kings 8:27; 2 Chronicles 2:6). His presence includes—but is not limited to—heaven and earth (Psalm 113:4-6; Isaiah 66:1; Jeremiah 23:23,24).

God Is All-Knowing

Because God is all-knowing, He does not learn. He knows all things, both actual and possible. He knows all things *past* (Isaiah 41:22), *present* (Hebrews 4:13), and *future* (Isaiah 46:10). And because He knows all things, there can be no increase or decrease in His knowledge. Psalm 147:5 affirms that God's "understanding has no limit." God's knowledge is *infinite* (Psalm 33:13-15; 139:11,12; 147:5; Proverbs 15:3; Isaiah 40:14; 46:10; Acts 15:17,18; 1 John 3:20; Hebrews 4:13).

God Is All-Powerful

God is portrayed in Scripture as being omnipotent or all-powerful. He has the power to do all that He desires and wills.

Some 56 times, Scripture declares that God is *almighty* (for example, Revelation 19:6). God is abundant in strength (Psalm 147:5) and has incomparably great power (2 Chronicles 20:6; Ephesians 1:19-21). No one can hold back God's hand (Daniel 4:35). No one can reverse God (Isaiah 43:13), and no one can thwart Him (Isaiah 14:27). Nothing is impossible with God (Matthew 19:26; Mark 10:27; Luke 1:37), and nothing is too difficult for Him (Genesis 18:14; Jeremiah 32:17,27). The Almighty reigns (Revelation 19:6).

God Is Sovereign

God is sovereign in the sense that He rules the universe, controls all things, and is Lord over all (see Ephesians 1:20-22). There is nothing that can happen in this universe that is beyond the reach of His control. All forms of existence are within the scope of His absolute dominion. Psalm 50:1 makes reference to God as the Mighty One who "speaks and summons the earth from the rising of the sun to the place where it sets." Psalm 66:7 affirms that "he rules forever by his power." We are assured in Psalm 93:1 that "the Lord reigns" and "is armed with strength." He is sovereign over all things (Psalm 103:19). Isaiah 40:15 tells us that by comparison, "surely the nations are like a drop in a bucket; they are regarded as dust on the scales; he weighs the islands as though they were fine dust." Indeed, "before him all the nations are as nothing" (Isaiah 40:17). No one can stop God (Job 9:12), and no one can resist Him (Romans 9:19). God is said to be "the blessed and only Ruler, the King of kings and Lord of lords" (1 Timothy 6:15). He is truly sovereign.

God Is Holy

God's holiness means not just that He is entirely separate from all evil but also that He is absolutely righteous (Leviticus 19:2). He is pure in every way. God is separate from all that is morally imperfect. "God is light; in him is no darkness" (1 John 1:5). He is "majestic in holiness" (Exodus 15:11). No one is holy like the

Lord (1 Samuel 2:2). The Scriptures lay great stress upon God's holiness (Psalm 71:22; 99:9; 111:9; Isaiah 6:3; Habakkuk 1:12; Revelation 15:4).

God Is Just

That God is just means that He carries out His righteous standards justly and with equity. There is never any partiality or unfairness in God's dealings with people (Zephaniah 3:5; Romans 3:25,26). God is perfectly equitable. He will never pervert justice (Job 34:12). Justice is the very foundation of His throne (Psalm 89:14). God's justness is proclaimed emphatically in both the Old and New Testaments (see, for example, Genesis 18:25; Psalm 11:7; John 17:25; Hebrews 6:10).

These and other attributes revealed about God from the pages of the Bible show the falsehood of the Masonic view that God is essentially unknowable. For those who seek a definitive exposition on the knowability of God and His magnificent attributes, I suggest you pick up a copy of J. I. Packer's classic book, *Knowing God*.

God Is a Trinity

Contrary to the Masonic avoidance of the doctrine of the Trinity, God most certainly *is* a Trinity by nature. To speak of God in any way other than being a Trinity promotes a false view of God. C.S. Lewis once said that God Himself has revealed to us how we are to think of Him, and God Himself has revealed that He is a Trinity. For us to deny this doctrine or refuse to talk about it goes against the way the one true God of Scripture has revealed Himself. Christians who attend a Masonic Lodge and go along with denying or refusing to speak about the doctrine of the Trinity reveal clear evidence of their lack of commitment to the holy Scriptures. In fact, for them to do this is, in my view, apostasy.

Biblically, the doctrine of the Trinity is based on three clear lines of evidence: 1) there is only one true God; 2) there are three persons who are God; and 3) there is three-in-oneness in the Godhead.

Evidence for One God

The fact that there is only one true God is the consistent testimony of Scripture from Genesis to Revelation. God positively affirmed through Isaiah the prophet: "This is what the LORD says—Israel's King and Redeemer, the LORD Almighty: I am the first and I am the last; apart from me there is no God" (Isaiah 44:6). God also said, "I am God, and there is no other; I am God, and there is none like me" (46:9). These, and a multitude of other verses, make it clear that there is one—and only one—God (see also John 5:44; 17:3; Romans 3:29,30; 16:27; 1 Corinthians 8:4; Galatians 3:20; Ephesians 4:6; 1 Timothy 2:5; James 2:19).

Three Persons Who Are God

Though Scripture indicates there is only one God, in the unfolding of God's revelation to humankind it also becomes clear that there are three distinct persons who are called God in Scripture.

- *The Father Is God:* Peter refers to the saints "who have been chosen according to the foreknowledge of God the Father" (1 Peter 1:2).
- *Jesus Is God:* When Jesus made a postresurrection appearance to doubting Thomas, Thomas said: "My Lord and my God" (John 20:28). The Father said of the Son, "Your throne, O God, will last for ever and ever, and righteousness will be the scepter of your kingdom" (Hebrews 1:8).
- *The Holy Spirit Is God:* In Acts 5:3,4, we are told that lying to the Holy Spirit is equivalent to lying to God.

Moreover, each of the three persons on different occasions is seen to possess the attributes of deity. For example, all three are said to be *omnipresent:* the Father (Matthew 19:26), the Son (Matthew 28:18), and the Holy Spirit (Psalm 139:7). All three are *omniscient:* the Father (Romans 11:33), the Son (Matthew 9:4), and the Holy Spirit (1 Corinthians 2:10). All three are *omnipotent:* the Father (1 Peter 1:5), the Son (Matthew 28:18), and the Holy Spirit (Romans 15:19). Furthermore, *holiness* is ascribed to each person: the Father (Revelation 15:4), the Son (Acts 3:14), and the Holy Spirit (John 16:7–14). *Eternity* is ascribed to each person: the Father (Psalm 90:2), the Son (Micah 5:2; John 1:2; Revelation 1:8,17), and the Holy Spirit (Hebrews 9:14). And each of the three is individually described as *the truth:* the Father (John 7:28), the Son (Revelation 3:7), and the Holy Spirit (1 John 5:6).

Three-in-Oneness in the Godhead

In the New American Standard Bible, Matthew 28:19 reads: "Go therefore and make disciples of all the nations, baptizing them in the name of *the* Father and *the* Son and *the* Holy Spirit" (emphasis added). It is highly revealing that the word *name* in this verse is singular in the Greek, indicating that there is one God, but three distinct persons within the Godhead—*the* Father, *the* Son, and *the* Holy Spirit. Theologian Robert Reymond draws our attention to the importance of this verse for the doctrine of the Trinity:

> Jesus does not say, (1) "into the names [plural] of the Father and of the Son and of the Holy Spirit," or what is its virtual equivalent, (2) "into the name of the Father, and into the name of the Son, and into the name of the Holy Spirit," as if we had to deal with three separate Beings. Nor does He say, (3) "into the name of the Father, Son, and Holy Spirit," (omitting the three recurring articles), as if "the Father, Son, and Holy Ghost" might be taken as merely three designations of a single person. What He does say is this: (4) "into the name [singular] of *the* Father, and of *the* Son, and of *the* Holy Spirit," first asserting the unity of

the three by combining them all within the
bounds of the single Name, and then throwing
into emphasis the distinctness of each by intro-
ducing them in turn with the repeated article.[39]

In view of such facts, the Masons' refusal to refer to God as a
Trinity goes against the biblical portrayal of the one true God.
*Masons are going against the way God has revealed His nature
to be.* What this ultimately means is that the Masonic portrayal of
God is a false one.

___ Ask... ___

*Ask these questions after sharing the above defense of the
doctrine of the Trinity.*

• Would you agree that God has revealed to us how we are
  to think of Him?

• Since, according to the Bible, God has revealed Himself
  to be a Trinity, do you think it is a human prerogative to
  refuse to speak of Him according to how He has defined
  Himself?

• How do you think God looks upon such things?

Masons Are Guilty of Blasphemy

I could not close this chapter without noting that Masons are,
in some of their rituals, guilty of blasphemy—whether they are
aware of it or not. Blasphemy specifically involves irreverence
toward God and often entails the act of claiming for human beings
the attributes or prerogatives of deity. An example would be how,
in the 17th degree of the Scottish Rite, the "All-Puissant" opens
the "seven seals" in a Masonic ritual.[40] Yet the opening of the

"seven seals" is the prerogative of Christ alone, according to Scripture. We read in Revelation 5:1-5:

> Then I saw in the right hand of him who sat on the throne a scroll with writing on both sides and sealed with seven seals. And I saw a mighty angel proclaiming in a loud voice, "Who is worthy to break the seals and open the scroll?" But no one in heaven or on earth or under the earth could open the scroll or even look inside it. I wept and wept because no one was found who was worthy to open the scroll or look inside. Then one of the elders said to me, "Do not weep! See, the Lion of the tribe of Judah, the Root of David, has triumphed. He is able to open the scroll and its seven seals."

Blasphemy is thus being committed in the Masonic ritual inasmuch as a Mason (in the role of the "All-Puissant") claims the prerogative of doing something attributable *only* to Jesus Christ.

Masons also commit blasphemy when they use the holy names of God as common passwords or secret words. In the 14th degree of the Scottish Rite, for example, both *Jehovah* and *Adonai* are used as secret words. Likewise, in the 27th degree of the Scottish Rite, *Immanuel* is used as a mere password.[41] To so casually use such holy names of God as secret words or passwords shows great disrespect. Indeed, in Exodus 20:7 we read God's own commandment, "You shall not misuse the name of the LORD your God, for the LORD will not hold anyone guiltless who misuses his name."

_____ *Ask...* _____

- Do you understand that showing irreverence toward the God of the Bible and claiming the attributes of deity is a serious desecration of God's name?

- When the "All-Puissant" opens the "seven seals" in a Masonic ritual, does it bother you that Revelation 5:1-5 claims this as a prerogative of *Christ alone in heaven?* (Be ready to read aloud from Revelation 5:1-5.)

- When the names *Jehovah* and *Adonai* are used as secret words or passwords in the 27th degree of the Scottish Rite, how is this *not* a violation of God's commandment in Exodus 20:7: "You shall not misuse the name of the LORD your God, for the LORD will not hold anyone guiltless who misuses his name"?

Masons Are Also Guilty of Idolatry

One scholar has noted that idolatry "does not consist in bodily kneeling before a material image; it consists in worshiping God under any other conception of him than that which is set before us in the gospels....Idolatry is indeed a deadly thing."[42] By this definition, there can be no doubt that Freemasonry engages in idolatry, for it sets forth a conception of God other than that found in the gospel (it is a view that associates the God of the Bible with the false deities of Islam and Hinduism, as well as Baal worship). Truly, Masonic idolatry is deadly since eternal salvation is found *only* in the one true God of the Bible.

8

Masonry's Connection to Paganism and the Mystery Religions

As I researched this book, I daily came across references in Masonic literature to various Egyptian deities affiliated with one or another of the ancient mystery religions. Various Masonic authorities have written a great deal about how much the Masonic ritual is either rooted in or has borrowed from some of these ancient rites. One noteworthy example is American Mason Albert Mackey, who, in his *Encyclopedia of Freemasonry*, wrote:

> Egypt has always been considered as the birthplace of the mysteries. It was there that the ceremonies of initiation were first established. It was there that truth was first unveiled in allegory, and the dogmas of religion were first imparted under symbolic forms....To Egypt, therefore, Masons have always looked with peculiar interest as the cradle of that mysterious

science of symbolism whose peculiar modes of teaching they alone, of all modern institutions, have preserved to the present day....The first degree, as we may term it, of Egyptian initiation was that into the mysteries of *Isis*....The mysteries of *Serapis* constituted the second degree of the Egyptian initiation....The mysteries of *Osiris*...were the consummation of the Egyptian system.[1]

These three Egyptian deities—*Isis*, *Serapis*, and *Osiris*—are mentioned regularly in Masonic literature.[2] Other Egyptian deities, such as the great sun god *Re*, *Apis* (the sacred bull god), *Thoth*, *Phtha*, *Hermes*, *Orpheus*, and *Horus*, among many others, are also regularly cited.[3] Albert Pike makes mention of "the 12 great gods of Egypt."[4] Not surprisingly, he suggests that Masonry is "a successor of the mysteries," and is "identical with the ancient mysteries."[5] Vindex affirms that "Freemasons today will recognize an affinity with these ancient mysteries."[6] Freemasonry is "the heir and legitimate successor of the ancient mysteries."[7] In the *Holy Bible—Masonic Edition*, we read, "It is admitted that Masonry is descended from the ancient mysteries."[8]

Though my historical research indicates that there is no *direct historical lineage* that can be traced from the ancient mystery religions to the Freemasonry of today, it does seem clear that modern Masonry has borrowed some of its ideas and rituals from these old religions. As John Ankerberg and John Weldon put it, "The ancient pagan mystery religions practiced in Egypt, Asia Minor, and later in Greece appear to have formed the religious basis of much Masonic teaching, symbol, and ritual, although no direct link can be established."[9] Martin Wagner argues that "Freemasonry is the religion of the mysteries translated into a new and more modern ceremonial....It is couched in terms of operative [stone craft] Masonry and explained by legendary narratives of King Solomon and his architect. But the religion is the same. That has remained unchanged. The form and manner of expressing it have changed."[10]

These mystery religions, like modern Freemasonry, stressed oaths of secrecy, secret rites of initiation, brotherhood, religious quest, and immortality. They worshiped pagan deities, promoted occultism of various sorts, and engaged in a variety of bizarre and sometimes abhorrent rituals involving numerous deities.[11]

Researcher Ron Campbell notes that these ancient mysteries were of two kinds—the Lesser and the Greater. The Lesser Mysteries were always preparatory for the higher degrees. "An initiate into these Lesser Mysteries was called a Mystes, which comes from the Greek word meaning 'to shut the eyes.' As a Mystes, the candidate was considered blind; but when he was initiated into the Greater Mysteries, he was called an Epopt, or 'one who saw.'"[12] By various rites and ceremonies, the neophyte was led from darkness to light, from ignorance to knowledge and hope in the afterlife.[13]

_____REASONING FROM THE SCRIPTURES_____

An extremely important point that Christians must not miss is that Egypt's worship of such deities as Re, Apis, Isis, Osiris, Serapis, and others was going on during the time of Moses. Indeed, as will be demonstrated in what follows, the ten plagues inflicted on the Egyptians by God through the hand of Moses served as a judgment against these gods and the entire religious system of Egypt. Since that is the case, this ultimately means that *Freemasons, in their ritual, have borrowed heavily from a false religious system that was judged horrifically by the one true God of the Bible.*

In making my case, I begin with the recognition that Moses said to God, "Who among the gods is like you, O LORD? Who is like you—majestic in holiness, awesome in glory, working wonders?" (Exodus 15:11). One must ask why Moses, especially in view of the polytheism he was exposed to as a child in Egypt, gave his sole allegiance to the God of the Bible above all the other gods. The Bible, of course, gives us the answer: Moses had a "close encounter" with the one true God. He experienced the one with whom there is no rival!

A key emphasis throughout the first five books of the Bible is that the one true God of the Bible, whose name is *Yahweh*, is incomparable. I've discussed this aspect of God in varying degrees of detail in some of my previous books (see *Miracles Around Us* for the fullest treatment[14])—but it demands at least a brief treatment here precisely because Masons often appeal to false Egyptian deities and the mystery religions in support of their own rituals. The material in this chapter is presented with a view to helping you demonstrate to a Mason the folly of such a practice. *Masons desperately need to see that the God of the Bible has no rival, and the mystery religions they cite in support of their ritual are "dead in the water" before the one true God.*

Demonstrating Incomparability

Moses expressed the incomparability of Yahweh in two different ways, the most common being by *negation*. This was usually couched in terms like, "There is no one like the LORD [Yahweh] our God" (Exodus 8:10; see also 9:14). Having been exposed to all the gods of Egypt during his childhood, Moses was surely qualified to make such judgments, especially after experiencing Yahweh's superior power as miraculously manifested in the beginning of the Exodus account (and later, of course).

A second way Moses expressed the incomparability of Yahweh was by using rhetorical questions. He often asked, "Who among the gods is like you, O LORD?" (Exodus 15:11). The implied answer is, "No one in all the universe."

Even to the present day, scholars are unsure about the total number of gods the Egyptians worshiped. Most lists contain somewhere in the neighborhood of 80 deities.[15] The dedication of the Egyptians to their gods is evident even to the casual observer as he tours modern Egypt. Beautiful temples honoring different gods fill the landscape. The ancient Egyptians took their many gods seriously.

In Egyptian religion, the god at the very top of the totem pole was the sun god, *Re*. Next in line was the Pharaoh of Egypt, who was considered to be the son of Re.[16] Inasmuch as Re was considered superior to all other gods, his son—the Pharaoh—was also considered to possess unmatched power as a god. This adds a whole new dimension to the Exodus account. It is as if a contest occurs between the true God on the one side and the false gods of Egypt's mystery religions on the other side (see Numbers 33:4).

As the Exodus account makes clear, Pharaoh reacted to the various displays of Yahweh's incomparability (as manifested in the ten plagues) by hardening his heart against Yahweh. He was, no doubt, stunned in disbelief that a "foreign.God" could come into his territory, make shambles of all the gods of his land, and make him (the mighty son of Re!) appear impotent before his own people. Furthermore, the representatives of this "foreign God" (Moses and Aaron) were both in the neighborhood of 80 years old when they encountered Pharaoh.[17] How dare the youthful Pharaoh's power and authority be challenged by a couple of old guys!

Perhaps one of the greatest passages of Scripture where the incomparability of Yahweh is seen is in Exodus 7–11. In this passage, Moses confronted Pharaoh on behalf of Yahweh regarding the redemption of His people. This meeting may have taken place at one of the temples associated with some aspect of the Nile's sacredness.[18] Pharaoh may even have been worshiping or performing a sacred rite in one of these temples when Moses approached.

Pharaoh wouldn't listen to Moses' message, so God inflicted ten plagues to get his attention. Scholars have noted that the number ten is the number of completeness, indicating God's thorough judgment of Egypt. These plagues likely took place over a nine-month period, beginning in August (when the Nile rises) and ending in April (the Passover month).

It all started this way. Moses and Aaron appeared before the Pharaoh of Egypt and said: "This is what the LORD, the God of Israel, says: 'Let my people go, so that they may hold a festival to me in the desert'" (Exodus 5:1). Pharaoh then asked the question of the century: "Who is the LORD [Yahweh], that I should obey him and let Israel go?" (verse 2). The Pharaoh was aware that he himself was the son of Re and considered to be a great god.[19] He also knew there were scores of gods who were worshiped in varying degrees by his people. But *who was Yahweh* that Pharaoh should obey Him? Pharaoh's question would soon be answered.

As we survey the ten plagues, keep in mind God's oft-repeated twofold purpose in sending these plagues on the Egyptians: *To the Jews*—"You will know that I am the LORD your God, who brought you out from under the yoke of the Egyptians" (Exodus 6:7). *In regard to the Egyptians*—"by this you will know that I am the LORD" (7:17); "...in order that you may know that I, the LORD, am in the midst of the land" (8:22); "...so that you may know that there is no one like Me in all the earth" (9:14 NASB); "...that you may know that the earth is the LORD'S" (9:29); "...and the Egyptians will know that I am the LORD" (14:4; 14:18). Obviously, the true God did not want His purpose to be misunderstood. He wanted it to be utterly clear that there is one, and only one, true God in the universe. He wanted it to be clear that the gods of the Egyptian mystery religions were *false gods*. Pharaoh asked the question, "Who is Yahweh?" Yahweh answered big-time![20]

The First Plague

Because Pharaoh had refused to let the Israelites go, Moses informed him that the water of the Nile would be turned into blood (Exodus 7:17). The streams, canals, ponds, and reservoirs that were connected to the Nile would also be turned to blood (verse 19).

Without question, this plague would have jolted every Egyptian in the land. This was because they venerated the Nile and all things associated with it. The river Nile was worshiped by the Egyptians under various names and symbols. It was considered the Father of life, and in view of the fact that its water was the lifeblood of Egypt, the blow must have been devastating.[21] So revered was the Nile by the Egyptians that hymns were written in its honor. One such hymn begins, "Hail thee, Oh Nile, that issues from the earth and comes to keep Egypt alive!"[22]

This judgment presents the beginning of Moses's demonstration of the true God's miraculous power over the many false gods of Egypt.[23] Besides being a judgment against Pharaoh (the godking), this blood plague also constituted a judgment against the Egyptian sacred river god, *Nilus*.[24] Since Nilus was worshiped by every Egyptian, this action struck the very heart of Egyptian religion.

Other false gods affected included *Khnum*, the "guardian of the Nile sources," and *Hapi*, "the spirit of the Nile." Furthermore, Osiris was believed to be a great god of the underworld whose bloodstream was the Nile river.[25] How ironic that God turned the Nile into *real* blood.

Not only did the fish in the river die, but "the river smelled so bad that the Egyptians could not drink its water" (Exodus 7:21). What a contrast this is to the Egyptian "Hymn to the Nile," which triumphantly proclaimed that the Nile River is "the bringer of good, rich in provisions, creator of all good, lord of majesty, sweet of fragrance"!

Still other gods that would have been affected in lesser degrees include *Neith* (a God who took great interest in the "Lates," the largest fish to be found in the Nile), and *Hathor* (protector of the "Chromis," a slightly smaller fish in the Nile).[26] To say the least, this plague convincingly demonstrated the total impotence of the gods of Egypt in the face of the incomparable Yahweh.

Apparently the Egyptian sorcerers were able to turn small quantities of water into blood (though it would have been more beneficial if they had been able to turn the blood back into water) (Exodus 7:22). The water they turned to blood was likely in small quantities taken from water holes dug in the ground since the water of the Nile had already been completely turned into blood (see verse 24). Pharaoh seemed satisfied with his magician's duplication, and his heart continued to harden against Moses and Aaron.

The Second Plague

The second plague resulted in a massive swarm of frogs (see Exodus 8:1-15). This plague is particularly significant in view of the Egyptian veneration of these creatures. The sacredness of the frog to the Egyptians is evident in the many amulets that have been discovered that are shaped like frogs. Bible scholar John Davis observes, "The common presence of the frog to the Egyptians was not something loathsome or to be abhorred. The frogs, to a large degree, represented fruitfulness, blessing, and the assurance of the harvest."[27]

So honored were frogs by the Egyptians that they were deified, and the Egyptians made a representation of the goddess *Heqt* in the image of a frog. Heqt was considered an emblem of fertility, and it was believed that she assisted Egyptian women in the bearing of children.[28] The Egyptian attitude is also evident in the fact that the intentional killing of a frog was punishable by death.[29] When this plague was inflicted on the Egyptians, it must have been abominable for them in that everywhere they stepped, they crushed a frog.

Not willing to be outdone, Pharaoh's magicians were called in to demonstrate that the gods of Egypt were equal to Yahweh. The magicians were able to bring up frogs upon the land (Exodus 8:7), but they proved incapable of removing the plague. Accordingly, Pharaoh requested Moses to "pray to the LORD" (Yahweh) that the plague would be removed. Pharaoh even promised that Israel would be permitted to leave Egypt and sacrifice to Yahweh.

To further demonstrate the incomparability of Yahweh, Moses asked Pharaoh to specifically name the time when he wanted the plague to end. Pharaoh asked Moses to have it removed the following day. Moses answered, "It will be as you say, so that you may know there is no one like the LORD [Yahweh] our God" (Exodus 8:10).

Why didn't Pharaoh ask for the plague to terminate immediately? More than likely, he hoped the frogs would go away on their own, under which circumstance he would be under no obligation to Moses or Yahweh. Nevertheless, despite the fact that there was relief and the plague ended the following day, Pharaoh again hardened his heart and refused to honor the promise he made to Moses. He could not bring himself to admit that Yahweh was indeed the incomparable One with no rival.

The Third Plague

The third plague resulted in a devastating swarm of gnats (Exodus 8:16-19). Such gnats were so small that they were nearly invisible to the human eye, but they delivered a very painful and irritating sting.[30] The bite of such an insect caused a sore to develop, and numerous bites would cover a person's skin with small sores.

It is not clear what specific deities this plague was directed against (with the exception of the god-king, Pharaoh). It is possible, however, that this plague was intended to humiliate the official priesthood in Egypt. Such priests were well-known for their physical purity and attention to bodily care. "They were circumcised, shaved the hair from their heads and bodies, washed frequently, and were dressed in beautiful linen robes."[31] Such gnats would have likely made their existence especially miserable. Furthermore, their prayers would have been made ineffective by their own personal impurity which resulted from the bites all over their bodies. This would have resulted in a paralysis of the entire Egyptian religious system.

Up to this point, the Egyptian magicians had been duplicating the miracles of Moses. But this is not the case with the present plague. As Bible scholar Alan Cole observes, "Here, for the first time, the sorcerers fail. At last they know that Moses and Aaron are not producing conjuring tricks, by sleight of hand, as presumably they themselves have been doing all along. They admit that this is God at work."[32] Upon the infliction of this plague, the Egyptians have begun to discover the incomparable nature of Yahweh.

The Fourth Plague

The fourth plague resulted in an overwhelming swarm of flies (Exodus 8:20-32). The bloodsucking "gadfly" or "dogfly" was abhorred in Egypt and may have been partially responsible for the great deal of blindness in the land.[33]

That this plague was supernatural is clear from the fact that the land of Goshen (where the Israelites were staying) was untouched by the swarm (Exodus 8:22). The plague was directed only against Pharaoh and the other false gods of Egypt.

Among the false gods this judgment was directed against was *Beelzebub*, the god of the flies.[34] This god was thought to have the power to prevent flies. But as has been true all along, Beelzebub was nowhere to be found.

Again, in view of the cleanliness which was necessary for proper Egyptian worship, the putrid conditions brought about by the unclean flies would have been a great hindrance to the idolatrous priests of Egypt. The plague likely brought religious worship in Egypt to another total standstill.

In view of Pharaoh's complete inability to cope with the situation, he called for Moses and Aaron and offered them the first of four compromises. He said he would allow them to sacrifice to Yahweh, but only on the condition that they would do it within the boundaries of Egypt (Exodus 8:25). This, of course, was not acceptable to Moses. Pharaoh then offered a second compromise in which he said he would allow them to go into the wilderness, assuming that they would not go very far (verse 28). Moses went along with this, but warned Pharaoh not to continue dealing deceitfully with the people of God. He then promised Pharaoh that the plague would end the following day.

However, once freed from the devastation of this plague, Pharaoh again hardened his heart against Yahweh and went back on his promise (Exodus 8:32). It seemed nearly impossible for this god-king to succumb to a foreign God, especially in view of the fact that all of Egypt was watching how their mighty leader was reacting to this outside invasion.

The Fifth Plague

The fifth plague resulted in many animals becoming diseased (Exodus 9:1-7). To further substantiate the miraculous nature of this plague, the Lord announced a set time for the beginning of this disaster and this time was precisely fulfilled as announced, according to Exodus 9:6. Furthermore, not a single one of the Israelites' animals was afflicted.

The Egyptians believed every animal to be sacred in view of the fact that various gods were thought to inhabit their bodies. Legend has it that when the giants made war on the gods, the gods were all obliged to flee to Egypt and take refuge in the bodies of animals. Such were therefore sacred, protected, and worshiped. It was with such knowledge that "the Persians unfairly won a battle against the Egyptians in the days of Cambyses by driving a 'screen' of sacred animals ahead of them, at which no Egyptian bowman would shoot."[35]

It is because of this belief that the Egyptians often created images of the gods in the forms of animals. For example, the god *Jupiter* was adored in the form of a ram; *Apollo* in the form of a crow; *Bacchus* as a goat; *Juno* as a heifer; *Diana* as a cat; *Venus* as a fish; and so forth.[36]

Further support for the Egyptian veneration of animals is found in the necropolis of sacred bulls that was discovered near Memphis, an area well-known for its worship of both *Ptah* and the sacred *Apis* bulls. (The Apis bull was thought to be the sacred animal of the god Ptah.) At any one given time, there was only one sacred Apis bull. As soon as one died, another was chosen to take its place. Such sacred bulls were supposedly recognized by 28 distinctive marks that identified them as divine and indicated that they were to become objects of worship.[37]

Among other gods affected by this plague are *Hathor* (a goddess of love, beauty, and joy represented by the form of a cow) and *Mnevis* (a sacred bull venerated at Heliopolis and often associated with the sun-god Re).[38] Such gods were powerless when this deadly disease was inflicted by the hand of the mighty Yahweh.

The Sixth Plague

The sixth plague resulted in both men and beasts breaking out with boils and sores (Exodus 9:8-12). This was a severe inflammation that caused the flesh to burn and swell.[39] The infections described may have been similar to those which Job suffered (Job 2:7).

Egyptians were well aware of the ever-present possibility of infectious diseases and sores. This is reflected in their belief that *Sekhmet*, a lion-headed goddess, had the power of both creating epidemics and bringing them to an end. According to John Davis, "a special priesthood was devoted to [*Sekhmet*] called *Sunu*."[40]

Following this plague, the magicians were apparently called in again to attempt to vindicate the power of the gods of Egypt and to show that Yahweh's power was not unique. However, they were not only unable to duplicate this miracle but were apparently not even able to appear in the royal court because of the severity of this plague upon their own bodies (Exodus 9:11).

The Egyptians no doubt sought relief from their sores from many of the Egyptian deities charged with the responsibility of healing. Among these were *Imhotep*, who was considered the god of medicine and the guardian of healing sciences, and *Isis*, who was considered a goddess capable of healing.[41] Neither Pharaoh, the other false gods, nor the priests were able to undo what the incomparable Yahweh did.

The Seventh Plague

The seventh plague resulted in a very heavy hail falling on the land (Exodus 9:13-35). This plague was preceded by a specific explanation to Pharaoh from God through Moses and Aaron: "This time I will send the full force of my plagues against you and against your officials and your people, so you may know that there is no one like me in all the earth" (9:14). Furthermore, said Yahweh, "I have raised you up for this very purpose, that I might show you my power and that my name might be proclaimed in all the earth" (verse 16). There was to be no misunderstanding as to the significance of what was about to occur.

Moses and Aaron also issued a warning: "Give an order now to bring your livestock and everything you have in the field to a place of shelter, because the hail will fall on every man and animal that has not been brought in and is still out in the field, and they will die" (Exodus 9:19). This warning was heeded by many of Pharaoh's officials (verse 20), a fact that was no doubt distressing to the god-king of Egypt. How humiliating it must have been for him as he witnessed how his followers were giving heed to Moses and Aaron.

As was true earlier, the supernatural element of this judgment is clear because no hail fell whatsoever in the land of Goshen (Exodus 9:26). This could not be explained away as a natural storm.

Among the gods this judgment was directed against are *Shu*, the Egyptian God of the atmosphere,[42] and Isis and Osiris, gods whose roles included overseeing agriculture.[43] Also included would be *Nut* (the sky goddess whose task it was to ensure the blessings of the sun and warmth), and *Seth* (a deity responsible for watching after crops).[44] All of these were thought to have the power necessary to prevent such catastrophes from occurring. But they were impotent in the shadow of the almighty Yahweh.

The violent rain and hail were so severe that Pharaoh had to call again on Moses and Aaron. This time Pharaoh the god-king made three concessions to them. In Exodus 9:27 we read: 1) he acknowledged that he had sinned; 2) he acknowledged that Yahweh is righteous (quite a concession since he denied the existence of Yahweh in Exodus 5:2); and 3) he admitted that he and his people were wicked and had acted wrongly. His confession was probably undergirded with a high degree of insincerity much like that of Saul (1 Samuel 15:24) and Nebuchadnezzar (Daniel 4:37).

In any event, relief from this plague did not change the heart of Pharaoh, and he continued to resist as he had on previous occasions (Exodus 9:34,35). His heart continued to harden against Yahweh. He still could not bring himself to admit that his own power and authority were no match for the true God.

The Eighth Plague

The eighth plague resulted in a massive locust swarm (Exodus 10:1-20).[45] Such a swarm would have been devastating to Egypt. Individual locusts have the capability of eating their own weight daily. This particular type of locust swarm would have had a density of 100,000,000 to 200,000,000 locusts per square mile, with the potential of destroying hundreds of square miles of land. Such locusts possess the ability to flap their wings nonstop for 17 hours, and can cruise at an airspeed of up to 12 miles an hour. With an average density of 130,000,000 locusts per square mile, the collective movement of the swarm ranges from a few miles to more than 60 miles in a single day.[46]

In addition to Pharaoh, this was also apparently a judgment against *Serapis*, the Egyptian god that was supposedly able to protect the land from locusts.[47] Yet Serapis was nowhere to be found on this sober day in Egypt. As was true with the earlier plagues, this one was inflicted by Yahweh "that you may know that I am the LORD" (Exodus 10:2). (They will also know at the same time that the false gods of the mystery religions of Egypt are not gods at all.)

Then Pharaoh again called Moses and Aaron and offered them a third compromise. He was willing to let the *men* in Israel worship, but not their wives or their children (Exodus 10:10,11). This was not acceptable to Moses and Aaron, and they were driven out of Pharaoh's presence (verse 11).

It did not take long for Pharaoh to realize that he was confronted with a crisis of unparalleled proportions. He accordingly called Moses and Aaron back again "quickly" and offered another confession, even asking for forgiveness this time (Exodus 10:16,17). Like the earlier occasions, he probably did this more out of expediency than out of sincerity.

Moses subsequently prayed that the plague would end, "and the LORD changed the wind to a very strong west wind, which caught up the locusts and carried them into the Red Sea" (Exodus 10:19). Still, despite Yahweh's display of grace in ending the plague, Pharaoh's heart continued to harden and he would not let the Israelites go.

The Ninth Plague

The ninth plague resulted in darkness enveloping the land of Egypt for three days. The darkness was so thick that it could actually be felt (Exodus 10:21,22). Yet the Israelites had light where they lived—clearly indicating the selective nature of God's judgment.

This judgment was clearly against the Egyptian sun god, Re. Regarding this mighty Egyptian deity, Bible scholar C.J. Labuschagne explains: "The sun-god was not only regarded as the creator, father, and king of the gods, but his singular and exceptional character as creator and sustainer of all living things caused him to be looked upon as the most excellent, most distinguished god in the pantheon, and to be praised as the god who was stronger, mightier, and more divine than the other gods."[48] John Davis adds that "his faithfulness in providing the warmth and light of sun day after day without fail caused them to express great joy over the faithfulness of this deity."[49] A hymn entitled "A Universalist hymn to the Sun" proclaims: "Hail to thee, beautiful Re of every day, who rises at dawn without ceasing."[50] This judgment of darkness in the land dealt a blow to the strongest god in Egypt.

Imagine how Pharaoh must have felt when he witnessed the impotence of the god who was considered his father.

Of course, Re was not the only god affected by this plague. Other gods included *Aten* (the deified sun disc), *Atum* (the god of the setting sun), *Khepre* (who was another form of the sun god Re), *Hathor* and *Nut* (sky goddesses), and *Thoth* (a moon god of Hermopolis).[51]

In desperation, the Pharaoh again called on Moses and Aaron and put forth a compromise. He put forth to let the children of Israel go and worship God in the desert, but with the stipulation that their flocks and herds be left behind (Exodus 10:24). This was unacceptable to Moses and Aaron because the Israelites needed the animals to offer sacrifices to God (verses 25,26).

Through this encounter, Pharaoh's heart continued to harden, and the Egyptian leader refused to let the Israelites go. Allowing the Israelites to go with no assurance that they would return was just too much for him. He became enraged and demanded that Moses once for all leave the royal court, saying: "The day you see my face you will die" (Exodus 10:28). Moses responded, "Just as you say....I will never appear before you again" (verse 29).

Moses and Aaron *did* appear before Pharaoh again in Exodus 12:31, at Pharaoh's summoning. In this latter encounter, Pharaoh ordered Moses and the Israelites to leave Egypt. We may thus understand Moses' words in Exodus 10:29 to refer to the fact that Moses and Aaron would not be *initiating* any appearances before Pharaoh to bring messages from God.

The Tenth Plague

The tenth and final plague resulted in the death of the firstborn of all the land (Exodus 11:1–12:36). God issued a sober pronouncement to the Egyptians: "I will pass through Egypt and strike down every firstborn—both men and animals—and I will bring judgment on all the gods of Egypt. I am the LORD" (12:12).

This judgment was particularly devastating to Pharaoh in view of the fact that his firstborn would have eventually sat on his father's throne.[52] Furthermore, Pharaoh's son (by an act of the gods) was considered to have divine properties just like his father.[53] From an Egyptian point of view, it is hard to conceive of any stronger demonstration of the incomparability of Yahweh.

In addition to Pharaoh, this was a judgment against *all* the gods of Egypt. After all, as noted above, Yahweh said that through this judgment He would "bring judgment on *all* the gods of Egypt" (Exodus 12:12, emphasis added).

Among the gods who were judged are *Ptah*, the Egyptian god of life[54]; *Min*, the god of procreation and reproduction; *Isis*, a god and symbol of fecundity with the power to produce offspring; and *Hathor*, one of seven deities who was believed to attend the birth of children. Furthermore, the death of the *Apis* bull, a firstborn animal with supposedly divine qualities, would have had a tremendous impact on the worshipers and priests of the temple.[55] All the firstborn in Egypt died as an irrefutable demonstration and proof that no god in Egypt had the power to stand against Yahweh, the incomparable one.

Following this awful judgment, Pharaoh finally gave in and declared to Moses and Aaron that the children of Israel should leave. He made no qualifications and asked for no concessions. He also requested of Moses: "And also bless me" (Exodus 12:32). This is an amazing request, especially in light of the fact that Pharaoh considered himself to be a god. It took ten plagues, but Yahweh answered the question Pharaoh asked in Exodus 5:2: "Who is the LORD [Yahweh], that I should obey him and let Israel go?"

Why Masons Should Take Notice

As noted previously, Masonic leaders often make reference to such Egyptian deities as Isis, Serapis, Osiris, Re, Apis, Thoth, Phtha, Hermes, Orpheus, Horus, and many others. They often boast how Masonry is descended from the ancient Egyptian mystery religions. I think you will agree that the information set forth in this chapter shows the seriousness of this issue.

Many "Christian Masons" may be completely unaware of these facts relating to the ancient gods of Egypt. After sharing the information in this chapter with them, challenge them to *act* on it and leave the Masonic Lodge.

Some Masons may respond that what they are doing is just "symbolic," nothing to get really excited about. My late colleague, Dr. Walter Martin of the Christian Research Institute, responded quite forcefully to such an idea. Consider his words:

> In the [Masonic] temple in Los Angeles, which I took the trouble to visit, there is a statue of Moses, and then there is a statue of Zoroaster, and then there is one of Osiris, and then there are statues of Egyptian gods and goddesses. Now, my objection would be based on this, that when you put a representative of the God of the Bible in the midst of the pagan world, which God judged for its evil, condemned them as vile, depraved, and wicked, then I think that you would have gone over the borderline of just *symbol*. You're playing with a very dangerous spiritual fire.[56]

Martin went on to argue that such an attitude is totally incongruent with the apostle Paul's words in 2 Corinthians 6:14-17:

> Do not be yoked together with unbelievers. For what do righteousness and wickedness have in common? Or what fellowship can light have with darkness? What harmony is there between Christ and Belial? What does a believer have in common with an unbeliever? What agreement is there between the temple of God and idols? For we are the temple of the living God. As God has said: "I will live with them and walk among

them, and I will be their God, and they will be my people." "Therefore *come out from them and be separate*, says the Lord. Touch no unclean thing, and I will receive you" (emphasis added).

What Masons have done in bringing these false gods of Egypt into their ritual is an outrage to God's holy name, especially for those who claim to be Christians. *Repentance is in immediate order.* God's message—not just to Masons, but to all people everywhere—is this: *There is none like me in all the earth; therefore, come out from them and be separate, says the Lord God Almighty.*

___ Ask... _____

- Did you know that when God, through the hand of Moses, inflicted the ten plagues upon Egypt, He was actually judging such false Egyptian gods as Isis, Serapis, Osiris, Apis, Thoth, Phtha, Hermes, Orpheus, and Horus?

- When God turned the Nile River into blood, are you aware of the fact that He was judging the Egyptian sacred river god known as Nilus?

- When God cast darkness upon the land, wasn't this a judgment on the Egyptian sun god, Re?

- Did you know that when God caused an overwhelming swarm of flies, this was a judgment on the Egyptian god of the flies, Beelzebub?

- What do you think these judgments indicate about the true God's attitude toward false Egyptian deities?

- Since the Masonic Lodge regularly cites these deities in its literature, what do you think the true God's attitude is toward the Lodge?

- Would you please open your Bible and read aloud from 2 Corinthians 6:14-17? What do you make of these words?

9

Whatever Happened to Jesus?

The deity of Christ is either completely denied or greatly downplayed within Masonic circles. Those who are Christians within the Masonic Lodge may consider Jesus to be the divine Son of God, but they typically choose not to use his name when praying.[1] Masons are instructed: "Prayers in the lodges should be closed with expressions such as 'in the Most Holy and Precious name we pray,' using no additional words which would be in conflict with the religious beliefs of those present at meetings."[2] Since not all Masons believe in Jesus, calling on Jesus might be offensive to some.

Further, if the name of Jesus were invoked during prayer, then others from different religious persuasions would pray in the name of their deity. Since Masons try to avoid religious disputes, specifically referring to *any* name—including that of Jesus—is avoided. Prayers offered within the walls of the Masonic Lodge are universal in nature. "In its language citizens of every nation may converse; at its altars men of all religions may kneel; to its creed disciples of every faith may subscribe."[3] In *Morals and Dogma*, Albert Pike writes:

> The chaplain of the Masonic Lodge who prays as the voice of the lodge does not pray in the name of the Carpenter of Nazareth or the name of Jehovah or the name of Allah. He prays to the Grand Artificer or the Great Architect of the Universe. Under that title men of all faiths may find each his own deity. Failure to mention any deity by name is not denial, but merely the practice of a gracious courtesy, so that each man for whom prayer is offered can hear the name of his own deity in the all inclusive title of Great Architect.[4]

For the most part, Jesus is regarded by many Masons as a great moral teacher and ethical philosopher. He is in the same league with other great men, such as Socrates. Pike comments that "none can deny that Christ taught a lofty morality."[5] Similar to other great religious leaders, Jesus stood for morality and virtue. Masons typically cite a number of sayings of Jesus from the Bible to illustrate His high morality:

- "By this all men will know that you are my disciples, if you love one another" (John 13:35).
- "Love your enemies and pray for those who persecute you" (Matthew 5:44).
- "Blessed are the pure in heart, for they will see God" (Matthew 5:8).
- "Do not store up for yourselves treasures on earth, where moth and rust destroy, and where thieves break in and steal. But store up for yourselves treasures in heaven, where moth and rust

do not destroy, and where thieves do not break in
and steal" (Matthew 6:19,20).

* "Do to others what you would have them do to
  you, for this sums up the Law and the Prophets"
  (Matthew 7:12).

Some Masons go so far as to say that the very reason Jesus
was put to death was because of His morality: "Whatever higher
attributes the Founder of the Christian Faith may, in our belief,
have had or not have had, none can deny that He taught and practiced a pure and elevated morality, even at the risk and to the ultimate loss of his life."[6] Indeed, "the gospel of love He sealed with
His life....He expired uttering blessings upon humanity."[7]
Although Jesus is admired, any suggestion that Jesus is the "only
way" to God is outright rejected by Masons. Such a position is
viewed as intolerant, and intolerance is not a characteristic
allowed within the halls of Masonic Lodges. Masons believe there
are many acceptable paths to God, all based on attaining a high
level of morality.

According to some Masonic interpreters, Jesus taught that we
are to be tolerant. Richard Thorn comments:

> Many people consider those of a different religion
> to be their enemies. Jesus said to love our ene-
> mies. Freemasonry teaches us to accept other
> people, and to respect their religious beliefs. It
> does not teach that all religions are equal, only
> that we should respect them. My religious con-
> cepts were formed long before I became a Mason,
> but I consider Freemasonry to be a work of the
> Lord Jesus Christ, raised up to emphasize that part
> of his teaching so often neglected by the church:
> to love your enemy.[8]

In similar fashion, Pike writes: "The great commandment of Masonry is this: 'A new commandment give I unto you: that ye love one another! He that saith he is in the light, and hateth his brother, remaineth still in the darkness.'"[9] By this, of course, Pike is referring to loving and accepting and fellowshiping with one another in brotherly love, despite vast religious differences.

REASONING FROM THE SCRIPTURES

Stripping Out References to Jesus

It is highly revealing that when Scripture verses are quoted in the Masonic Lodge, the name of Jesus is always deleted.

First Peter 2:5 (NASB) actually reads, "...to offer up spiritual sacrifices acceptable to God *through Jesus Christ*." The Masonic ritual reads, "...to offer up spiritual sacrifices acceptable to God."[10]

Second Thessalonians 3:6 reads, "*In the name of the Lord Jesus Christ*, we command you, brothers, to keep away from every brother who is idle and does not live according to the teaching you received from us." The Masonic ritual reads, "Now we command you, brethren, that ye withdraw yourself from every brother that walketh disorderly, and not after the tradition which ye received from us."[11]

Second Thessalonians 3:12 (NASB) reads, "Now such persons we command and exhort *in the Lord Jesus Christ* to work in a quiet fashion and eat their own bread." The Masonic ritual reads, "Now them that are such, we command and exhort, that with quietness they work and eat their own bread."[12]

How can "Christian" Masons in good conscience go along with such a practice? Especially in view of the clear teaching of Deuteronomy 4:2: "Do not add to what I command you and *do not subtract from it*, but keep the commands of the LORD your God that I give you" (emphasis added). In the same spirit, Revelation 22:18,19 tells us, "I warn everyone who hears the words of the prophecy of this book: If anyone adds anything to them, God will add to him the plagues described in this book. And *if anyone takes words away from this book of prophecy*, God will take away from him his share in the tree of life and in the holy city, which are described in this book" (emphasis added). There is no doubt that the Masonic deletion of Jesus' name from Scripture verses violates the spirit of these commands of God.

____ *Ask...* ____

After emphasizing God's commands in Deuteronomy 4:2 and Revelation 22:18-19, ask the following questions.

- Please read aloud from 1 Peter 2:5.

- Since Scripture forbids subtracting from God's Word, how do you tolerate omitting the words "through Jesus Christ" from 1 Peter 2:5 in the Masonic ritual?

- Please read aloud from 2 Thessalonians 3:6.

- Since Scripture forbids subtracting from God's Word, how do you ignore the omitting of the words "in the name of the Lord Jesus Christ" from 2 Thessalonians 3:6 in the Masonic ritual?

- Please read aloud from 2 Thessalonians 3:12.

- Since Scripture explicitly forbids subtracting from God's Word, how do you justify supporting the omitting of the words "in the Lord Jesus Christ" from 2 Thessalonians 3:12 in the Masonic ritual?

- Do you want to be part of an organization that does this? Do you know that God promises judgment against those who do such things?

Stripping the name of Jesus from Bible verses is especially heinous in view of the fact that *all of Scripture exalts the name of Jesus*. Philippians 2:10,11, for example, tells us that Christ was given a name above every name, "that at the name of Jesus every knee should bow, in heaven and on earth and under the earth, and every tongue confess that Jesus Christ is Lord." It is significant that the apostle Paul in this verse was alluding to Isaiah 45:22-24: "I am God, and there is no other. By myself I have sworn, my mouth has uttered in all integrity a word that will not be revoked: Before me every knee will bow; by me every tongue will swear." Paul was drawing on his vast knowledge of the Old Testament to make the point that what is true of Yahweh (in His exaltation) is also true of Christ (in His exaltation). *Jesus is the exalted One.*

In keeping with this, the Bible indicates that the Father raised Jesus from the dead "and seated him at his right hand in the heavenly realms, far above all rule and authority, power and dominion, and every title that can be given, not only in the present age but also in the one to come" (Ephesians 1:20,21). Jesus is on the center stage of glory—both now and forever! To purposefully delete His name from Bible verses is thus abominable.

The Jesus of Hinduism and Islam

Both Hinduism and Islam hold diminished views of Jesus Christ. While Jesus is respected in Hinduism, His words are said to reflect Vedic philosophy. In other words, Jesus' teachings are said to reflect Hinduism. It is suggested that Christians have misunderstood the messages of Jesus and that Hindu sages have a better grasp of them.[13]

What does Hinduism teach in regard to Christ? Among other things, Jesus is *one of many* holy men that communicated spiritual truth. He certainly was not humankind's only Savior, nor was He uniquely the Son of God. Rather He was a great master, in a league with other great masters.[14] It is also believed that there were holy men who were greater than Jesus. Prabhupada, who founded the Hare Krishna movement (an offshoot of Hinduism), is said to be an example. Some have suggested that Jesus may have been an *avatar* (an incarnation of a god), but He is nevertheless lower than the great Brahman (the "ultimate God that permeates all reality").

Some Hindus have suggested that Jesus was not perfect. They respect and honor Him, but His imperfection is evident in the anger He showed in driving moneychangers out of the temple and in causing the fig tree to wither. Still, despite such imperfections, He is viewed as a great sage.

Hindus often teach that Jesus did not suffer on the cross, for He was a man who had attained enlightenment and was beyond the possibility of physical pain. Maharishi Mahesh Yogi said, "It's a pity that Christ is talked of in terms of suffering."[15]

Quite obviously, the Hindu view of Christ differs with the Bible at many points. First, from the Bible it is abundantly clear that Jesus not only suffered on the cross but the whole reason Jesus was born as a human being was to go to the cross to suffer for the sins of humankind (see Isaiah 53:3-5; Matthew 16:21; Luke 9:22; Acts 1:3). Further, Hindus have wrongly attributed imperfection to Jesus simply because He expressed righteous indignation against that which was evil, such as profiting monetarily in God's temple. (Indeed, to *not* display righteous anger against that which is evil would be an imperfection.) Contrary to the claim that Jesus was imperfect, the Scriptures indicate that Jesus *was* perfect, was "without sin" (Hebrews 4:15), and "had no sin" (2 Corinthians 5:21). He is said to be "holy, blameless, pure" (Hebrews 7:26). He has been "made perfect forever" (Hebrews 7:28).

In view of such different interpretations of Jesus, *how can Christians worship together with Hindus in a Masonic Lodge?*

Islam, too, holds a diminished view of Jesus Christ. Muslims believe Jesus was one of the foremost prophets of God. He was a sinless man who was a messenger of God—bringing truth to His age. But He *was not* the Son of God. He was not God in human flesh. He is to be honored, but no more so than any other prophet of Allah. He is a *lesser* prophet than Muhammad.

Muslims say Jesus did not die on the cross, but rather ascended directly into heaven. (Judas was allegedly crucified in His place.) It would have been unthinkable, Muslims say, that Allah would have allowed one of his prophets to be crucified. Therefore, the crucifixion of Christ is viewed as a disrespectful doctrine.

Islam denies the very central teachings on Jesus that are at the very heart of the Bible—especially His deity and His salvific mission involving His death on the cross for the sins of humankind. In view of such differences, *how can Christians worship together with Muslims in a Masonic Lodge?*

___ *Ask...* ___

- Did you know that Hindus teach that Jesus was not humankind's only Savior, and that He was not the unique Son of God?

- If you discovered that Hindus teach that Jesus was *lesser* than certain Hindu holy men, such as Prabhupada, the founder of the Hare Krishna movement, what would you do?

- Can you honor God and worship with Hindus, knowing they believe Jesus had imperfections?

- Have you considered the fact that Hindus teach that Jesus did not suffer on the cross?

- Christianity teaches that Jesus *is* the unique Son of God (John 3:16), *is* the only Savior of humankind (John 14:6; Acts 4:12; 1 Timothy 2:5), *is* perfect in every way (Hebrews 7:26), *is* exalted above all human beings (Philippians 2:5-11), and *did* suffer on the cross (Matthew 16:21). Is it not clear that Hindus and Christians hold radically different views about Jesus?

- How, then, can you engage in spiritual fellowship and worship under the same roof as Hindus?

- Does it concern you that Muslims teach that Jesus was "just a prophet," lesser than the prophet Muhammad?

- Did you know Muslims believe that Jesus was not crucified on the cross?

- Since Christianity teaches that Jesus *is* not just a prophet but *is* God-incarnate (John 1:1,18), *is* exalted above all humans—including Muhammad (Philippians 2:5-11), and *was* crucified on the cross (Matthew 27:22-54), isn't it clear that Muslims and Christians hold radically different views about Jesus?

- How, then, can you engage in spiritual fellowship and worship under the same roof as Muslims?

"Love One Another" Doesn't Mean "Ignore False Doctrine"

It is true that Jesus was the most loving human being that ever lived. It is also true that one of His primary teachings is that we should love one another, and we should even love those who are our enemies. Yet Jesus was most certainly not saying that we should ignore false doctrine. He continually warned His followers about the possibility of spiritual and religious deception. He did not say to overlook religious differences that conflict with His teachings; rather, He said to *beware of them* in order to *avoid* them. For example:

- Jesus warned His followers, "Watch out for false prophets. They come to you in sheep's clothing, but inwardly they are ferocious wolves. By their fruit you will recognize them" (Matthew 7:15,16).

- Jesus also warned His followers: "Watch out that no one deceives you. For many will come in my

> name, claiming, 'I am the Christ,' and will
> deceive many.... And many false prophets will
> appear and deceive many people" (Matthew
> 24:4,5,11).

Further, we must recognize that those Christ criticized most severely during His three-year ministry were the religious leaders of Israel who were inflicting oppressive religious beliefs on the common people. Though Jesus was the most loving person who ever lived, He had some rather scathing words for these false leaders. In Matthew 23, Jesus called them "hypocrites" (verse 13), "blind guides" (verse 16), "blind fools" (verse 17), "blind men" (verse 19), and "whitewashed tombs, which look beautiful on the outside but on the inside are full of dead men's bones and everything unclean" (verse 27).

Being loving to one another does not in any way mean we are to ignore or overlook false religious teachings, teachings that go against the Word of God. Inasmuch as the teachings of the Masonic Lodge *do* go against the Word of God at numerous points, it is certainly not unloving for Christians to point out their error. To *not* share truth with someone who has been led astray is to be unloving.

_____ *Ask...* _____

- Even though Jesus was the most loving person who ever lived, did you know that He also went to great measures to warn His followers about false prophets and false Christs? (Be ready to read from Matthew 7:15,16 and 24:4,11.)

- Did you know that Jesus reserved His harshest words for false religious leaders? (Be ready to read from Matthew 23:13-17.)

• From Jesus' perspective, do you think "loving one another" means that we should ignore or overlook false teachings?

Jesus Was More Than a Moral Teacher

Contrary to the view of many Masons, Jesus was not just a good teacher or ethical example. No mere moral teacher would claim that the destiny of the world lay in His hands or that people would spend eternity in heaven or hell depending on whether they believed in Him (John 6:26-40). The only example this would provide would be one of lunacy. And for Jesus to convince people that He was God (John 8:58) and the Savior of the world (Luke 19:10) when He really was not, would be the ultimate *immorality*. To say Jesus was *just* a good, moral teacher and nothing more is unreasonable. C.S. Lewis put it so well:

> A man who was merely a man and said the sort of things Jesus said would not be a great moral teacher. He would either be a lunatic—on the level with the man who says he is a poached egg—or else he would be the Devil of Hell. You must make your choice. Either this man was, and is, the Son of God: or else a madman or something worse.[16]

___ *Ask...* ___

• Would a person who was merely a "good, moral teacher," and nothing more, tell people they would spend eternity in heaven or hell depending on whether they believed in him? (Be ready to read aloud from John 6:26-40.)

- Would it be "moral" for a person to claim that he was the Savior of all humankind, if he were not?

- Can I get your opinion on a statement made by C.S. Lewis? (Read the previous quote from Lewis.)

Prayer Should *Always* Be in the Name of Jesus Christ

The New Testament is clear that our prayers to God are to be in the name of Jesus Christ. In John 14:13,14, Jesus spoke to the disciples about the issue of prayer and said, "I will do whatever you ask *in my name*, so that the Son may bring glory to the Father. You may ask me for anything *in my name*, and I will do it" (emphasis added). In John 15:16, Jesus said, "Whatever you ask of the Father *in My name*, He may give to you" (NASB, emphasis added). In John 16:23,24 Jesus said, "I tell you the truth, my Father will give you whatever you ask *in my name*. Until now you have not asked for anything *in my name*. Ask and you will receive, and your joy will be complete" (emphasis added). More broadly, Colossians 3:17 tells us: "And whatever you do, whether in word or deed, do it all *in the name of the Lord Jesus,* giving thanks to God the Father through him" (emphasis added).

The reason our prayers are to be in the name of Jesus Christ is that Jesus is the one and only mediator between God and humanity: "For there is one God and one mediator between God and men, the man Christ Jesus" (1 Timothy 2:5). To leave Jesus out of the equation is to cut ourselves off from access to God.

Another related issue regarding prayers in Masonic Lodges centers on who the others are praying to. When prayers are offered in the name of the "Great Architect of the Universe," this ultimately means that Hindus and Muslims are interpreting the prayers as being in the name of their respective gods, which, as demonstrated in an earlier chapter, are pagan deities. No Christian should participate in a prayer in which some of the people present are praying to false gods.

___ *Ask...* _____

- Would you please read aloud from John 14:13,14? John 16:23,24? Colossians 3:17?

- Should *all* prayers be offered to God by Christians in the name of Jesus Christ?

- How do you think prayer relates to the apostle Paul's statement in 1 Timothy 2:5: "For there is one God and one mediator between God and men, the man Christ Jesus"?

- Does it bother you that when you participate in a prayer in the Lodge, some of the people present are using the *same* prayer to worship pagan deities?

Jesus Died for Our Sins

To suggest that Jesus died as a result of His commitment to high morality and ethical living completely distorts biblical teaching. The Bible says that Jesus, the divine Savior, "gave himself as a ransom for all men" (1 Timothy 2:6). The word *ransom* refers to something given in exchange for another as the price of redemption. The idea is that of substitution—Christ taking our place. Christ died to satisfy the demands of the offended righteousness of God. Our Savior died in the sinner's place. He died as the sinner's substitute (Matthew 20:28). By so doing, He provided a salvation for human beings that they had virtually no hope of procuring for themselves.

Jesus affirmed that it was for the very *purpose of dying* that He came into the world (John 12:27). Moreover, He perceived His death as being a sacrificial offering for the sins of humanity; He said His blood "is poured out for many for the forgiveness of sins" (Matthew 26:28). Jesus took His sacrificial mission with utmost seriousness. He knew that without Him, humanity would certainly perish (Matthew 16:25) and spend eternity apart from God in a place of great suffering (Luke 16:22-28).

Jesus described His mission this way: "The Son of Man did not come to be served, but to serve, and to give his life as a ransom for many" (Matthew 20:28). "The Son of Man came to seek and to save what was lost" (Luke 19:10).

In John 10, Jesus compares Himself to a good shepherd who not only gives His life to save the sheep (John 10:11), but He lays His life down of His own accord (see John 10:11,18). This is precisely what Jesus did at the cross—He laid His life down as a sacrificial offering for the sins of humanity (Matthew 26:53).

Certainly this is how others perceived His mission. When Jesus began His three-year ministry and was walking toward John the Baptist at the Jordan River, John said, "Look, the Lamb of God, who takes away the sin of the world!" (John 1:29). John's portrayal of Christ as the Lamb of God is a graphic affirmation that Jesus Himself would be the sacrifice that would atone for the sins of humanity.

Christ was our substitute. He took our place. He took our sin upon Himself and provided salvation for us. He did not die as a result of His own morality; He died as a result of *our immorality*. He died to make our salvation possible.

____ *Ask...* ____

- Can you show me one verse in the Bible where it says that Jesus died on the cross as a result of His high morality, as Masons often claim?

- Would you please read 1 Timothy 2:6? John 12:27? Matthew 26:26-28?

- What do these verses tell us about why Jesus really died?

- Can you see that Jesus died not because of *His* high morality but because of *our* low morality—that is, He died for our sins in order to make salvation possible?

Jesus Christ Is the *Only* Way

The Jesus of the Bible is unique in every way, especially in view of the fact that He is absolute deity (see John 1:1; 8:58; 10:30; 20:28). Jesus did not just claim to have "a way" to God, like the founders of the other world religions. Jesus claimed *to be* God. Moreover, Jesus and His message were inseparable. The reason Jesus' teachings had absolute authority was that He *was* and *is* God. This is not the case with the leaders of the other world religions. Buddha taught that his ethical teachings were what are important, not himself. He emphasized that these ethical teachings were important *whether or not he himself existed.* But Jesus said, "Verily, *I* say unto you…"(KJV) with the very authority of God.

Jesus claimed that what He said took precedence over all others. He said He is humanity's *only* means of coming into a relationship with God (John 14:6). This was confirmed by those who followed Him. Peter asserted, "Salvation is found in no one else, for there is no other name under heaven given to men by which we must be saved" (Acts 4:12). The apostle Paul affirmed, "For there is one God and one mediator between God and men, the man Christ Jesus" (1 Timothy 2:5).

While God's way of salvation is *narrow* (that is, by faith in Christ alone), God's heart is infinitely *wide.* He is full of love for *all* people—men and women, rich and poor, fat and thin, kings and peasants, the social elite and social outcasts (see Ezekiel 18:23; Isaiah 45:22; 1 Timothy 2:3,4). He offers the *same* gift to everyone. It is a *singular* gift, a gift of salvation in Jesus Christ. Jesus wants *all people* to receive this wonderful present (see Matthew 28:19; John 3:17), as did the apostles (Acts 26:28,29; Romans 1:16).

In view of this wonderful gift of salvation in Jesus Christ, it is truly foolish to dishonor His name as Masons have done. Jesus affirmed that those who do not honor Him cannot honor the Father who sent Him (John 5:23). We are told in 1 John 2:23 that "no one who denies the Son has the Father." Of particular signif-icance to those Christians who choose to attend Masonic Lodges and participate in the devaluing of Jesus Christ, Jesus asserted in Luke 9:26: "If anyone is ashamed of me and my words, the Son of Man will be ashamed of him when he comes in his glory and in the glory of the Father and of the holy angels."

_____ *Ask...* _____

- Did you know that in John 14:6 Jesus said, "I am the way and the truth and the life. No one comes to the Father except through me"?

- The apostle Peter, speaking of Jesus, said: "Salvation is found in no one else, for there is no other name under heaven given to men by which we must be saved" (Acts 4:12). When Peter said "no other name," does that include Allah, the god of the Muslims, and Brahman, the "all-permeating" deity of Hinduism?

- Is the Masonic Lodge correct in saying that Jesus is not the only way of salvation?

- How do you interpret Jesus' words in John 5:23: "He who does not honor the Son does not honor the Father, who sent him"?

- How does 1 John 2:23 apply to practices in the Lodge: "No one who denies the Son has the Father; whoever acknowledges the Son has the Father also"?

Jesus Is Absolute Deity

Masons often speak of God as being the Great Architect of the Universe, one of His names being Jehovah or Yahweh. But what they fail to recognize is the biblical teaching that *Jesus is Yahweh*. The scriptural support for this idea is abundant, and you need to be able to demonstrate this to Masons.

A comparison of the Old and New Testaments provides powerful testimony to Jesus' identity as Yahweh. Support for this is found, for example, in Christ's crucifixion. In Zechariah 12:10, Yahweh is speaking prophetically: "They will look on me, the one they have pierced." Though Yahweh is speaking, this is obviously a reference to Christ's future crucifixion.[17] We know that "the one they have pierced" is Jesus, for He is described this same way by the apostle John in Revelation 1:7.

The Septuagint provides us with additional insights on Christ's identity as Yahweh. The Septuagint is a Greek translation of the Hebrew Old Testament that dates prior to the birth of Christ. It renders the Hebrew phrase for "I AM" (God's name) in Exodus 3:14 as *ego eimi*.[18] On a number of occasions in the Greek New Testament, Jesus used this term as a way of identifying Himself as God.[19] For example, in John 8:24 (NASB) Jesus declared: "Unless you believe that I am [*ego eimi*] He, you will die in your sins." The original Greek for this verse does not have the word *He*. The verse is literally: "Unless you believe that I am, you will die in your sins."

Then, according to verse 28, Jesus told the Jews: "When you lift up the Son of Man, then you will know that I am [*ego eimi*] He." Again, the original Greek reads: "When you lift up the Son of Man, then you will know that I am" (there is no *He*). Jesus purposefully used the phrase as a means of pointing to His identity as Yahweh.[20]

It is also highly revealing that Old Testament passages about Yahweh were directly applied to Jesus in the New Testament. For instance, in Isaiah 44:24 we find Yahweh speaking about His exclusive role in the creation of the universe: "I am the LORD [Yahweh], who has made all things, who alone stretched out the heavens, who spread out the earth by myself." Clearly, Yahweh is the *sole creator* of the universe. Yet, the New Testament just as clearly tells us that Jesus Christ is the agent of creation. John 1:3 affirms of Jesus, "Through him all things were made; without him nothing was made that has been made." Likewise, Colossians 1:16 affirms of Christ, "For by him all things were created: things in heaven and on earth,

visible and invisible, whether thrones or powers or rulers or authorities; all things were created by him and for him." This can only
mean one thing: *Jesus and Yahweh are equal.*

Further, Isaiah 40:3 informs us: "In the desert prepare the way
for the LORD [Yahweh]; make straight in the wilderness a
highway for our God [Elohim]." Mark's Gospel tells us that
Isaiah's words were fulfilled in the ministry of John the Baptist
preparing the way for Jesus Christ (Mark 1:2-4).

Still another illustration is Isaiah 6:1-5, where the prophet
recounts his vision of Yahweh "seated on a throne high and
exalted" (verse 1). The angels surrounding the throne said, "Holy,
holy, holy is the LORD [Yahweh] Almighty; the whole earth is full
of his glory" (verse 3). Isaiah also quotes Yahweh as saying: "I am
the LORD; that is my name! I will not give my glory to another"
(42:8). Later, the apostle John, under the inspiration of the Holy
Spirit, wrote that Isaiah "saw Jesus' glory" (John 12:41).

Additionally, the Old Testament tells us that Yahweh is the
divine shepherd of God's people. Psalm 23:1 says, "The LORD
[Yahweh] is my shepherd." Yet in the New Testament we are told
that Jesus is the good shepherd (John 10:1-16), the Chief Shepherd (1 Peter 5:4), and the great Shepherd (Hebrews 13:20).

Christ's deity is further confirmed for us in that many of the
actions of Yahweh in the Old Testament are performed by Christ
in the New Testament. For example, in Psalm 119 we are told
about a dozen times that it is Yahweh who gives and preserves
life. But in the New Testament, Jesus claims this power for Himself: "For just as the Father raises the dead and gives them life,
even so the Son gives life to whom he is pleased to give it" (John
5:21). Later in John's Gospel, when speaking to Lazarus' sister
Martha, Jesus said: "I am the resurrection and the life. He who
believes in me will live, even though he dies; and whoever lives
and believes in me will never die" (John 11:25,26).

In the Old Testament, the voice of Yahweh was said to be "like
the roar of rushing waters" (Ezekiel 43:2). Likewise, we read of
the glorified Jesus in heaven: "His feet were like bronze glowing

in a furnace, and his voice was like the sound of rushing waters" (Revelation 1:15). What is true of Yahweh is just as true of Jesus.

It is also significant that in the Old Testament, Yahweh is described as "an everlasting light," one that would make the sun, moon, and stars obsolete: "The sun will no more be your light by day, nor will the brightness of the moon shine on you, for the LORD [Yahweh] will be your everlasting light, and your God will be your glory. Your sun will never set again, and your moon will wane no more; the LORD [Yahweh] will be your everlasting light, and your days of sorrow will end" (Isaiah 60:19,20). Jesus will do the same for the future eternal city in which the saints will dwell forever: "The city does not need the sun or the moon to shine on it, for the glory of God gives it light, and the Lamb is its lamp" (Revelation 21:23).

David F. Wells, in his book *The Person of Christ*, points us to even further parallels between Christ and Yahweh:

> If Yahweh is our sanctifier (Exodus 31:13), is omnipresent (Psalm 139:7-10), is our peace (Judges 6:24), is our righteousness (Jeremiah 23:6), is our victory (Exodus 17:8-16), and is our healer (Exodus 15:26), then so is Christ all of these things (1 Corinthians 1:30; Colossians 1:27; Ephesians 2:14). If the gospel is God's (1 Thessalonians 2:2, 6-9; Galatians 3:8), then that same gospel is also Christ's (1 Thessalonians 3:2; Galatians 1:7). If the church is God's (Galatians 1:13; 1 Corinthians 15:9), then that same church is also Christ's (Romans 16:16). God's Kingdom (1 Thessalonians 2:12) is Christ's (Ephesians 5:5); God's love (Ephesians 1:3-5) is Christ's (Romans 8:35); God's Word (Colossians 1:25; 1 Thessalonians 2:13) is Christ's (1 Thessalonians 1:8; 4:15); God's Spirit (1 Thessalonians 4:8) is Christ's (Philippians 1:19); God's

peace (Galatians 5:22; Philippians 4:9) is Christ's (Colossians 3:15; cf. Colossians 1:2; Philippians 1:2; 4:7); God's "Day" of judgment (Isaiah 13:6) is Christ's "Day" of judgment (Philippians 1:6, 10; 2:16; 1 Corinthians 1:8); God's grace (Ephesians 2:8, 9; Colossians 1:6; Galatians 1:15) is Christ's grace (1 Thessalonians 5:28; Galatians 1:6; 6:18); God's salvation (Colossians 1:13) is Christ's salvation (1 Thessalonians 1:10); and God's will (Ephesians 1:11; 1 Thessalonians 4:3; Galatians 1:4) is Christ's will (Ephesians 5:17; cf. 1 Thessalonians 5:18). So it is no surprise to hear Paul say that he is both God's slave (Romans 1:9) and Christ's (Romans 1:1; Galatians 1:10), that he lives for that glory which is both God's (Romans 5:2; Galatians 1:24) and Christ's (2 Corinthians 8:19, 23; cf. 2 Corinthians 4:6), that his faith is in God (1 Thessalonians 1:8, 9; Romans 4:1-5) and in Christ Jesus (Galatians 3:22), and that to know God, which is salvation (Galatians 4:8; 1 Thessalonians 4:5), is to know Christ (2 Corinthians 4:6).[21]

Clearly, then, Jesus is Yahweh (or Jehovah[22]) and is eternally self-existent—coequal and coeternal with God the Father and God the Holy Spirit. Before time began, Christ was "I AM." He was before all things. Like the Father and the Holy Spirit, He is everlastingly the Living One.

In view of such facts, it is patently obvious that Masons are committing a great atrocity when they prevent Jesus from being mentioned within the halls of their Lodges. Dr. Alva McClain put it so well:

If Masonry does not confess Jesus Christ, then Masonry does not confess the true God. And if

> Masonry does not confess the true God, then Masonry confesses a false God. And if Masonry confesses a false God, let us be plain and call Masonry what it really is, by its own utterances, in the light of the Bible—nothing but paganism and idolatry![23]

By contrast, McClain writes,

> If a man confesses Jesus Christ, he is confessing the true God. If he worships Jesus Christ, he is worshipping the true God. If a man refuses to confess Jesus Christ as God, he is denying the true God. If he refuses to worship Jesus Christ, he is refusing to worship the true God.[24]

Walton Hannah, another critic of Freemasonry, agrees with McClain and tells us that "Christianity is an exclusive faith. To offer worship to God in forms that reject Christ with the specific intention of including people who likewise reject Christ is an act of apostasy for which no amount of mental reservation can altogether atone."[25] Indeed, "All worship which deliberately excludes Christ is pagan."[26]

Jesus once affirmed, "He who is not with me is against me, and he who does not gather with me scatters" (Matthew 12:30). By refusing to acknowledge Jesus Christ within Masonic Lodges, are not Masons openly demonstrating that they are not "with" Christ, thereby showing that they are in fact "against" Christ? This is a solemn issue not to be taken lightly.

___ *Ask...* ___

- The Masonic Lodge acknowledges that *Yahweh* is one of the names of the Great Architect of the Universe, right?

- Did you know there is abundant biblical evidence that equates Jesus and Yahweh? (Be ready to share some of this evidence. Spend plenty of time on this. It is crucial information that the Mason desperately needs to know.)

- If Jesus *is* Yahweh, as Scripture indicates, are Masons denying the true God if they deny Jesus Christ?

- When Masons deny the true God, aren't they confessing a *false* god?

- If Masons are confessing a false god, are they guilty of idolatry?

10

Redefining Sin and Salvation: Part 1

Masons do not like the idea that human beings are "fallen" and need to be redeemed by trusting in Christ alone. In fact, one Mason spoke of the evangelical view of salvation as "an outworn and bigoted theology of 'salvation only in the blood of Christ.'"[1] Masons much prefer the view that salvation is attained by ethical living.

Many Masons deny the Christian doctrine of original sin and reject any suggestion that human beings are depraved.[2] Mason H.L. Haywood comments that man "is not a perfect being...nor is he a debased, rotted creature, wallowing in mire until touched by the arbitrary grace of some supernatural power."[3] Masonry does not teach that "human nature is a depraved thing, like the ruin of a once proud building."[4] Rather, human beings are just imperfect. They make mistakes. If a person works hard at keeping the principles and teachings of the Masonic Lodge (that is, if he lives *ethically*), he will finally be ushered into the Grand Lodge Above, where the Supreme Architect of the Universe resides.[5] L. James Rongstad comments:

> Masonry teaches its adherents that the candidate coming into the lodge has a "rough and imperfect nature." That is why Masonry uses the [symbols of the] Ashlar, Gavel, Square, and Compass—to remind the members that they ever must work out their imperfections in order to be found acceptable to the "Supreme Grand Master" and to achieve a life in paradise, the "Grand Lodge Above."[6]

The Masonic Lodge advocates that human beings can, in and of themselves, improve their somewhat flawed or unpolished character and behavior and attain the moral perfection necessary to go to heaven.[7] W.L. Wilmhurst writes, "Human nature is perfectible by an intensive process of purification and initiation."[8] Masonry's purpose is thus "to make good men better."[9] Albert G. Mackey, in his *Encyclopedia of Freemasonry*, writes that all Masons "unite in declaring it to be a system of morality, by the practice of which its members may advance their spiritual interest, and mount by the theological ladder from the Lodge on earth to the Lodge in heaven."[10]

Moral and spiritual perfection are said to lie within every human being and may be discovered and surfaced through the education that takes place in the Masonic Lodge. Haywood writes:

> To Masonry man is a being that can be educated. This is implied in the Masonic ritual from end to end, and is taken for granted in every phase of Masonic teachings. The candidate comes in the dark, ignorant, a child, needing to be led about by a guide, and cared for by patient guardians. At the end of initiation he stands on his own feet, he sees the light, he has in him a new vision, a new nature....This view of human nature is optimistic.[11]

Freemasonry allegedly provides what every human being needs in order to attain moral perfection. This heightened morality is evidenced in the fact that Masons are typically involved in charity and engage in civic duties.[12] In short, Freemasonry helps men become better people, who themselves help the world become a better place.

Masons often speak of the transformation the initiate goes through in terms of a "new birth." Indeed, "initiation is, as it were, a death to the world and resurrection to a new life."[13] The candidate stands "on the threshold of this new Masonic life, in darkness, helplessness, and ignorance. Having been wandering amid the errors and covered over with the pollutions of the outer and profane world, he comes inquiringly to our doors, seeking the new birth, and asking a withdrawal of the veil which conceals divine truth from his uninitiated sight."[14] As a result of Masonic initiation—

> ...the candidate should become a new man: he should have a new range of thought; a new feeling about mankind; a new idea about God; and new confidence in immortality; a new passion for brotherhood; a new generosity and charity. The whole purpose of the ritual, of the symbols, of all that is done and said, is solemnly to bring about such a transformation in the man.[15]

We are told that "the whole ceremony is in itself an attempt to create a new nature in the candidate."[16] Without this "new birth" one cannot enter "into the Secret Kingdom of the Rites."[17] The candidate "comes as one whose old self must die in order that a new self may be born; but this new life into which the candidate is born *is not in any sense supernatural.*"[18] The "new man" that results from this "new birth" sets out on a path of *earning* entrance into the Celestial Lodge Above *by ethical living*.

The Masonic view of salvation is works-oriented from beginning to end. A man *earns* salvation by living according to whatever holy book he subscribes to (the Christian Bible, the Hindu Vedas, or the Muslim Koran, for example). William Hammond writes, "Through the fellowship of a moral discipline Masons are taught to qualify for the fellowship of eternal life."[19]John Robinson writes, "The Masonic leaning is to encourage the individual to advance toward the hope of resurrection and immortality through personal merit and acts of charity." [20] Jack Harris, a former Worshipful Master Mason, affirms that "in all the rituals that I taught for eleven years, Masonry did teach how to get to heaven. They taught it with the apron that I wore, by my purity [of] life and conduct....Never at any Masonic ritual did they point out that Jesus is the way of salvation." [21]

One of the closing prayers used in the Lodge includes words that point to the works-oriented salvation of Freemasonry: *"May we so practice thy precepts,* that we may finally obtain thy promises, and find an entrance through the gates into the temple and city of our God."[22] Likewise, the following words are often spoken at a Masonic burial service: "May the present instance of mortality remind us of our own approaching fate, and, by drawing our attention toward Thee, *may we be induced so to regulate our conduct here* that when the moment of dissolution shall arrive at which we must quit this brief scene, we may be received into Thine everlasting kingdom, there to enjoy that uninterrupted and unceasing felicity which is allotted to the souls of just men made perfect."[23]

The lambskin, as noted earlier in this book, is often used by Masons as a symbol of the purity necessary in life to gain entrance into the Grand Lodge Above. Raymond Lee Allen writes, "In all ages the lamb has been deemed an emblem of innocence; he, therefore, who wears the Lambskin as a badge of Masonry is continually reminded of that purity of life and conduct which is necessary to obtain admittance into the Celestial Lodge Above, where the Supreme Architect of the Universe presides."[24]

Hammond agrees and notes, "Associated with innocency and white by nature, it is accepted by the Craft as an emblem of virtue. It serves as a constant reminder of the ideal cleanliness of conduct Masons should ever strive to emulate."[25]

_____REASONING FROM THE SCRIPTURES_____

Man Is a Sinner

The Masonic contention that human beings can in themselves move toward spiritual perfection is seriously misled. Though Masons deny it, the reality is that *every* human being is born into this world in a state of sin. When Adam and Eve sinned, it did not just affect them in an isolated way. It affected the entire human race.

The apostle Paul said that "sin entered the world through one man, and death through sin, and in this way death came to all men, because all sinned" (Romans 5:12). Indeed, "through the disobedience of the one man the many were made sinners…" (Romans 5:19; see also 1 Corinthians 15:21,22).

In Psalm 51:5, David said, "Surely I was sinful at birth, sinful from the time my mother conceived me." According to this verse, human beings are born into the world in a state of sin. The sin nature is passed on *from conception*. This is why Ephesians 2:3 says that human beings are "by nature objects of wrath." Every one of us is born into this world with a sin nature.

From a scriptural perspective, since the time of Adam and Eve every human being is born into the world "totally depraved." This does not mean that human beings are as bad as they can be, or that they commit all the sins that are possible, or that they are incapable of doing kind and benevolent things to others. What it does mean is that every human is contaminated in every part of his or her being by sin, and there is nothing that any human being can do to earn merit before a just and holy God.

The great C.H. Spurgeon once said, "He who doubts human depravity had better study himself."[26] Spurgeon was no doubt thinking of such verses as Romans 3:10-12, which tell us: "There is no one righteous, not even one; there is no one who understands, no one who seeks God. All have turned away, they have together become worthless; there is no one who does good, not even one." In Isaiah 64:6, we read: "All of us have become like one who is unclean, and all our righteous acts are like filthy rags; we all shrivel up like a leaf, and like the wind our sins sweep us away."

Jesus said, "For out of the heart comes evil thoughts, murder, adultery, sexual immorality, theft, false testimony, slander..." (Matthew 15:19). While Freemasonry focuses attention on *external* ethics, the fraternity can do nothing to cure the ills of the *inner* human heart. Only Christ can do that. People's lives do not need an external Masonic tune-up, they need a brand-new engine. They need to become new creatures (2 Corinthians 5:17), and that can only happen with a personal relationship with Christ (John 3:3-5, 18).

Scripture asks, "Can the Ethiopian change his skin or the leopard its spots? Neither can you do good who are accustomed to doing evil" (Jeremiah 13:23). We need a change *from within*. Apologists John Ankerberg and John Weldon are right when they say: "According to the Bible, man cannot simply get out the 'Gavel' and knock off the rough edges of human nature. Sin is far more deeply ingrained in man than that. Simply chipping off a few rough edges will not solve the sin problem or give one right standing before God."[27]

Let us not forget that Jesus taught that people without exception are utterly sinful. He taught that human beings have a grave sin problem that is altogether beyond their means to solve. He taught that human beings are evil (Matthew 12:34) and that man is capable of great wickedness (Mark 7:20-23). Moreover, He said that man is lost (Luke 19:10), that he is in need of repentance before a holy God (Mark 1:15), and that he needs to be born again (John 3:3,5,7). Jesus often spoke of sin in metaphors that illustrate the havoc sin can wreak in one's life. He described sin as blindness (Matthew 23:16-26), sickness (Matthew 9:12), being enslaved in bondage (John 8:34), and living in darkness (John 8:12; 12:35-46). Jesus also taught that sin is a *universal* condition; all people are guilty before God (Luke 7:37-48).

Jesus further taught that both inner thoughts and external acts render a person guilty (Matthew 5:28). He affirmed that God is fully aware of every person's sins, both external acts and inner thoughts; nothing escapes His notice (Matthew 22:18; Luke 6:8; John 4:17-19). In view of such facts, moral perfection among human beings hardly seems attainable.

Even for those who become Christians, there still remains a fountain of evil continually producing irregular and evil desires (read the book of Romans for proof of this). This warfare inside each Christian will be terminated only by death or the second coming of the Lord. While growth in Christlikeness and sanctification will take place during this life (see, for example, Titus 2:12), moral *perfection* will not be attainable on this side of eternity. We read in 1 John 1:8, "If we claim to be without sin, we deceive ourselves and the truth is not in us."

____ *Ask...* _____

- What did the apostle Paul mean when he wrote, "Sin entered the world through one man, and death through sin, and in this way death came to all men, because all sinned" (Romans 5:12)?

- What do you think Paul meant when he wrote that "through the disobedience of the one man the many were made sinners" (Romans 5:19)?

- Doesn't this indicate that *all* human beings are born into the world with a sin nature?

- Is it possible for human beings to attain moral perfection in light of these Scriptures? (Read aloud from Romans 3:10-12: "There is no one righteous, not even one; there is no one who understands, no one who seeks God. All have turned away, they have together become worthless; there is no one who does good, not even one.")

- What do you think about C.H. Spurgeon's comment, "He who doubts human depravity had better study himself"?

Making "Good Men Better"

If a right relationship with God simply requires good ethics, then any religion will do just fine. Hinduism? Islam? Take your pick. After all, aside from Christianity, the other world religions consistently set forth a system of salvation that is based on ethics—that is, making human beings into better people. But Christianity paints man's problem as being much worse than a mere ethics problem.

The Bible portrays all human beings as spiritually *dead* (in "transgressions and sins"(Ephesians 2:1). To put it another way, while the other religions seek to take *good* people (or, more accurately, *bad* people) and make them *better*, Christianity seeks to take *dead* people and make them spiritually *alive*. There's a world of difference between the two. If it is true that we are spiritually dead, this means there is nothing *we* can do in and of ourselves to remedy our situation. *Dead people are helpless.* We need external help. And that help has come in the person of Jesus Christ, who died on the cross for our sins and makes those who believe in Him *spiritually alive*, "resurrected" as it were, into a brand-new life. Because of Jesus, "God raised us up with Christ and seated us with him in the heavenly realms in Christ Jesus" (Ephesians 2:6). "Therefore, if anyone is in Christ, he is a new creation; the old has gone, the new has come!" (2 Corinthians 5:17).

___ Ask... _____

- Did you know that the non-Christian religions focus primarily on ethics? They focus on how to make *bad* people *better*.

- Do you see that Christianity, by contrast, seeks to take *dead* people and make them spiritually *alive*? (Be ready to explain what you mean.)

The Biblical Doctrine of Justification

Contrary to the works system of salvation in the Masonic Lodge, the Bible indicates that we become "justified" the moment we trust in Christ. Biblical justification is a singular and instantaneous event in which God *declares* the believing sinner to be righteous. Justification viewed in this way is a judicial term in which God makes a *legal pronouncement.* It is not based on performance or good works. It involves God's pardoning of sinners and making them absolutely righteous at the moment he or she trusts in Christ for salvation (see Romans 3:25,28,30; 8:33,34; Galatians 4:21–5:13; 1 John 1:7–2:2).

Here is the theological backdrop. Humankind's dilemma of falling short of God's glory (Romans 3:23) pointed to the need for a solution. Man's sin—his utter unrighteousness—was such that there was no way of his coming into a relationship with God on his own. Humankind was guilty before a holy God, and this guilt of sin put a barrier between us.

The solution is found in what is often called *forensic justification.* This means that man is once-for-all pronounced not guilty before God; the word also means that man is once-for-all pronounced righteous before God. "Forensic" comes from a Latin word meaning "forum." In the ancient Roman forum, a court could meet and make judicial or legal declarations. Forensic justification, then, involves God's *judicial declaration* of the believer's righteousness before Him. The believer is legally acquitted of all guilt and the very righteousness of Christ is imputed to his account.[28] Henceforth, when God sees the believer He sees him in all the righteousness of Christ.

Note that this declaration is something external to man. It does not hinge on man's personal level of righteousness. It does not depend on anything that man does. *It is solely based on God's declaration.* It is a once-for-all judicial pronouncement that takes place the moment a sinner places faith in Christ. Even while the person is yet a sinner and is experientially not righteous, he is nevertheless righteous *in God's sight* because of forensic justification.

This view of justification has support from the Old Testament. For example, in Deuteronomy 25:1 we read of judges who *"justify the righteous* and condemn the wicked" (NASB, emphasis added). The word *justify* here clearly means "declare to be righteous" just as *condemn* means "declare to be guilty." (See also, for example, Job 27:5 and Proverbs 17:15.) And when the apostle Paul (an Old Testament scholar par excellence) used the word *justify* in the book of Romans, he did so against this Old Testament backdrop.[29]

Now, as previously noted, at the moment someone places personal faith in Christ, God makes an incalculable "deposit" of righteousness into that person's personal, spiritual bank account. It is a once-for-all act on God's part. It is irrevocable, it is a done deal. It cannot be lost. God's word is final. And this pronouncement on God's part ensures that *the believing sinner will never receive just punishment for the sins committed during life.* This is the wonderful gift of salvation.

Romans 3:24 tells us that God's declaration of righteousness is given to believers "freely by his grace." The word *grace* literally means "unmerited favor." It is because of God's unmerited favor that believers can freely be "declared righteous" before God. *Righteousness cannot be earned.* This does not mean, however, that God's declaration has no objective basis. God did not just decide to overlook man's sin or wink at his unrighteousness. Jesus died on the cross for us. He died in our stead. He paid for our sins. Jesus ransomed us from death by His own death on the cross (2 Corinthians 5:21).

There has been a great exchange. As the great Reformer Martin Luther said, "Lord Jesus, you are my righteousness, I am your sin. You have taken upon yourself what is mine and given me what is yours. You have become what You were not so that I might become what I was not."[30]

A key blessing that results from being declared righteous is that we now have peace with God (Romans 5:1). The Father sees believers through Jesus Christ. And because there is peace between the Father and Jesus Christ, there is also peace between the Father and believers, since believers are "in Christ."

If we were to look through a piece of red glass, everything would appear red. If we were to look through a piece of blue glass, everything would appear blue. If we were to look through a piece of yellow glass, everything would appear yellow. Likewise, when we believe in Jesus Christ as our Savior, God looks at us *through the Lord Jesus Christ*. He sees us in all the white holiness of His Son. Our sins are imputed to the account of Christ, and Christ's righteousness is imputed to our account. For this reason, the Scriptures indicate that there is now no condemnation—literally, *no punishment*—for those who are in Christ Jesus (Romans 8:1).

Biblical Christians believe in justification *by faith in Christ alone*, and not by personal works (Romans 4:1-25; Galatians 3:6-14). God justifies "the one who has faith in Jesus" (Romans 3:26 NASB). Indeed, "we maintain that a man is justified by faith apart from works of the Law" (Romans 3:28 NASB). Our works just won't cut it; we are told that "no one is good—except God alone" (Mark 10:18). "All our righteous deeds are like a filthy garment" (Isaiah 64:6 NASB). Even when we think we are doing good works, they are actually filthy rags. Galatians 2:16 tells us, "Man is not justified by observing the law, but by faith in Jesus Christ. So we, too, have put our faith in Christ Jesus that we may be justified by faith in Christ and not by observing the law, because by observing the law no one will be justified." By trusting in Christ alone, we are given what we could never earn: *a right relationship with God.* "Abraham believed God, and it was credited to him as righteousness" (Romans 4:3). "Having been justified by faith, we have peace with God through our Lord Jesus Christ" (Romans 5:1 NASB).

Good works, however, are a by-product of salvation (Matthew 7:15-23; 1 Timothy 5:10,25). Good works result from the changed purpose for living that salvation brings (1 Corinthians 3:10-15). We are not saved *by* our works, but in order *to do* good works. We do works not to get salvation, but because we have *already received* it. Good works are a *consequence* of justification, not a *condition* for it.

The attempt to earn justification before God by one's righteous and charitable deeds is a doctrine with many casualties along the spiritual highway. Stephen Merritt speaks of an experience he had as a member of the Lodge that drove home this fact to him:

> Again and again I found Masons dying without God and without hope. I was called to the bedside of one member of my lodge who was thought to be dying. He gave me the grip as I sat down by him. He said he was dying and was now in great distress for his soul. I tried to have him look to Christ. But he reproached me, saying I had led him astray. I had told him in the lodge, as Master, that a moral life was enough. He said, "You told me then that it was all right if I was an upright man, and obeyed the precepts of the lodge, but I am leaning on a broken reed; and now I am dying without God. I lay this to your charge, Worshipful Master. I leaned on you and now I am dying."
>
> I groaned in agony and fell on my knees and cried to God to spare the man's life. My heart was almost broken. God heard and spared the

man, but he has since died a Christian. He was converted, and told me I must get out of the lodge; that I could not be consistent as a Christian and a Mason. But I did not see it. Ministers and other good men are in the lodge. They help to make it a dilution and a snare. The times of such ignorance God winked at, but now every man is commanded to repent of lodge folly.[31]

Let this story be a warning. Every one of us will one day die. Before that day arrives, let us see to it that our relationship with God is not foolishly built on what we perceive to be righteous or charitable deeds (our "good works" are actually filthy rags in God's sight), but solely based on faith in Christ, who died on our behalf. Jesus has done it all. By the grace of God, we are given a salvation we could never earn by simply trusting in Christ (John 3:16; Acts 16:31; Ephesians 2:8,9). Masons need to hear and accept this truth or face the severe consequences.

___ *Ask...* ___

- How do you respond to Stephen Merritt's words?

- In view of the biblical teaching that righteous deeds cannot earn salvation, do you really trust the Masonic Lodge's teaching that personal righteousness will get you into heaven? (Be ready to share from Galatians 2:16; Romans 3:28; 5:1.)

- Isn't it infinitely more appealing and realistic to trust in Christ for salvation, involving God's declaration of "not guilty" regarding your sins and the imputation of Christ's own righteousness to your life? (Be ready to explain in detail the biblical view of justification.)

The Biblical "New Birth"

Contrary to the Masonic view that the "new birth" is not a supernatural event but rather refers to a new Masonic life based on Masonic light, Scripture indicates that the true "new birth" *is a supernatural event* that involves a spiritual birth. Being "born again" literally means to be "born from above." It refers to the act of God by which He gives eternal life to the person who believes in Christ (Titus 3:5).

Being "born again" places one into God's eternal family (1 Peter 1:23). Just as a *physical* birth places a new baby into a family, so a *spiritual* birth places one into the family of God. In John 3, Jesus spoke about the need to be born again with a man named Nicodemus. Here we find a Pharisee, a Jewish leader, who would have been trusting in his physical descent from Abraham for entrance into the Messiah's kingdom. The Jews believed that because they were physically related to Abraham, they were in a privileged position before God.

Jesus, however, denied such a possibility. Parents can transmit to their children only the nature which they themselves possess. Since each human parent has a sin nature, each parent transmits this same nature to their children. All people are born in sin. And what is sinful cannot enter the kingdom of God (John 3:5). The only way one can enter God's forever family is to experience a spiritual rebirth, and this is precisely what Jesus emphasized to Nicodemus.

The moment we place our trust in Jesus, the Holy Spirit infuses our dead human spirits with the eternal life of God and we are reborn spiritually. One moment we are spiritually dead; the next moment we are spiritually alive. At the moment of the new birth, the believer receives a new spiritual nature or capacity that expresses itself in spiritual concerns and interests. Formerly uninterested in the things of God, the new believer now is concerned with the things of God—His Word, His people, His service, His glory, and above all, God Himself.

Contradictory Views of Salvation

In closing this chapter, it is important to note that the salvation offered by Hinduism and Islam is radically different than that offered by Christianity. The relevance of this fact seems obvious, but at the risk of sounding redundant, I ask now what I have asked in earlier chapters: How can a Christian in good conscience worship under the same roof with Hindus and Muslims when their views of salvation radically differ from what Christianity teaches?

In Hinduism, the soul and salvation are interpreted in terms of reincarnation and the law of karma. *Samsara* refers to the cycle of death and rebirth in Hinduism. The fate of the soul in each lifetime is said to be governed by the law of karma. If one builds up good karma during one's life, one will be born in the next life in a favorable state. If one builds up bad karma during one's life, one will be born in the next life in a less desirable state. This allegedly goes on life after life after life.

The goal, in Hinduism, is to eventually break free from the wheel of karma and merge with the Universal Soul. This deliverance from samsara leads to immortality. *Moksha* is the Hindu term used for the liberation of the soul from the wheel of karma.[32] This is salvation in Hinduism. At this point, the person becomes *one* with Brahman (God or the Universal Soul which is believed to permeate all reality).

In Islam, by contrast, salvation is found in complete surrender to Allah. This is in keeping with the meaning of *Islam* ("submission") and *Muslim* ("one who submits"). Salvation is based on obedience to Allah. Human effort is pivotal in the Islamic view of salvation.

In contrast to Islam and Hinduism, Christianity teaches that at the moment one trusts in Christ, one is spiritually born again (John 3:5), declared righteous (Romans 3:24), reconciled to God (2 Corinthians 5:19), forgiven (Hebrews 10:17), and adopted into God's forever family (Romans 8:14,15). Salvation is a free gift of God received by faith in Jesus Christ (John 3:16; Acts 16:31). The differences between Christianity, Hinduism, and Islam could not be greater! Christians should never worship in harmony with proponents of these religions.

_____ *Ask...* _____

- Did you know that Hinduism's view of salvation involves reincarnation over many lifetimes until the person allegedly becomes increasingly perfect, thereby enabling him to eventually break free from the process and "merge" with the Universal Soul?

- Did you know that Islam, by contrast, argues that salvation comes only by personal surrender and obedience to Allah?

- Since both of these contradict the biblical view of salvation, how can proponents of each of these religions worship under the same roof together? If one of these is right, the others must be wrong.

11

Redefining Sin and Salvation: Part 2

In the previous chapter we saw that Masons believe righteous works and charitable deeds are necessary to gain entrance into the Celestial Lodge Above. We continue our examination of this issue, focusing on a representative sampling of some of the primary Scripture verses Masons cite.

JAMES 2:17-26: *Faith Without Works Is Dead*

Masonic View: Albert Pike urges, "Do not forget the words of the apostle James."[1] He then alludes to the following words from James' epistle:

> In the same way, faith by itself, if it is not accompanied by action, is dead. But someone will say, "You have faith; I have deeds." Show me your faith without deeds, and I will show you my faith by what I do....You see that a

> person is justified by what he does and not by
> faith alone. In the same way, was not even Rahab
> the prostitute considered righteous for what she
> did when she gave lodging to the spies and sent
> them off in a different direction? As the body
> without the spirit is dead, so faith without deeds
> is dead (James 2:17,18,24-26).

Pike thus argues that a man is justified *by what he does*. This is where Masons are said to really shine. They do lots of good works and engage in many charitable acts. As Vindex puts it, Masonry "not only believes in deeds, it performs deeds, and in this alone we are justified in the eyes of God."[2]

Biblical View: In this passage James is basically answering the question, "How can someone tell whether or not a person has true faith?" And all that follows in chapter 2 answers this question.

James begins by asking, "What use is it, my brethren, if someone says he has faith but he has no works? Can that faith save him?" (James 2:14). Notice the oft-neglected little word "says." The people who make an empty profession of faith show their lack by the absence of works. But James shows that true faith results in works, which become *visible evidences of faith's invisible presence.* In other words, good works are the "vital signs" indicating that faith is alive.

Keep in mind that James was writing to Jewish Christians, "to the twelve tribes" (James 1:1), who were in danger of giving nothing but lip-service to Jesus. Apparently some of these Jewish Christians had made a false claim of faith. It is this spurious boast of faith that James was condemning. *Claiming* to have faith is insufficient. Genuine faith is evidenced by works. Indeed,

> workless faith is worthless faith; it is unproduc-
> tive, sterile, barren, dead! Great claims may be
> made about a corpse that is supposed to have
> come to life, but if it does not move, if there are

> no vital signs, no heartbeat, no perceptible pulse,
> it is still dead. The false claims are silenced by
> the evidence.[3]

The fact is, apart from the spirit, the body is dead. It is a life-less corpse. By analogy, apart from the evidence of good works, faith is dead. It is lifeless and nonproductive. This is what James is teaching in these verses.

It is important not to miss the fact that the object of faith in James' theology is Jesus Christ. James, himself a servant of Jesus Christ, makes reference to his spiritual brothers as "believers *in our glorious Lord Jesus Christ*" (2:1, emphasis added). It is not just faith in some "Great Architect of the Universe" of which James speaks, but faith in the Lord Jesus Christ. This is an extremely important point to emphasize to the Mason.

___ *Ask...* ___

- Do you agree that James 2:26 indicates that apart from the spirit, the body is dead?

- By analogy, can we agree that apart from the evidence of good works, faith is dead?

- Can you see from James 2:26 that good works are the "vital signs" indicating that faith is alive?

Note: The Mason may well agree with these initial points, but these are simply preparatory to the main point you want to make.

- Did you know that in James' theology, the object of faith is not the "Great Architect of the Universe" but rather Jesus Christ? It is faith specifically *in Jesus* that saves, not faith in the broadly defined deity of the Masonic Lodge. (Be ready to share James 2:1.)

JAMES 1:27: "Acceptable" Religion Requires Righteous Works

Masonic View: In James 1:27, we read, "Religion that God our Father accepts as pure and faultless is this: to look after orphans and widows in their distress and to keep oneself from being polluted by the world." Since Masons engage in many good works, they believe they fulfill the spirit of this verse.[4]

Biblical View: A fundamental rule of interpreting the Bible is that *Scripture interprets Scripture.* James 1:27 cannot be isolated from all the other verses in the Bible that speak about religion and a right relationship to God. In this verse, James was providing a needed corrective to a situation in the early church. Some orphans and widows had indeed been overlooked, so James emphasized the necessity of watching after them. But by saying what he did in verse 27, James was not also saying that salvation comes by good deeds and not by faith. His big point throughout his epistle is that faith in Christ *is the necessary condition* for salvation, but it is the *kind* of faith that naturally leads to good works. Good works are a by-product of salvation (Matthew 7:15-23; 1 Timothy 5:10,25). Good works *result* from the changed purpose for living that salvation brings (1 Corinthians 3:10-15). We are not saved *by* our works, but we are saved in order *to do* good works. We do works not to *get* salvation, but because we have *already received it.* Works are a *consequence* of being saved, not a *condition* for it.

___ Ask... _____

- Though it is good to be righteous and charitable, James, in his epistle, indicates that good works do not yield salvation in themselves. Did you know that James emphasized the absolute necessity of faith for salvation? (Be ready to share the true meaning of James 2:14-26.)

- Did you know that in James' theology, good works *follow* faith? We are not saved by our works, but we are saved in order *to do* good works. We do works not to get salvation, because we have already received it. Works are a consequence of being saved, not a condition for it.

LUKE 10:30-37: *The Good Samaritan*

Masonic View: This passage contains Jesus' words about the Good Samaritan to an expert in the law:

> Jesus said: "A man was going down from Jerusalem to Jericho, when he fell into the hands of robbers. They stripped him of his clothes, beat him and went away, leaving him half dead. A priest happened to be going down the same road, and when he saw the man, he passed by on the other side. So too, a Levite, when he came to the place and saw him, passed by on the other side. But a Samaritan, as he traveled, came where the man was; and when he saw him, he took pity on him. He went to him and bandaged his wounds, pouring on oil and wine. Then he put the man on his own donkey, took him to an inn and took care of him. The next day he took out two silver coins and gave them to the innkeeper. 'Look after him,' he said, 'and when I return, I will reimburse you for any extra expense you may have.'
>
> "Which of these three do you think was a neighbor to the man who fell into the hands of robbers?"
>
> The expert in the law replied, "The one who had mercy on him."
>
> Jesus told him, "Go and do likewise."

Masons often assert that the true test of religion is the good works that result from the religion, as we see in the story of the Good Samaritan. Richard Thorn argues that Masons shine in this regard.[5]

Biblical View: This passage has nothing to do with salvation. It *only* deals with how to treat other people. More precisely, Jesus was teaching that when you see someone in need, and you have the means of helping that person in need, then you should help that person. Certainly we can be thankful that Masons are interested in helping other people. However, if the Mason thinks that by helping other people, he is earning entrance into the Celestial Lodge Above, then that is wrong. As pointed out earlier, good works have nothing to do with salvation; good works *follow* salvation. We are not saved *by* our works, but in order *to do* good works.

This same Jesus that told the story about the Good Samaritan constantly taught that *it is only by personal faith in Him* that one can be saved. Consider:

- In John 5:24, Jesus said, "I tell you the truth, whoever hears my word and believes him who sent me has eternal life and will not be condemned; he has crossed over from death to life."

- In John 11:25, Jesus said, "I am the resurrection and the life. He who believes in me will live, even though he dies."

- In John 12:46, Jesus said, "I have come into the world as a light, so that no one who believes in me should stay in darkness."

If salvation were not by faith alone, then Jesus' message in the Gospel of John—manifest in the above quotations—would be deceptive. If righteous works and charitable deeds were necessary for salvation, it would have been deceitful of Jesus to say so many times that there is only one condition for salvation—*faith*.

_____ *Ask...* _____

- Would it surprise you to know that I commend Masons for doing charitable works?

- When Jesus taught that we should be like the Good Samaritan in helping others, do you think He was saying that *by doing* good a person can go to heaven?

- If yes, how do you reconcile this with the fact that the same Jesus who told the story of the Good Samaritan asserted over and over again that it is *only* by personal faith in Him that a person can be saved? (Be ready to share John 5:24; 11:25; 12:46.)

MATTHEW 7:24-27: *The Necessity of Doing God's Will*

Masonic View: In Matthew 7:24-27, which is part of Jesus' Sermon on the Mount, we read:

> Therefore everyone who hears these words of mine and puts them into practice is like a wise man who built his house on the rock. The rain came down, the streams rose, and the winds blew and beat against that house; yet it did not fall, because it had its foundation on the rock. But everyone who hears these words of mine and does not put them into practice is like a foolish man who built his house on sand. The rain came down, the streams rose, and the winds blew and beat against that house, and it fell with a great crash.

Masons argue that Jesus, in this section of the Sermon on the Mount, is pointing to the importance of *doing* the will of God. Those who hear God's words and do them are likened to a wise man who built his house upon a rock. "It is only in *doing* that man submits to the will of God."[6] Masons, it is argued, engage in *doing* God's work.

Biblical View: I find it most interesting that Masons would cite this verse, since they seem to pay little attention to many of Jesus' words in the New Testament. For example:

- Instead of believing what Jesus has to say about man being fallen in sin, Masons believe man is not fallen. (See my discussion of this in chapter 10.)

- Instead of believing that human beings are spiritually lost (Luke 19:10), Masons say that human beings are essentially good people who can be made into better people.

- Instead of believing that Jesus is the only way to salvation (John 14:6), Masons say members of any religion can be saved regardless of who they worship.

- Whereas Masons are completely silent on the doctrine of hell, Jesus taught that this is the destiny of all who reject Him (see Matthew 25:46).

Masons certainly cannot "do" God's will when they so blatantly reject much of what Jesus reveals in Scripture. Related to this, it is interesting to note that Jesus taught, "The work of God is this: to believe in the one he has sent" (John 6:29). If doing God's work is the most important thing, as Masons say, then they should turn to Jesus and believe in Him alone for salvation.

Ask...

- Did you know that in John 6:29 Jesus said, "The work of God is this: to believe in the one he has sent"?

- If doing God's will is so important to Masons, why don't they turn to Jesus and believe in Him alone for salvation?

MATTHEW 25:35-40: *The Necessity of Charitable Works*

Masonic View: In Matthew 25:35-40, Jesus emphasizes the importance of helping others in need. He is portrayed, at this future judgment, giving an invitation of eternal life to the righteous who helped others:

> "For I was hungry and you gave me something to eat, I was thirsty and you gave me something to drink, I was a stranger and you invited me in, I needed clothes and you clothed me, I was sick and you looked after me, I was in prison and you came to visit me." Then the righteous will answer him, "Lord, when did we see you hungry and feed you, or thirsty and give you something to drink? When did we see you a stranger and invite you in, or needing clothes and clothe you? When did we see you sick or in prison and go to visit you?" The King will reply, "I tell you the truth, whatever you did for one of the least of these brothers of mine, you did for me."

By virtue of the fact that Masons engage in charitable works toward other people, they believe they fulfill the spirit of Jesus' words in Matthew 25.[7] Indeed, "here, in the words of our blessed Lord himself is described one of the acts of mercy and charity which will lead us to heaven, and here, too, Freemasonry has nothing to fear by comparison with any other body in the world."[8]

Biblical View: As noted previously, a basic interpretive principle is that *Scripture interprets Scripture*. Ephesians 2:8,9 indicates that salvation comes only by faith in Christ and is based entirely on the grace of God, and other Scriptures support this view. But, of course, authentic faith expresses itself in good works (see verse 10). Indeed, the lives people live form the *test* of the faith they profess. Those who are truly saved give evidence of that salvation in the works they perform.

This is certainly the case of the "sheep" mentioned in Matthew 25:31-34. Many Bible scholars have noted that these verses deal with the situation on earth immediately following the second coming of Christ (see verse 31). After His second coming, Christ will gather all people and separate the "sheep" from the "goats" based on how they have treated the "brothers." Who are the brothers? Many expositors believe these brothers are the 144,000 Jews mentioned in Revelation 7 and 14, who will apparently be engaged in evangelism all over the earth during the future Tribulation period. Who are the sheep? These are believers who give *evidence* of their faith by treating the 144,000 brothers kindly, giving them drink, and food, and clothing, and such. The "goats," by contrast, *are not believers* because they give no evidence of faith in their lives.

Other biblical commentators believe these "brothers" may be Jews in general, as opposed to the specific group of 144,000. *The Bible Knowledge Commentary* suggests:

> The expression "these brothers" must refer to a third group that is neither sheep nor goats. The only possible group would be Jews, physical brothers of the Lord. In view of the distress in the Tribulation Period, it is clear that any believing Jew will have a difficult time surviving (cf. 24:15-21). The forces of the world dictator will be doing everything possible to exterminate all Jews (see Revelation 12:17). A Gentile going out of his way to assist a Jew in the Tribulation will mean that Gentile has become a believer in

Jesus Christ during the Tribulation. By such a
stand and action, a believing Gentile will put his
life in jeopardy. *His works will not save him; but
his works will reveal that he is redeemed.*[9]

Matthew 25:31-46, then, is dealing with a very specific context
(the Tribulation period), and should not be taken to be a general
description of what God requires for someone to be saved. Since
Scripture interprets Scripture, we may conclude that a person is
saved by faith in Christ (Acts 16:31; John 3:16), and this faith gives
evidence of itself in many ways, including treating people kindly
(see James 2:14-26). The Matthew 25:35-40 passage cannot be log-
ically cited in support of a works system of salvation.

LEVITICUS 25:35: *Almsgiving Required*

Masonic View: In Leviticus 25:35 we read, "If one of your
countrymen becomes poor and is unable to support himself
among you, help him as you would an alien or a temporary resi-
dent, so that he can continue to live among you." Masons sometimes cite this verse and suggest that almsgiving "is intimately
interwoven with the whole superstructure of Freemasonry, and
its practice is inculcated by all the principles of the Order....No
true Mason can live for himself alone; he must live for others who
need his assistance."[10]

Biblical View: It is true that this verse urges a spirit of generosity in reaching out to help those who are less fortunate. And
there is no debate that Masons have done generous, charitable
work. Yet there are two points to make when Masons cite this
verse.

First, if the Mason were seeking to engage in charitable works
as an end in itself, that would be one thing. But it is clear from
reading Masonic literature that Masons seek to engage in righteous living and charitable deeds *as a means of earning entrance
into the Celestial Lodge Above.* This is where the problem is from
a biblical viewpoint. Scripture is emphatic that no amount of good

works can contribute in even a small way toward a person's salvation. As the apostle Paul put it in Ephesians 2:8,9, "It is by grace you have been saved, through faith—and this not from yourselves, it is the gift of God—not by works, so that no one can boast." We are told, "He saved us, not because of righteous things we had done, but because of his mercy" (Titus 3:5). Scripture assures us, "No one will be declared righteous in his sight by observing the law" (Romans 3:20). So, while charity is a good thing, it does nothing in terms of salvation. Faith in Christ is necessary for those who seek their ultimate destiny in heaven.

A second point that must be made is that if Masons are going to cite a verse from Leviticus on good deeds, then why don't they focus on other verses in Leviticus that admonish us to avoid pagan deities and follow the one true God of the Bible. Leviticus 19:4 says, "Do not turn to idols or make gods of cast metal for yourselves. I am the LORD your God." Leviticus 26:1 commands, "Do not make idols or set up an image or a sacred stone for yourselves, and do not place a carved stone in your land to bow down before it. I am the LORD your God." Similar admonitions are found in the New Testament (see 1 Corinthians 5:10,11; 6:9; 10:14; Galatians 5:20; and 1 Peter 4:3).

As noted earlier, Freemasonry teaches that God's true name is Jabulon, which combines the names of Yahweh, Baal, and Osiris, the last two of which are pagan deities. I noted earlier that Baal worship is perhaps the epitome of evil idol worship in the ancient world, involving such things as ritual prostitution (Judges 2:17; Hosea 4:12-14; Deuteronomy 23:17), self-mutilation (1 Kings 18:28), and the sacrificing (ritual murder) of little children (Jeremiah 19:4,5). The worship of "Jabulon" is abominable and flies in the face of God's commandments in Leviticus and elsewhere.

GENESIS 28:12: *A Ladder to Heaven*

Masonic View: In Genesis 28:12 we read of Jacob, "He had a dream in which he saw a stairway resting on the earth, with its top reaching to heaven, and the angels of God were ascending and descending on it." Mackey argues that this stairway or ladder is "a symbol of moral and intellectual progress" involving "a succession of steps, of gates, of decrees...."[11] That's why the stairway or ladder is a symbol of the progress one makes in a Masonic Lodge, both *mentally* (in receiving Masonic light) and *morally* (in acting upon that light). The ladder represents the "progressive upward course to be traveled by earthly sojourners."[12]

Biblical View: Genesis 28:12 does not deal with the moral and/or intellectual progress that takes place within a Masonic Lodge. This passage merely illustrates communication between heaven and earth, with angels ascending and descending on the stairway. Commentator Donald Grey Barnhouse notes, "Jacob must have been thinking of the distance between him and God, and of his need to bridge that distance. God was not slow to answer."[13] In context, God is communicating from heaven to earth (*to Jacob*) that He will honor the covenant He made with Israel (see verses 13-16). Masons are going beyond Scripture, practicing eisogesis (reading a meaning into the text), to interpret this stairway as something humans metaphorically climb by progression in a Masonic Lodge.

_____ *Ask...* _____

- Is there any indication in the context of this verse that *humans* climb this ladder?

- Does it seem reasonable to you that Jacob may have been thinking of the distance between himself and God and the need to bridge that distance?

- Wouldn't this dream of the ladder, which originated with God, meet this need?

- Contextually, do you agree that God is communicating from heaven to earth (to Jacob) that He will honor the covenant He made with Israel? (Consult the broader context of Genesis 28.)

AMOS 7:7,8: *The Plumb Line—A Symbol of Purity*

Masonic View: Amos 7:7,8 says, "This is what he showed me: The Lord was standing by a wall that had been built true to plumb, with a plumb line in his hand. And the LORD asked me, 'What do you see, Amos?' 'A plumb line,' I replied. Then the Lord said, 'Look, I am setting a plumb line among my people Israel; I will spare them no longer.'"

This metaphor is taken from the custom of using a line in measuring a plot of land, and in dividing portions of it among several people.[14] Masons often cite the plumb line in Amos 7 as a way of symbolizing the purified character that is necessary to enter into the Celestial Lodge Above. Mackey tells us that "the plumb admonishes us to walk uprightly in our several stations, before God and man, squaring our actions by the square of virtue, and remembering that we are traveling upon the level of time to that undiscovered country from whose bourne no traveler returns."[15]

Biblical View: This passage is written in specific reference to the nation of Israel. In using the term *plumb line,* Scripture is telling us that God's people had been "built" according to God's perfect standards, and they were expected to be true to those standards, but in reality they were completely "out of plumb" when tested (see 2 Kings 21:13).[16] In Amos 7, the nation is being called to repentance, called to get back on the right course.

Though Masons use this verse to symbolically refer to walking uprightly, the more appropriate application to draw is that Freemasonry should be measured according to God's perfect standard (the plumb-line of the Word of God). Where it is found wanting, it should commit to change. The Masonic view of God, Jesus Christ, sin, and salvation should all be measured against the plumb line of Scripture and then altered to fit the biblical view. Such an action would require that worship under the same roof with members of pagan religions (i.e., Hindus and Muslims) should cease, just as God called the Israelites not to fellowship with pagan religions and nations (see Leviticus 19:4; 26:1; Judges 2:11-13; 1 Chronicles 5:25; Ezekiel 16:28-30; 23:5-7).

___ *Ask...* ___

- Since the plumb line metaphorically represents God's perfect standard, would you mind if we sat down together and measured the Masonic view of God, Jesus Christ, sin, and salvation against the plumb line of Scripture? (Take one issue at a time. See chapters 7, 9, and 10 for important information to share on these doctrines.)

DEUTERONOMY 28:14: *Do Not Deviate from the Path*

Masonic View: In Deuteronomy 28:14 we read, "Do not turn aside from any of the commands I give you today, to the right or to the left...." Masons sometimes cite this verse using the "plumb" as a symbol of not deviating from the right path.[17]

Biblical View: Taken in its entirety, this verse reads: "Do not turn aside from any of the commands I give you today, to the right or to the left, *following other gods and serving them*" (emphasis added). The significance of the last part of the verse increases in view of the fact that the god of the Masonic Lodge is not the God of the Bible. Indeed, as demonstrated in chapter 7—"God: The Great Architect of the Universe"—God's Masonry name is said to be *Jabulon*, a hybrid involving Yahweh, Baal, and Osiris. To worship Jabulon is to worship a pagan deity, which violates the injunction in Deuteronomy 28:14. A key aspect of not "turning to the right or left" involves not participating in any way with a pagan deity. Whether they realize it or not, Masons *have* participated with a pagan deity.

___ *Ask...* ___

- Would you please read aloud Deuteronomy 28:14?

- Do you not agree that "turning to the right or left" in this verse specifically involves a command not to follow pagan deities?

- Since Masonry teaches (in the Royal Arch degree) that God's true name is Jabulon, which is a hybrid name involving Yahweh, Baal, and Osiris, how is this verse applicable to Masonry? (Be ready to point out the evils of Baal worship and God's injunction to not serve pagan dieties.)

LUKE 9:62: *Continuing Masonic Education Needed*

Masonic View: Masonic education involving the reception of Masonic light, which is necessary for entering the Celestial Lodge Above, is viewed as a perpetual and ongoing process. Mackey cites Luke 9:62 in making this point: "No one who puts his hand to the plow and looks back is fit for service in the kingdom of God." He argues:

> There is in Speculative Masonry always a progress, symbolized by its peculiar ceremonies of initiation. There is an advancement from a lower to a higher state—from darkness to light—from death to life—from error to truth. The candidate is always ascending; he is never stationary; never goes back; but each step he takes brings him to some new mental illumination—to the knowledge of some more elevated doctrine.[18]

Biblical View: Contextually, this verse builds on a situation involving a man who wanted to bury his father before engaging in proclaiming the kingdom of God. The man said to Jesus, "I will follow you, Lord; but first let me go back and say good-by to my family" (Luke 9:61). It is at this point that Jesus said, "No one who puts his hand to the plow and looks back is fit for service in the kingdom of God."

Jesus is painting a picture that would have been very familiar to His first-century hearers. The plows used in that day were primitive, constituting a piece of wood with a handle at one end and a metal tip at the other end to break up soil. If a man engaged in handling the plow took his eyes off his work and looked backward, it would cause the furrow he was plowing to become crooked, which wasn't good. Holding the metal tip in such a way that it produced the desired results while plowing required constant attention.

Contrary to the Masonic interpretation, which sees this passage as referring to continuing Masonic education, the point Jesus was really making was that anyone who wishes to engage in *service to Him* must give his whole heart to the matter and not be double-minded, with one foot in service to the kingdom and one foot in the affairs of this world. There should be no divided interests. The person who would follow Jesus and engage in kingdom work needs a firm hand and a steady eye on the forward-moving plow.

Jesus stressed this truth to those who followed Him because in the days to come they would be subjected to harsh persecution by the religious leaders of Israel. Jesus was telling His followers to settle their priorities now—or they would never go the distance.

___ *Ask...* _____

First summarize the context by reading Luke 9:57-61.

- Contextually, isn't Jesus saying that anyone who wishes to engage in *service to Him* must give his whole heart to the matter and not be double-minded, with one foot in service to the kingdom and one foot in the affairs of this world?

- Why do you think Jesus stressed this truth to those who would follow Him? (If the Mason is not sure, discuss the harsh persecution followers would soon face by the religious leaders of Israel.)

- Does this verse *really* refer to pursuing Masonic education? (If he says yes, respectfully ask him to prove it from the context.)

DANIEL 12:2: *Resurrection Is Assured*

Masonic View: In Daniel 12:2 we read, "Multitudes who sleep in the dust of the earth will awake: some to everlasting life, others to shame and everlasting contempt." Masons sometimes use this verse in support of their assurance that they will be resurrected from the dead.[19]

Biblical View: Masons are right in saying that Daniel 12:2 gives all people an assurance of resurrection—but some will be resurrected *as believers*, who will spend eternity with Christ in heaven (participating in "everlasting life"), and some will be resurrected *as unbelievers* who will spend eternity in hell ("shame and everlasting contempt"). Jesus taught that it is not just the saved who are resurrected, but the unsaved as well (see John 5:28,29).

Scripture clarifies this by telling us that there are two types of resurrection, respectively referred to as the "first resurrection" and the "second resurrection" (Revelation 20:5,6,11-15). The first resurrection is the resurrection of Christians, while the second resurrection is the resurrection of the wicked. We are told, "Blessed and holy are those who have part in the first resurrection....They will be priests of God and of Christ and will reign with him for a thousand years" (verse 6). These are people who have trusted in Christ alone for salvation. All those who have *refused* to trust in Christ, however, are excluded from this first resurrection.

The "second" resurrection will be an awful spectacle, for all the unsaved of all time will be resurrected, judged at the Great White Throne judgment, and then cast alive into the Lake of Fire (Revelation 20:11-15). They will be given bodies that will last forever, but bodies that are subject to pain and suffering. Like the devil and his angels, they will exist forever in the Lake of Fire.

These resurrections are a powerful reminder of the importance of sharing God's truth with Masons.

12

Masonry's Great Omission: The Judgment and Hell

A blaring omission from all Masonic literature is the doctrine of a future judgment *and* the doctrine of hell. Although Masons make no mention of judgment or hell, the Bible is full of references to these subjects. What is particularly relevant is that Scripture portrays Jesus Christ as being the Judge of Christians (at the "Judgment Seat of Christ") *as well as* unbelievers (at the "Great White Throne" judgment). Christians will be evaluated according to their level of faithfulness to God during their earthly sojourn. Based on how they fare, they will receive or lose rewards—but *all* Christians remain saved and go to heaven. Unbelievers will be judged, then cast into the Lake of Fire, where they will spend eternity. In view of the sobering reality of these judgments, those who strip the name of Jesus Christ from Masonic literature and proceedings have clearly not taken "the long look" in considering the ultimate consequences of their actions.

Mason H.L. Haywood once said that "our Fraternity leaves it to each individual to fashion his own conceptions of the Beyond."[1] However, this claim does not represent the way things *truly* are at the Masonic Lodge. The literature and rituals of Freemasonry often speak of the Celestial Lodge Above (heaven), and this Celestial Lodge is viewed as the ultimate destiny of *all* Masons as a result of their good works. By contrast, hell is not mentioned *in a single ritual or ceremony* of the three degrees of the Blue Lodge, the 10 degrees of the York Rite, or the 30 degrees of the Scottish Rite. The result of this is that many Masons think they will automatically go to heaven when they die. They are never told the penalty for rejecting God's true salvation in Jesus Christ. This, in itself, constitutes a "teaching" on the afterlife by the Masonic Lodge. It is teaching by omission. Here's what Albert Mackey has to say regarding the afterlife:

> To teach the doctrine of immortality is the great object of the Third Degree. In its ceremonies we learn that life here is a time of labor, and that, working at the construction of a spiritual temple, we are worshiping the Great Architect, for whom we build that temple. But we learn also that, when that life is ended, it closes only to open upon a newer and higher one, where, in a second temple and a purer Lodge, the Mason will find eternal truth. Death, therefore, in Masonic philosophy, is the symbol of initiation completed, perfected, and consummated.[2]

No concern of a future judgment or the possibility of hell is even hinted at in such statements. Mackey simply affirms that "the life of man, regulated by morality, faith, and justice, will be rewarded at its closing hour by the prospect of eternal bliss."[3]

In view of this, I would be remiss not to address in this book what Scripture has to say about the future judgment and hell. All

Masons need to understand the sobering teachings of Scripture on this subject. They need to be told the "rest of the story."

The Judgment of Humankind

Though many people prefer to avoid any mention of the subject, the fact remains that *every* human being will face judgment. From Scripture, we can affirm that the purpose of the Christian's judgment is altogether different from that of the non-Christian's judgment. The Christian is evaluated not in relation to salvation (which is absolutely secure) but in relation to receiving or losing rewards from God. The non-Christian, however, is judged as a precursor to his being cast into the Lake of Fire.

Before tackling this issue, we must firmly establish in our minds that God is a God of judgment. In recent years this idea has fallen out of favor, which is reflected in Masonic writings. Most people prefer to focus almost exclusively on the love of God. Certainly it is true that God *is* a God of love, but He is also a *holy and righteous Judge*. This has always been true.

In his modern classic *Knowing God*, popular writer J. I. Packer sums it up this way:

> The reality of divine judgment, as a fact, is set forth on page after page of Bible history. God judged Adam and Eve, expelling them from the Garden and pronouncing curses on their future earthly life (Genesis 3). God judged the corrupt world of Noah's day, sending a flood to destroy mankind (Genesis 6–8). God judged Sodom and Gomorrah, engulfing them in a volcanic catastrophe (Genesis 18–19). God judged Israel's Egyptian taskmasters, just as He foretold He would (see Genesis 15:14), unleashing against them the terrors of the ten plagues (Exodus 7–12). God judged those who worshiped the golden calf, using the Levites as His executioners

(Exodus 32:26-35). God judged Nadab and Abihu for offering Him strange fire (Leviticus 10:1ff.), as later He judged Korah, Dathan, and Abiram, who were swallowed up in an earth tremor. God judged Achan for sacrilegious thieving; he and his family were wiped out (Joshua 7). God judged Israel for unfaithfulness to Him after their entry into Canaan, causing them to fall under the dominion of other nations (Judges 2:11ff.; 3:5ff.; 4:1ff.).[4]

In the New Testament, we find that judgment falls on the Jews for rejecting Jesus Christ (Matthew 21:42,43), on Ananias and Sapphira for lying to God (Acts 5:1-11), on Herod for his self-exalting pride (Acts 12:21-23), and on Christians in Corinth who were afflicted with illness in response to their irreverence in connection with the Lord's Supper (1 Corinthians 11:29-32). God truly *is* a God of judgment. For us to forget or ignore this fact is to do so at our own peril. God will hold all of us accountable for the things done in this life.

Judgment Is According to the Light Given

As a foundational principle, it is important to grasp that God's judgment of each person will be based upon that particular person's response to the revealed will of God. Certainly God will take into account the fact that people have different degrees of knowledge of God's will (and, thus, their ability to fulfill that will). Jesus spoke of this when He said, "The one who does not know and does things deserving punishment will be beaten with few blows. From everyone who has been given much, much will be demanded; and from the one who has been entrusted with much, much more will be asked" (Luke 12:48). Each person's knowledge of God's will is always taken into consideration (see Matthew 11:21-24).

We may rest assured that God's judgment is utterly fair. In the face of the many injustices that characterize life in the present age, we can rest in the certainty that God knows all, that He is not mocked, and that He has appointed a day in which He will judge the world in righteousness (Acts 17:31).

For the Mason who knows what the Bible teaches about Jesus Christ, knows what the Bible teaches about God, and knows what the Bible teaches about how one is saved (the gospel of Jesus Christ), the judgment will be strict. Despite his knowledge, the Mason has chosen to remain within an institution that sets forth deviant forms of these pivotal Christian doctrines and worships alongside those who participate in pagan religions.

The Judgment of Believers

All Christians will one day stand before the Judgment Seat of Christ (Romans 14:8-10). At that time, each Christian's life will be examined in regard to deeds done while in the body. Personal motives and intents of the heart will also be weighed.

The idea of a "Judgment Seat" relates to the athletic games of Paul's day. "After the races and games concluded, a dignitary or even the emperor himself took his seat on an elevated throne in the arena. One by one the winning athletes came up to the throne to receive a reward—usually a wreath of leaves, a victor's crown."[5] In the case of Christians, each of us will stand before Christ the Judge and receive (or lose) rewards. Christ's judgment of us will not be in a corporate setting like a big company being praised or scolded by the boss. Rather it will be *individual* and *personal*. "We will all stand before God's judgment seat" (Romans 14:10). Each of us will be judged on an individual basis.

This judgment has nothing to do with whether or not the Christian will remain saved. Those who have truly placed faith in Christ *are* saved, and nothing threatens that. Believers are eternally secure in their salvation. This judgment has to do with the reception or loss of rewards.

I should note, in passing, that some "Christian Masons" have trusted in Christ, yet still choose to attend a Masonic Lodge. These men will be judged at the Judgment Seat of Christ. Other

"Christian Masons" may just be "cultural Christians" who have not truly trusted in Christ. This latter group will participate in the "Great White Throne" judgment, which is the judgment of unbelievers.

It seems to be the testimony of Scripture that some Christians at the judgment may have a sense of deprivation and suffer some degree of forfeiture and shame. Indeed, certain rewards may be forfeited that otherwise might have been received, and this will involve a sense of loss. The fact is, Christians differ radically in holiness of conduct and faithfulness in service. God in His justice and holiness takes all this into account. Some believers will be without shame and others *with* shame at the Judgment Seat of Christ. Second John 8 warns us, "Watch out that you do not lose what you have worked for, but that you may be rewarded fully." In 1 John 2:28, John wrote about the possibility of a believer actually being ashamed at Christ's coming. What will it be like for the "Christian Mason"? Will he forfeit rewards as a result of participating in a God-dishonoring Masonic Lodge? I believe the answer can only be yes.

Tried by Fire

In 1 Corinthians 3:11-15 we read,

> No one can lay any foundation other than the one already laid, which is Jesus Christ. If any man builds on this foundation using gold, silver, costly stones, wood, hay or straw, his work will be shown for what it is, because the Day will bring it to light. It will be revealed with fire, and the fire will test the quality of each man's work. If what he has built survives, he will receive his reward. If it is burned up, he will suffer loss; he himself will be saved, but only as one escaping through the flames.

Notice that the materials Paul mentions in this passage range from very combustible to not combustible at all. Obviously the hay and straw are the most combustible, then comes wood, then precious metals and stones. It also seems clear that some of these materials are useful for building while others are not. If you construct a house made of hay or straw, it surely will not stand long. (And it can burn to the ground very easily.) But a house constructed with solid materials such as stones and metals will stand and last a long time.

What do these building materials represent? Pastor Douglas Connelly insightfully suggests that "gold, silver, and costly stones refer to the fruit of the Spirit in our lives; they refer to Christ-honoring motives and godly obedience and transparent integrity. Wood, hay, and straw are perishable things—carnal attitudes, sinful motives, pride-filled actions, selfish ambition."[6] This is relevant, I believe, to Freemasonry. Freemasonry is not Christ-honoring but rather Christ-obscuring and Christ-diminishing. While Masons pridefully point to all the great things they have done (such as hospitals they have paid for), the key question is: Will such good deeds burn up like hay at the judgment? It is a sobering question.

Fire in Scripture sometimes symbolizes the holiness of God (see Leviticus 1:8; Hebrews 12:29). And there are clear cases in the Bible in which fire portrays God's judgment upon that which His holiness has condemned (see Genesis 19:24; Mark 9:43-48). God will examine our works, and they will be tested against the fire of His holiness. If our works are built with good materials, such as precious metals and stones, they will stand. But if our works are built with less valuable materials—wood, hay, or straw—they will burn.

Perhaps the image is intended to communicate that those works performed with a view to glorifying God and Jesus Christ are the works that will stand. Works performed with a view to glorifying self, performed in the flesh, are those that will be burned up. Inasmuch as Freemasonry does not glorify the true

God (it sets forth a common-denominator deity palatable to people of all faiths) and does not glorify Jesus Christ (*strips His name from all Masonic rituals*), I would not want to be in the shoes of a Christian Mason at the Judgment Seat of Christ.

Scripture indicates that some Christians will suffer such loss that practically all—*if not all*—of their works go up in flames. The apostle Paul describes this person as being saved, "but only as one escaping through the flames" (1 Corinthians 3:15). Theologian Merrill F. Unger explains it this way:

> Imagine yourself waking out of sleep to find your house ablaze. You have no time to save a thing. You flee with only the night clothes on your back. Even these are singed away by the flames that engulf you. You escape with literally nothing but your life....In this fashion believers who have lived carnally and carelessly or who have worked for self and self-interest instead of for the Lord will find that all their works have been burned up. They shall have no reward. No trophies to lay at Jesus' feet! No crowns to rejoice in that day of judgment![7]

The Scope of the Judgment Includes Actions

The Christian's judgment will focus on his personal stewardship of the gifts, talents, opportunities, and responsibilities given to him in this life. The very character of each Christian's life and service will be utterly laid bare under the unerring and omniscient vision of Christ, whose eyes are "like a blazing fire" (Revelation 1:14).

Numerous Scripture verses reveal that each of our actions will be judged before the Lord. The psalmist said to the Lord, "Surely you will reward each person according to what he has done" (Psalm 62:12; see also Matthew 16:27). In Ephesians 6:8, we read that the Lord "will reward everyone for whatever good he does, whether he is slave or free."

Christ's judgment of our actions will be infallible. There will be no confusion on His part. His understanding of the circumstances under which we committed acts on earth will be fully understood by Him. As John Wesley once put it, "God will then bring to light every circumstance that accompanied each word and action. He will judge whether they lessened or increased the goodness or badness of them."[8]

Christian Masons may think they will fair well regarding this aspect of judgment. After all, their actions include participating in many charitable acts. However, as noted above, God will bring to light every circumstance that accompanies each action. In the Masonic Lodge, good works are typically done with a view to earning entrance into the Celestial Lodge Above. This clearly goes against Scripture, which teaches that works have nothing to do with salvation (Ephesians 2:8,9). Salvation comes solely through faith in Christ (Acts 16:31). In view of this, the Mason would do well to ponder the fact that actions human beings may judge benevolent and good may not fare so well before Christ's all-penetrating eyes.

The Scope of the Judgment Includes Thoughts

At the Judgment Seat of Christ, it will not just be our *actions* that will come under scrutiny. Our *thoughts* also count. In Jeremiah 17:10, God said, "I the LORD search the heart and examine the mind, to reward a man according to his conduct, according to what his deeds deserve." The Lord "will bring to light what is hidden in darkness and will expose the motives of men's hearts" (1 Corinthians 4:5). The Lord is the one "who searches hearts and minds" (Revelation 2:23). Contrary to the Masonic mindset, which focuses on external actions (doing good things), Christ goes deeper by examining every thought of the mind. John Wesley once wisely wrote:

In that day, every inward working of the human soul will be discovered—every appetite, passion, inclination, and affection, with all the various combinations of them, and every temper and disposition that constitutes the whole complex character of each individual. Who was righteous, who was unrighteous, and in what degree every action, or person, or character was either good or evil will be seen clearly and infallibly.[9]

The Scope of the Judgment Includes Words

Finally, the believer's judgment will include all the words he has spoken. Christ once said that "men will have to give account on the day of judgment for every careless word they have spoken" (Matthew 12:36). This is an important aspect of judgment, for tremendous damage can be done through the human tongue (see James 3:1-10).

John Blanchard reminds us that "if even our careless words are carefully recorded, how can we bear the thought that our calculated boastful claims, the cutting criticisms, the off-color jokes, and the unkind comments will also be taken into account. Even our whispered asides and words spoken in confidence or when we thought we were 'safe' will be heard again."[10]

- Will Christian Masons have to give an account for the words they spoke at the Masonic initiation ceremony in terms of them being in darkness and seeking the light of Masonry? *Undoubtedly.*

- Will Christian Masons have to give an account for their omission of Jesus' name, even in Scripture passages that are quoted in the Masonic Lodge? *Yes.*

• Will Christian Masons have to give an account
for the blood oaths they spoke? *Absolutely.*

These questions and responses are not included to condemn Masons. My heartfelt concern is that many Christians who have joined a Masonic Lodge may not have fully considered the ultimate consequences of their membership. There will be a judgment, and there will be accountability!

The Judgment of Unbelievers

Unlike Christians, whose judgment deals only with rewards and loss of rewards, unbelievers face a horrific judgment that leads to their being cast into the Lake of Fire. The judgment that unbelievers face is called the Great White Throne judgment (Revelation 20:11-15). Christ is the divine Judge, and those who are judged are the unsaved dead of all time This event takes place at the end of the millennial kingdom, Christ's 1000-year reign on planet Earth that follows His Second Coming.

Those who face Christ at this time will be judged on the basis of their works (Revelation 20:12,13). They get to this judgment because they are unsaved. This judgment will not separate believers from unbelievers, for all who will experience it will have already made the choice during their lifetimes to reject the God of the Bible. Once they are before the divine Judge, they are judged according to their works not only to justify their condemnation but to determine the degree to which each person should be punished throughout eternity.

When Christ opens the Book of Life, no name of anyone present at the Great White Throne judgment is in it. Their names do not appear in the book since they rejected the *source* of life—Jesus Christ. Because they rejected the source of life, they are cast into the Lake of Fire, which constitutes the "second death" and involves eternal separation from the one true God. This makes the Masonic stripping of the name of Jesus Christ from Lodges even more serious. Moreover, the omission of the doctrine of hell in Masonic

Lodges leads Masons to falsely believe that such could never be their destiny.

The Reality of Hell

The Scriptures use a variety of words to describe the horrors of hell—including fire, fiery furnace, unquenchable fire, the lake of burning sulfur, the Lake of Fire, everlasting contempt, perdition, the place of weeping and gnashing of teeth, eternal punishment, darkness, the wrath to come, exclusion, torments, damnation, condemnation, retribution, woe, and the second death. It is not pleasant to focus on such horror, but it will provide a better grasp of the biblical portrayal of hell.

The Lake of Burning Sulfur/The Lake of Fire

In Revelation 19:20, we read that the beast and the false prophet—two malevolent foes who come into power during the future Tribulation period—will be "thrown alive into the fiery lake of burning sulfur." This takes place *before* the beginning of Christ's Millennial Kingdom (that 1,000-year period following the Second Coming of Christ in which Christ will physically rule on earth).

At the end of the Millennial kingdom—1,000 years *after* the beast and the false prophet were thrown into the lake of burning sulfur—the devil will also be "thrown into the lake of burning sulfur.... *They will be tormented day and night for ever and ever*" (Revelation 20:10, emphasis added). Notice that the beast and false prophet are not burned up or annihilated at the time the devil is thrown into the lake of burning sulfur. They are *still burning* after 1,000 years. These sinister beings, along with unbelievers of all times, will be punished day and night for eternity (Revelation 20:14,15).

Eternal Fire

Jesus often referred to the eternal destiny of the wicked as "eternal fire." For example, Jesus warned: "If your hand or your foot causes you to sin cut it off and throw it away. It is better for you to enter life maimed or crippled than to have two hands or two feet and be thrown into eternal fire" (Matthew 18:8).

Following His Second Coming, when He separates the sheep (believers) from the goats (unbelievers), Jesus will say to the goats: "Depart from me, you who are cursed, into the eternal fire prepared for the devil and his angels" (Matthew 25:41). This verse reveals a very important fact: The "eternal fire" (or the Lake of Fire) was not originally created for mankind. It was initially created for the devil and his host of fallen angels (demons). But fallen man will join the fallen angels in this horrendous place of suffering.

What precisely is the "fire" of hell? Some believe it is literal. And that may very well be the case. Others believe "fire" may be a metaphorical way of expressing the great wrath of God. Scripture tells us: "The LORD your God is a consuming fire, a jealous God" (Deuteronomy 4:24); "God is a consuming fire" (Hebrews 12:29); "his wrath is poured out like fire" (Nahum 1:6); "Who can stand when he appears? For he will be like a refiner's fire..." (Malachi 3:2). God said, "My wrath will break out and burn like fire because of the evil you have done—burn with no one to quench it" (Jeremiah 4:4). How awful is the anger of God!

Fiery Furnace

Scripture also refers to the destiny of the wicked as a "fiery furnace." Jesus said that at the end of the age the holy angels will gather all evil-doers and "throw them into the fiery furnace, where there will be weeping and gnashing of teeth" (Matthew 13:42). There is a difference between fiery furnaces on earth and the fiery furnace of hell. On earth, when one throws debris into a furnace, the debris is utterly consumed and turns to ashes. This is not the case for those who suffer eternally in hell, for they never turn to ashes. They are not annihilated. This is a terrible thing to ponder, but the Scriptures are clear that the wicked suffer *eternally* in hell (Mark 9:47,48).

What is meant by "weeping and gnashing of teeth"? "Weeping" carries the idea of "wailing, not merely with tears, but with every outward expression of grief."[11] This weeping will be caused by the environment, the company, the remorse and guilt, and the shame that is part and parcel of hell. People "gnash their teeth" when they are angry. In his well-received book *Whatever Happened to Hell?* British evangelist John Blanchard says:

> The wicked will be angry at the things which gave them pleasure on earth but now give them pain in hell; angry at the sins that wrecked their lives; angry at themselves for being who they are; angry at Satan and his helpers for producing the temptations which led them into sin; and, even while compelled to acknowledge his glory and goodness, angry at God for condemning them to this dreadful state.[12]

Destruction

Jesus warned in Matthew 7:13, "Enter through the narrow gate. For wide is the gate and broad is the road that leads to destruction, and many enter through it." The ultimate destruction to which Jesus refers is that which is wrought in hell.

Second Thessalonians 1:8,9 tells us: "He will punish those who do not know God and do not obey the gospel of our Lord Jesus. They will be punished *with everlasting destruction* and shut out from the presence of the Lord and from the majesty of his power."

The Greek word translated "destruction" in this verse carries the meaning "sudden ruin" or "loss of all that gives worth to existence." The word refers not to annihilation but rather indicates separation from God and the lack of everything worthwhile in life. Just as "endless life" belongs to Christians, so "endless destruction" belongs to those opposed to Christ.[13]

Eternal Punishment

Jesus affirmed that the wicked "will go away to eternal punishment, but the righteous to eternal life" (Matthew 25:46). Notice that the eternality of the punishment of the wicked *equals* the eternality of the life of the righteous. *One is just as long as the other.* This points to the "forever" nature of the punishment of the wicked. It never ceases. This punishment is emphasized all throughout Scripture. The fire of hell, for example, is called an "unquenchable fire" (Mark 9:43 NASB); the worm of the wicked "does not die" (Mark 9:48); and the "smoke of their [sinners] torment rises for ever and ever" (Revelation 14:11).

Of particular significance is the reference in Revelation 20:10 to the devil, the beast, and the false prophet being tormented in the Lake of Fire "for ever and ever." This is significant because the Greek word translated "for ever and ever" is used elsewhere in Revelation in reference to the endless worship of God (Revelation 1:6; 4:9; 5:13). The word is also used of the endless life of God (4:10; 10:6). Further, the word is used in reference to Christ's endless kingdom (11:15).[14] The suffering of evil-doers is endless.

Exclusion from God's Presence

Unquestionably the greatest pain suffered by those in hell is that they are forever excluded from the presence of God. If ecstatic joy is found in the presence of God (Psalm 16:11), then utter dismay is found in the absence of His presence.

At the future judgment, some people will falsely claim to be Christians and will claim to have served Christ during their years on earth. But Christ will say to them, "I don't know you or where you come from. Away from me, all you evildoers!" (Luke 13:27). Such individuals will find themselves separated from God's presence for eternity. They will be "shut out from the presence of the Lord and from the majesty of his power" (2 Thessalonians 1:9). There is no doubt that some Masons who profess to be Christians will be among this group.

At the judgment of the sheep (believers) and goats (unbelievers), Christ will command the goats: "Depart from me, you who are cursed, into the eternal fire prepared for the devil and his angels" (Matthew 25:41; see also verses 31-40,42-46). What terrible words to hear from the lips of the King of kings and Lord of lords.

Degrees of Punishment in Hell

The Scriptures clearly indicate that there are degrees of punishment in hell. Certainly an Adolf Hitler will suffer eternally much more than a Christ-rejecting moralist (a category that fits many Masons). The "sentence" will be commensurate with one's sin against the light which one has received. Note the following passages that indicate levels of punishment:

- "I tell you the truth, it will be *more bearable* for Sodom and Gomorrah on the day of judgment than for that town" (Matthew 10:15, emphasis added).

- "For the Son of Man is going to come in his Father's glory with his angels, and then he will *reward each person according to what he has done*" (Matthew 16:27, emphasis added).

- "That servant who knows his master's will and does not get ready or does not do what his master wants will be *beaten with many blows*. But the one who does not know and does things deserving punishment will be *beaten with few blows*. From everyone who has been given much, much will be demanded; and from the one who has been entrusted with much, much more will be asked" (Luke 12:47-48, emphasis added).

- "Another book was opened, which is the book of life. The dead were judged *according to what they had done* as recorded in the books. The sea gave up the dead that were in it, and death and Hades gave up the dead that were in them, and each person was judged *according to what he had done*" (Revelation 20:12,13, emphasis added).

- "Behold, I am coming soon! My reward is with me, and *I will give to everyone according to what he has done*" (Revelation 22:12, emphasis added).

Clearly the wicked will be judged according to the things they have done in this life. Some will be punished more severely than others, depending on what they have done. The biblical God is a God of perfect justice.

Whether one is "beaten with few blows" or "beaten with many blows," *all* the occupants of hell are ultimately there according to their own will. As C. S. Lewis pointed out in his book *The Great Divorce*, the condemned who populate hell are those to whom God finally says, "*Your* will be done."

Indeed, these individuals reject the only thing that would keep them out of hell—*believing in Jesus Christ as Lord and Savior*. Any human soul that freely refuses the Source of all life and joy will find death and misery in hell. Masons must be made to see that by shoving Jesus out of their Lodges, they are pushing away the single Person who can save them from such a hideous destiny.

13

Occultism in Masonry

Christian apologists have often noted that there is a strong occult connection to some of the rituals in Freemasonry, though some Masons (particularly Christian Masons) may be unaware of this. Authoritative Masons acknowledge their heavy indebtedness to occultism. H.L. Haywood, for example, writes, "All our historians, at least nearly all of them, agree that Freemasonry owes very much to certain occult societies or groups that flourished—often in secret—during the late Middle Ages."[1]

The nineteenth through the twenty-eighth degrees of the Scottish Rite are deeply occultic, involving such things as the development of psychic powers, telepathy, altered states of consciousness, mysticism, Kabbalism (an occult art that began among the Jewish people in the first century A.D.), Rosicrucianism (a mystical brotherhood that involves pursuit of occultic powers and spirit contact), hermetic philosophy (alchemy), and the pursuit of esoteric truths.[2] The occult connection alone should be enough to dissuade Christians from participating in Freemasonry.

It is beyond the scope of this chapter to provide a detailed treatment of every aspect of occultism that is inherent in Freemasonry. For space purposes, I will limit my primary attention to Kabbalism, based on the Kabbalah (also spelled Kabalah, Cabala, Cabbala, Cabbalah, Kabala, Kabbala, Qabbala, and Qabbalah). This form of mystical occultism surfaces quite frequently in Masonic literature. For those seeking a broader treatment of the occultism in Freemasonry, good resources are available.[3]

Kabbalism is an occult philosophy and theology that developed among Jews in Babylonia, and later Italy, Provence, and Spain, between the sixth and thirteenth centuries A.D. Christian apologist Elliot Miller observes:

> The word "Cabala" means "to receive," and refers to heavenly revelation received by Jews and passed on to succeeding generations through oral tradition. At first it was used by the mainstream of Judaism, but eventually it became identified with those who believed that the Cabala was an esoteric, occult tradition that explained the true meaning of the Hebrew Scriptures, which was kept hidden from the masses and only made known to those who were spiritually ready to receive it.[4]

Kabbalah is essentially a mystical system that uses an occultic method of interpreting Scripture. Miller notes that intrinsic to Kabbalah is "the belief that Scripture is inspired, not only in its obvious interpretations, but even to the degree that, through the use of occult symbol interpretation, one could find hidden meanings in the very numerical and alphabetical interpretation of the texts."[5] The doctrines of the Kabbalists were derived through studying the Old Testament, albeit only after occultic interpretative methods were applied to it. *The Sorcerer's Handbook* tells us that the Kabbalah is "based on occult interpretations of the

Bible."[6] Indeed, according to the Kabbalah, "every letter in the Scriptures contains a mystery only to be solved by the initiated."[7] E.M. Storms tells us that the Kabbalah "is considered to be superior to the Bible, and Cabalists declare that the Bible is incomprehensible without their Cabala!"[8] Storms further notes:

> The Kabbalah teaches that the Bible as a whole is an allegory. Permeated with sexual imagery, the Kabbalah contains mystical rites and formulas. It intermingles sorcery and religion, providing the occultist with a great storehouse of magical words and symbols. Cabalists believe the hidden meanings of the Scriptures are unveiled by a specific means, including the manipulation of letters and numbers containing divine powers. The Cabala, comprised of magic, mysticism and supernatural lore, was used for calling upon angels and demons![9]

Just from the description of Kabbalism above, we can readily see similarities between this ancient form of occultism and Freemasonry. We do not have to merely theorize about a connection between these two schools of thought; Masons are quite open about the connection. Albert Pike, for example, confesses that "the Kabbala is the key of the occult sciences."[10] He sees Kabbalism in Masonry at every turn, which is why he encourages the Mason to familiarize himself with Kabalistic doctrine.[11] He says that "Masonry is a search after Light. That search leads us directly…to the Kabalah. In that ancient and little understood medley of absurdity and philosophy, the Initiate will find the source of many doctrines.…"[12] He notes that "the Kabalistic doctrine," like Freemasonry, "incessantly tends toward spiritual perfection."[13] He affirms that the adept can consult the Kabbalah for finding certain meanings.[14] He exults: "One is filled with admiration, on penetrating into the Sanctuary of the Kabalah, at seeing a doctrine so logical, so simple, and at the same time so absolute....This is the doctrine of the Kabalah, with which you will no doubt seek to make yourself acquainted."[15]

Albert Mackey likewise writes: "The Kabbala may be defined to be a system of philosophy which embraces certain mystical interpretations of Scripture, and metaphysical and spiritual beings....Much use is made of it in the advanced [Masonic] degrees, and entire rites have been constructed on its principles. Hence it demands a place in any general work on Masonry."[16]

Kabbalism has been called the parent of Freemasonry.[17] The Kabbalists "were syncretists in believing that at heart all the great religions are practically one, yet they sought to find common ground for Jews, Christians, and Muslims."[18] The similarities to the Masonic view is obvious.

The liturgy involved in the thirteenth degree of the Scottish Rite reads: "There are profounder meanings concealed in the symbols of this degree, connected with the philosophical system of the Hebrew Kabalists which you will earn hereafter, if you should be so fortunate as to advance. They are unfolded in the higher degrees."[19]

Now, I realize the Mason who joins the Blue Lodge and considers it just a fraternal organization may be completely unaware of much of the occultism practiced in the Lodge. In fact, John Ankerberg and John Weldon have commented that—

> most Masons who participate in the rituals do not understand their occult significance. If they pursue Masonry no further than unthinking participation in the rituals, it may be true for them that Masonry is not occultic. Such Masons are unaware of the occult meaning of many of the Masonic symbols and ritual and have chosen not to pursue the issue. But this is not true for all

Masons. Others do pursue the occult significance of Masonry.[20]

The occultic element of Freemasonry is disturbing, and we need to share this vital information on occultism with our Masonic friends. Particularly in regard to "Christian Masons," we can help them see that Kabbalism has been used in the past and is *still used today* for various kinds of magic, the conjuring of spirits, divination, and the development of psychic powers.[21] In view of the fact that God condemns *all* forms of occultism, this issue should be of grave concern to the men who have joined the Lodge.

_____REASONING FROM THE SCRIPTURES_____

The Problem with Mysticism

In responding to this mystical, occultic system which has thoroughly infiltrated the Masonic Lodge, I begin by pointing to the folly of relying on *any* form of mysticism to ascertain truth. Mysticism—such as that associated with the Kabbalah—is insufficient as a base on which to build our objective knowledge of God. As R.D. Clements put it, mysticism "is too uncertain in every way. The Christian points instead to history, and in particular to Jesus Christ, as the arena of God's personal, objective self-revelation and the proper ground for man's knowledge of God."[22]

The Bible stresses the importance of objective, certain, historical revelation. One example of how this is stressed in Scripture is John 1:18, where we are told, "No one has ever seen God, but God the One and Only [Jesus], who is at the Father's side, has made him known." In the empirical world of ordinary sense perceptions, Jesus was seen and heard by human beings as God's ultimate historical revelation to humankind. No wonder Jesus said, "If you really knew me, you would know my Father as well" (John 14:7). Jesus was an *objective* revelation of the Father.

The apostle Paul also stressed the importance of objective, historical revelation. In Acts 17:31, he warned the religious men of Athens of the reality of future judgment based on the objective evidence of the resurrection of Jesus Christ. Based on how people respond to this revelation, they will spend eternity in a real heaven or a real hell. The relevance of this to our present study is obvious: No Kabbalah-like Scripture-twisting will be able to avert a destiny in hell for the non-Christian Mason at the Great White Throne judgment.

It is also important to note that spiritual deception is not just possible but likely through all forms of mysticism. Those who place faith in mysticism, such as Kabbalah-influenced Masons, seem blind to the possibility of spiritual fraud. The question we must ask is: What if that which Masons assume to be genuine contact with God is in fact less than God, or, at worst, Satan, the great impersonator of God and the father of lies? Second Corinthians 4:4 tells us that "the god of this age [Satan] has blinded the minds of unbelievers, so that they cannot see the light of the gospel of the glory of Christ, who is the image of God." The fact that Masonic views on God, Jesus, sin, and salvation consistently contradict a straight reading of the Bible supports the idea that Satan may be behind them.

Kabbalistic Methodology Is Unreliable

In chapter 6, "The Bible: A 'Great Light' " I demonstrated that an esoteric method of interpreting Scripture is unreliable. All the points made in that chapter are applicable to Kabbalistic occultism. Before you review that chapter, make note of researcher Elliot Miller's point that "depending upon one's assumptions, one may apply Cabalistic methods to almost any piece of literature and draw almost any interpretation from it....The application of this method to the Bible has produced interpretations that are not supported by Scripture, and, in fact, are something directly opposed to it, in its obvious context."[23]

Masons may use the Bible in the rituals of the Masonic Lodge, but they most often make it say something other than intended by the God who inspired the Bible. By using Kabbalah-like methodology, the Bible can be made to say anything the Lodge may desire. But God goes by the book—*His* book, the Bible!.

God Condemns All Forms of Occultism

In Deuteronomy 18:9-12 we find that all forms of occultism are condemned and detestable to God:

> When you enter the land the LORD your God is giving you, do not learn to imitate the detestable ways of the nations there. Let no one be found among you who sacrifices his son or daughter in the fire, who practices divination or sorcery, interprets omens, engages in witchcraft, or casts spells, or who is a medium or spiritist or who consults the dead. Anyone who does these things is detestable to the LORD, and because of these detestable practices the LORD your God will drive out those nations before you.

God's stand against occultism and divination is consistent throughout Scripture. Exodus 22:18 instructs that sorceresses are to be put to death, a penalty that demonstrates how serious the sin of divination is. Leviticus 19:26 commands, "Do not practice divination or sorcery." Leviticus 19:31 instructs, "Do not turn to mediums or seek out spiritists, for you will be defiled by them. I am the LORD your God." We read in Leviticus 20:27, "A man or woman who is a medium or spiritist among you must be put to death. You are to stone them; their blood will be on their own heads." In 1 Samuel 28:3, we read that Saul rightly "expelled the mediums and spiritists from the land." Later we read that "Saul died because he was unfaithful to the LORD; he did not keep the word of the LORD and even consulted a medium for guidance" (1 Chronicles 10:13). In Acts 19:19, we read that many who converted to Christ in Ephesus destroyed all their paraphernalia formerly used for occultism and divination: "A number who had practiced sorcery brought their scrolls together and burned them publicly. When they calculated the value of the scrolls, the total came to fifty thousand drachmas." (A drachma was about a day's wage.)

In view of above, Masons have a choice to make. Will they honor God and leave the Masonic Lodge? Or will they remain in the Masonic Lodge *despite the fact that God condemns the occultism* that is a part of the Lodge?

The True Source Behind Occultism

Satan is the true source behind all forms of occultism, including Kabbalism. Scripture reveals a great deal about this diabolical being. Satan, though possessing creaturely limitations, is nevertheless pictured in Scripture as being extremely powerful and influential in the world. He is called the "ruler of this world" (John 12:31 NASB), "the god of this world" (2 Corinthians 4:4 NASB), and the "prince of the power of the air" (Ephesians 2:2 NASB). He is said to deceive the whole world (Revelation 12:9; 20:3). He is portrayed as having power in the governmental realm (Matthew 4:8,9), the physical realm (Luke 13:11,16; Acts 10:38), the angelic realm (Jude 9; Ephesians 6:11,12), and the ecclesiastical (church) realm (Revelation 2:9; 3:9). He is a powerful being who should be taken seriously

For the purposes of this chapter, I will limit our attention to a single aspect of Satan's work—the work of *deception*. I noted earlier that Satan is called the *father of lies* (John 8:44). The word father is used here metaphorically of the originator of a family or company of persons animated by a deceitful character. Satan was the first and greatest liar. It is a lie to say that the God of Christianity is one and the same as the god of Hinduism and the god of Islam. It is a lie to say that God's true name is *Jabulon*—a name that associates the biblical God with Baal and Osiris, pagan deities of the ancient world. It is a lie to say that Jesus was just a good, moral teacher. It is a lie to say that man has no sin nature and that man can merit the Celestial Lodge Above by good works. It is a lie to say that the Bible can be understood by using Kabbalistic esoteric methodology. These and other such ideas are no doubt rooted in the work of Satan, the father of lies.

In keeping with his deception, Satan may be viewed as the great counterfeiter.[24] It was Augustine who called the Devil *Simius Dei*—"the ape of God." Satan apes or mimics God in many ways. Generally the principle tactic Satan uses to attack God and His plan is to offer a counterfeit kingdom and program.[25] This is hinted at in 2 Corinthians 11:14, which states that Satan "masquerades as an angel of light." In what other ways does Satan act as "the ape of God"? Consider the following:

- Satan has his own church—the "synagogue of Satan" (Revelation 2:9).

- Satan has his own ministers—ministers of darkness that bring false sermons (2 Corinthians 11:4,5).

- Satan has formulated his own system of theology—called "doctrines of demons" (1 Timothy 4:1; Revelation 2:24).

- His ministers proclaim his gospel—"a gospel other than the one we preached to you" (Galatians 1:7,8).

- Satan has his own throne (Revelation 13:2) and his own worshipers (13:4).

- Satan inspires false Christs and self-constituted messiahs (Matthew 24:4,5).

- Satan employs false teachers who bring in "destructive heresies" (2 Peter 2:1).

- Satan sends out false prophets (Matthew 24:11).

- Satan sponsors false apostles who imitate the true followers of Jesus (2 Corinthians 11:13).

In view of such mimicking, one respected theologian concluded that "Satan's plan and purposes have been, are, and always will be to seek to establish a rival rule to God's kingdom. He is promoting a system of which he is the head and which stands in opposition to God and His rule in the universe."[26]

This is particularly relevant to our present subject matter, for the god of Masonry is a *counterfeit god,* the Jesus of Masonry is a *counterfeit Jesus,* and the gospel of Masonry is a *counterfeit gospel.* Further, Masonry offers a *counterfeit* system of interpreting the Bible known as Kabbalism. There is good reason to believe that these false teachings are rooted in the work of Satan, the master counterfeiter.

We certainly know that Satan is constantly about the business of misinterpreting God's Word and causing human beings to do the same. In the Garden of Eden, Satan, in the form of a serpent, said to Eve, "Did God really say...?" (Genesis 3:1). The fall of humankind was the result of that encounter. Satan also tried to twist Scripture when tempting Jesus, but was not successful (see Matthew 4:1-11). Satan's desire is to get people to believe that the Bible says something other than what it actually says. Kabbalism is a satanic masterpiece in this regard. By using such methodology, people can come up with such ideas as 1) all the religions are actually worshiping the same God; 2) Jesus is not God but is just a good, moral teacher; 3) man does not have a sin problem; and 4) salvation can be attained by good works.

The only way to battle these and other Satanic deceptions is through preaching the Word of God in dependence upon the Holy Spirit. As you witness to Masons with the Word, continually pray that God the Holy Spirit would remove the occultic veil of blindness from their eyes so they can understand the true gospel that can liberate them forever.

Note: It may be that some Christian Masons, upon learning of the occultic connection with Freemasonry, may choose to leave the Masonic Lodge. In the process, it is possible, and even likely, that they may experience an elevated level of spiritual warfare. Be sure to share with them the scriptural truths contained in appendix C: "Victory over Satan."

14

Should Christians Be Masons?

In 1992, Southern Baptist James Holly requested that the Southern Baptist Convention (SBC) conduct an investigation of Freemasonry. The SBC agreed, and in June of 1993 published its findings—the "Freemasonry Report." The report begins by commending the Masonic Order—

> for its many charitable endeavors such as the operation of 22 Shriners hospitals, 19 orthopedic hospitals, and 3 burns institutes with noteworthy success in treatment, research, and education, often providing free treatment to children under 18 years of age. Also, we commend support of the Foundation for the Prevention of Drug and Alcohol Abuse Among Children and the Eastern Star sponsorship of Masonic Homes for the Aged. These, with many other charitable and benevolent endeavors, are commendable.[1]

Yet the report also spoke of some extremely problematic aspects of Freemasonry. It noted that many tenets and teachings of Freemasonry are not compatible with Christianity or Southern Baptist doctrine, including:

> The prevalent use of offensive concepts, titles, and terms such as Worshipful Master for the leader of a lodge; references to their buildings as mosques, shrines, or temples; and the use of words such as Abaddon and Jah-Bul-On, the so-called secret name of God. To many, these terms are not only offensive but sacrilegious.
>
> ...The use of archaic, offensive rituals and so-called bloody oaths or obligations, among these being that promised by the Entered Apprentice.
>
> ...The reference to the Bible placed on the altar of the lodge as the furniture of the lodge, comparing it to the square and compass rather than giving it the supreme place in the lodge.
>
> ...The implication that salvation may be attained by one's good works, implicit in the statement found in some Masonic writings that Masonry is continually reminded of that purity of life and conduct which is necessary to obtain admittance into the Celestial Lodge Above where the Supreme Architect of the Universe presides.
>
> ...The refusal of most lodges (although not all) to admit for membership African-Americans.[2]

Strangely, despite its recognition of these severe doctrinal problems that are intrinsic to the Masonic Lodge, the report concluded:

> In light of the fact that many tenets and teachings of Freemasonry are not compatible with

Christianity and Southern Baptist doctrine, while
others are compatible with Christianity and
Southern Baptist doctrine, we therefore recommend that consistent with our denomination's deep
convictions regarding the priesthood of the believer
and the autonomy of the local church, membership
in a Masonic Order be a matter of personal conscience. Therefore, we exhort Southern Baptists to
prayerfully and carefully evaluate Freemasonry in
light of the Lordship of Christ, the teachings of the
Scripture, and the findings of this report, as led by
the Holy Spirit of God.[3]

The report, though recognizing significant incompatibilities
between Freemasonry and Christianity, concluded that membership in the Lodge is a matter of individual conscience! Tragically,
this evaluation by the Southern Baptist Convention has essentially served as an endorsement of the Masonic Lodge. In *The
Scottish Rite Journal*, a Masonic periodical, one Mason wrote:

Because of your support, the vote of the Southern
Baptist Convention is a historic and positive
turning point for Freemasonry. Basically, it is a
vitalization of our Fraternity by America's largest
Protestant denomination after nearly a year of
thorough, scholarly study. At the same time, it is
a call to renewed effort on the part of all Freemasons today to re-energize our Fraternity and move
forward to fulfilling its mission as the world's
foremost proponent of the Brotherhood of Man
under the Fatherhood of God.[4]

Keeping in mind the significant doctrinal aberrations documented throughout this book, to make joining the Masonic
Lodge merely a matter of personal conscience is a truly absurd

suggestion. Cult apologists George Mather and Larry Nichols agree, and point out that the Jehovah's Witnesses also hold to many "tenets and teachings...not compatible with Christianity and Southern Baptist doctrine [e.g., denial of the Trinity, deity of Christ, bodily resurrection, etc.], while others are compatible [e.g., belief in the inspiration and inerrancy of Scripture; a personal God; emphasis on honesty, integrity, industry, character; etc.]." Mather and Nichols thus ask: "Why, then, don't Southern Baptists allow participation and cooperation with the Witnesses 'as a matter of personal conscience'?"[5] They raise a good point. If it is okay to join a Masonic Lodge even in the face of the doctrinal problems intrinsic to Freemasonry, then why not worship alongside Jehovah's Witnesses, or Mormons, or other cultists?

The reality is that numerous Christian denominations have taken a public stand against Masonic organizations. These denominations include the Roman Catholic Church, the Methodist Church of England, the Wesleyan Methodist Church, the Russian Orthodox Church, the Synod Anglican Church of England, the Assemblies of God, the Church of the Nazarene, the Orthodox Presbyterian Church, the Reformed Presbyterian Church, the Christian Reformed Church in America, the Evangelical Mennonite Church, the Church of Scotland, the Free Church of Scotland, General Association of Regular Baptist Churches, Grace Brethren, Independent Fundamentalist Churches of America, The Evangelical Lutheran Synod, the Baptist Union of Scotland, The Lutheran Church Missouri Synod, the Wisconsin Evangelical Lutheran Synod, and the Presbyterian Church in America.[6]

The late General Booth, of the Salvation Army, also took a strong stand against Masonry. He addressed a letter to every officer in his organization in which he stated, "No language of mine could be too strong in condemning any Officer's affiliation with any society which shuts Him [Christ] outside its temples; and which in its religious ceremonies gives neither Him nor His name any place."[7] Booth was a man who spoke with conviction and acted upon that conviction.

The Problem of Biblical Illiteracy

I am convinced that one reason some Christians (though not all) join a Masonic Lodge is that they are biblically uninformed. L. James Rongstad writes, "When people are instructed into the lodge, they often are unable to recognize that lodge teachings contradict Christian teachings because they know too little of Christianity."[8] Likewise, John Ankerberg and John Weldon assert: "The principal reason many Christians have joined Freemasonry is out of simple ignorance—they do not know the contradictions between Masonry and Christianity. This indicates that the church must do a better job in educating her members concerning both Christian doctrine and the teachings of the Craft."[9]

Broadly speaking, many cult experts have noted that a key factor giving rise to the cult explosion in the United States is that churches have failed to make Bible doctrine and Bible knowledge a high priority. Walter Martin once said that the rise of the cults is "directly proportional to the fluctuating emphasis which the Christian church has placed on the teaching of biblical doctrine to Christian laymen. To be sure, a few pastors, teachers, and evangelists defend adequately their beliefs, but most of them—and most of the average Christian laymen—are hard put to confront and refute a well-trained cultist of almost any variety."[10]

There are many indications of the low priority placed on Bible doctrine in the local church today. This is evident in the unbiblical views held by many Christians. One poll indicated that one out of ten people who claim to be born again in America believe that sin is an outdated concept. Though this percentage is less than that of non-Christians (25 percent), it nevertheless represents a significant number of Christians who hold to an unorthodox view of sin.[11]

Regarding salvation, this same poll indicates that four out of ten American adults believe that leading a good life can earn them a place in heaven, wholly apart from a relationship with Christ.[12] What is of particular concern is the statistical finding that three out of ten "born-again" Christians agreed that good people go to heaven regardless of whether they have a personal relationship with Christ.[13] How can people who claim to be Christians be so far off-base when it comes to the fundamental doctrines of sin and salvation? This is the same problem we see in regard to Christians who attend the Masonic Lodge.

As long as the church continues to make doctrine a low priority, America's religious soil will remain richly fertilized for the continued growth of cultic weeds. The apostle Paul makes reference to "God's household, which is the church of the living God, the pillar and foundation of the truth" (1 Timothy 3:15). If the church fails to set forth and defend doctrinal truth, it fails to fulfill its God-appointed role.

Making the Right Decision

It is one thing to join a Masonic Lodge because of biblical illiteracy; but once a Christian becomes aware of the doctrinal problems in Freemasonry he is confronted with a decision: "Shall I remain in the Masonic Lodge despite the fact that I know its teachings clearly contradict and subvert God's Word? Or shall I break my oath and leave the Masonic Lodge, thus honoring the one true God?"

Making the right decision will be much easier when you review with your friend the problems focused on in this book. These are the points you will want to thoroughly cover with your Masonic acquaintance:

- When the candidate is going through the initiation ceremony, he is made to stand before the Worshipful Master and say something like: "I am lost in darkness, and I am seeking the light of Freemasonry."[14] This is the case even for the Christian who has already been delivered from the kingdom of darkness into the kingdom of light— Christ's kingdom (see Ephesians 5:8-11).

- When the candidate is going through the initiation ceremony, he is made to swear a horrible blood oath, saying, "Binding myself under no less penalty than that of having my throat cut across, my tongue torn out by its roots, and my body buried in the rough sands of the sea, at low-water mark, where the tide ebbs and flows twice in twenty-four hours, should I ever knowingly violate this my Entered Apprentice obligation."[15] No Christian has any business taking oaths that speak of cutting the throat or tearing out his tongue if he gives away the secrets of the Lodge (see Leviticus 5:4-6).

- The candidate is taught that the Bible is not God's *only* revelation to humankind, but it is simply one of many holy books that contain religious and moral truth. The Bible is said to be just a symbol of God's will.[16] Other "revelatory" books include the Hindu Vedas and the Muslim Koran. This is an outrage to the one true God, who has given us all the truth He desires us to have in the Bible (see 2 Timothy 3:16; 2 Peter 1:21).

- The candidate is taught that Jews, Christians, Hindus, Muslims, and those of other faiths are all worshiping the same God using different names. God is said to be "the nameless one of a hundred names."[17] This is so despite the fact that Christianity teaches a triune concept of God, Islam denies the Trinity and says God cannot have a son, and Hinduism involves virtually millions of gods.

- God's true name is said to be Jabulon—a name that associates the God of the Bible with Baal and Osiris, ancient pagan deities. Baal worship in particular is the epitome of evil idol worship in the ancient world and involved such things as ritual prostitution (Judges 2:17; Hosea 4:13,14), self-mutilation (1 Kings 18:28), and the sacrificing (ritual murder) of little children (Jeremiah 19:4,5).

• Freemasonry has strong connections to the ancient mystery religions, and often cites such false gods as Isis, Serapis, Osiris, Re, Apis, Thoth, Phtha, Hermes, Orpheus, and Horus.[18] These are the very gods that the true God Yahweh condemned and judged when inflicting the ten plagues on Egypt through the hand of Moses (see Exodus 7–12).

• Jesus is viewed not as God but rather as a good, moral teacher. His name is systematically stripped from prayers and from Scripture verses cited within the Masonic Lodge. By contrast, the Bible not only asserts the absolute deity of Christ (John 1:1; 8:58; 10:30; 20:28; Colossians 2:9), but tells us we should always pray in the name of Christ (John 16:24). Further, Christ Himself affirmed, "If anyone is ashamed of me and my words, the Son of Man will be ashamed of him when he comes in his glory and in the glory of the Father and of the holy angels" (Luke 9:26). To ignore Christ is to do so at our own peril.

• Man is viewed as not being sinful or born into the world with original sin. Rather, mankind is viewed as basically good with a few imperfections. This is so despite the fact that Scripture says man is fallen in sin and even his good acts are like filthy rags before God (Isaiah 64:6; see also Isaiah 53:5,6; Romans 3:23; 5:12).

- Man is said to be saved not by trusting in Christ but by engaging in good works and charitable acts. This flatly goes against the clear teaching of Scripture (see John 3:16; Acts 16:31; Romans 3:20-22; Ephesians 2:8,9).

- Masonry makes no mention of the future judgment or the reality of hell, thus implying that all Masons will end up in heaven. Jesus taught that those who reject Him will suffer in hell for eternity (Matthew 25:46; see also Matthew 5:29,30; Luke 16:23; 2 Peter 2:4; Revelation 20:13-15).

- Masonry involves various forms of occultism in its literature and rituals—including Kabbalism, Rosicrucianism, and alchemy. Scripture, by contrast, absolutely condemns all forms of occultism as detestable to God (Deuteronomy 18:10-12; see also Leviticus 19:31; 20:6; Jeremiah 27:9; Micah 5:12).

In view of how all these doctrines go against what God's Word reveals about these issues, it is obvious that the right decision for a Mason is to leave the Masonic Lodge. To not leave amounts to living in apostasy.

Christian author Walton Hannah writes, "I am firmly convinced that for a Christian to pledge himself to a religious (or even, to avoid begging the question, to a quasi-religious) organization which offers prayer and worship to God which deliberately excludes the name of our Lord and Savior Jesus Christ, in whose name only is salvation to be found, is apostatic."[19] He notes that this is something that the early Christians in the first century would have never succumbed to. "Christians in those days were willing to face death rather than cast a few grains of incense to the Emperor or other deities."[20]

The apostle Paul says that we should not fellowship with those who are disobedient to God. He affirms that God's wrath will come down upon them:

> Therefore do not be partners with them. For you were once darkness, but now you are light in the Lord. Live as children of light (for the fruit of the light consists in all goodness, righteousness and truth) and find out what pleases the Lord. Have nothing to do with the fruitless deeds of darkness, but rather expose them. For it is shameful even to mention what the disobedient do in secret. But everything exposed by the light becomes visible, for it is light that makes everything visible. This is why it is said: "Wake up, O sleeper, rise from the dead, and Christ will shine on you" (Ephesians 5:7-14).

Elsewhere, Paul instructs: "The sacrifices of pagans are offered to demons, not to God, and I do not want you to be participants with demons. You cannot drink the cup of the Lord and the cup of demons too; you cannot have a part in both the Lord's table and the table of demons. Are we trying to arouse the Lord's jealousy?" (1 Corinthians 10:20-22). This directly applies to Masonry, for Masonry involves Christians worshiping together with Muslims and Hindus, which are pagan religions that involve false deities. Paul says this cannot be. He commands:

> Do not be yoked together with unbelievers. For what do righteousness and wickedness have in common? Or what fellowship can light have with darkness? What harmony is there between Christ and Belial? What does a believer have in common with an unbeliever? What agreement is

there between the temple of God and idols? For we are the temple of the living God. As God has said: "I will live with them and walk among them, and I will be their God, and they will be my people." "Therefore come out from them and be separate, says the Lord. Touch no unclean thing, and I will receive you" (2 Corinthians 6:14-17).

In Isaiah 52:11, the followers of the one true God are exhorted: "Touch no unclean thing! Come out from it and be pure." Just as Israel was to abstain from participating with any pagan religions or heathenism, so those of us who call ourselves Christians are to abstain from such things. To worship in Lodges alongside of Hindus and Muslims and those of other religions is to engage in compromise and invites God's judgment.

Advice from Dwight L. Moody

I have long had tremendous respect for Dwight L. Moody, one of this country's most fruitful evangelists of times past. His words on leaving and staying out of the Masonic Lodge are stirring and challenging. I can think of no more appropriate way to end this chapter than to quote from this great evangelist:

I do not see how any Christian, most of all a Christian minister, can go into these secret lodges with unbelievers. They say they can have more influence for good; but I say they can have more influence for good by staying out of them, and then reproving their evil deeds. You can never reform anything by unequally yoking yourself with ungodly men. True reformers separate themselves from the world. "But," you say, "you had one of them in your church." So I had, but when I found out what it was I cleaned it out like a cage of unclean birds. [Here Moody was referring to a secret temperance union.] "But Mr. Moody," some say, "if you talk that way you will drive all the members of secret societies out of your meetings and out of your churches." But what if I did? Better men will take their places. Give them the truth anyway, and if they would rather leave their churches than their lodges, the sooner they get out of the churches the better. I would rather have ten members who are separated from the world than a thousand such members. Come out from the lodge. Better one with God, than a thousand without him. We must walk with God, and if only one or two go with us, it is all right. Do not let down the standard to suit men who love their secret lodges or have some darling sin they will not give up.[21]

15

Evangelism Among Masons

In this book a great deal of space has been devoted to addressing Masonic doctrines. In this closing chapter, which will be short and to the point, I offer some closing advice on evangelism.

These hints are largely gleaned from the many years of experience in which my late colleague Walter Martin personally witnessed to Masons and various cultists. I have adopted his methods as my own, and I acknowledge my indebtedness to him for the insights contained on the following pages.

Dr. Martin was firm that there are *dos* and *don'ts* when it comes to witnessing.[1] Here are a few key principles regarding evangelism among Masons.

Identify with the Masons

Do identify with the Masons. Martin says we must convince Masons that we consider them to be people in their own right—worthwhile, basically honest, and not trying to put something over on us. Lodge members are people *before* they are Masons. They have families, they have children, they have needs, they have frustrations and fears, and they are brothers and sisters *in Adam*, though not necessarily *in Christ*.[2] Acts 17:26 tells us that all people on earth, by virtue of being created by God, are offspring of God. In Adam, then, all of us share a common heritage.

In view of this, Martin suggests, we talk to Masons from the "family-of-Adam perspective," prayerfully hoping to bring them to the "family-of-God perspective."[3] If we can keep in mind that Masons are *people before they are Masons*—people with families, people who have the need for friendship, the need for love and security, people who laugh and cry—we will find it much easier to treat them with respect and kindness when we encounter them.

Labor Persistently with the Masons

Do labor persistently with the Masons. Never give up unless they decisively refuse further contact. Martin says, "Until they pull the plug, we need to hang in there remembering that the Lord blesses His Word."[4] Remember what God said in the book of Isaiah regarding His sovereign Word: "It shall not return unto me void, but it shall accomplish that which I please, and it shall prosper in the thing whereto I sent it" (Isaiah 55:11 KJV).

Keep in mind that God's Word is alive and powerful. Hebrews 4:12 says: "For the word of God is *living* and *active*. Sharper than any double-edged sword, it penetrates even to dividing soul and spirit, joints and marrow; it judges the thoughts and attitudes of the heart" (emphasis added). As you persist in sharing insights on the Word of God with the Mason, you can be sure that God is at work in his heart.

Answer the Questions of Masons

Do exhaust every effort to answer the questions of Masons. We must share not only *what* we believe as Christians, but *why* we believe it as well. We must be able to give convincing reasons for our beliefs. Dr. Martin notes that "the apostles were apologists [defenders of the faith] as well as evangelists. They not only proclaimed Christ, but when they were questioned, they had good, solid reasons for their faith."[5] This is why the apostle Peter said, "Always be prepared to give an answer to everyone who asks you to give the reason for the hope that you have. But do this with gentleness and respect" (1 Peter 3:15).

What happens if you don't know the answer to a question that a particular Mason brings up? Following Martin's lead (from his early days of witnessing), say: "That's a good question. I'm not sure what the answer is, but I'm going to do some research this week and find the answer. Can we talk about this the next time we meet?" The Mason will invariably go along with your request. Hopefully, this book will go a long way toward providing the answers you need.

Allow the Mason to Save Face

Do allow the Masons to save face. When you share your beliefs with Masons and defend your position from Scripture, there may come a time in your encounter when you sense you have "won the argument." When that moment arrives, make every effort to let love shine through and allow them to save face. Otherwise the Mason will resent you and fight you, even though he knows in his heart that you are right.

Martin suggests handling it this way: "When you sense that the person has lost the argument and is deflated, that's the time to be magnanimous and say to the person, lovingly: 'I realize that we can get awfully uptight in these areas if we let ourselves....Let's just think of ourselves as two people who want more than anything else to know the whole truth and the whole counsel of God. *Right*?' I haven't met a cultist yet who wouldn't say 'Right' in response."[6] Disarming the situation in this way will help lower defensive barriers and create an atmosphere in which honest discussion can occur.

Former cultists attest to the importance of taking a loving, disarming approach. One such individual points out that "empathy is so very important when reaching out to these misled individuals. Try to think of how you would want others to speak to you if you were the one who was misled. Then remember that 'all things whatsoever ye would that men should do to you, do ye even so to them' (Matthew 7:12)."[7]

No Spiritual Chips on the Shoulder

Don't approach Masons with a spiritual chip on your shoulder. Martin says that a "spiritual chip" communicates the feeling that you are looking down on the Mason because you have something he does not have. Such an attitude will turn him off as fast as anything you could imagine.[8]

Especially for Christians who have thoroughly prepared themselves by learning hard-hitting scriptural answers to Masonic errors (such as those contained in this book), the temptation may be to intellectually talk down at Masons instead of conversing with them. We need to be on our guard and make every effort, with God's help, to remain humble during our witnessing encounters. Watch out for spiritual pride; *it's deadly!*

Be Patient

Don't lose patience, regardless of how dense you may think the particular Mason you're talking to is. This is extremely important. Martin advises: "Remember how dense you and I were until the Lord managed to break through....Being patient means being willing to go over something ten times if necessary, believing that the Lord will bless your efforts."[9]

I can personally attest that these *dos* and *don'ts* will help you as you share the gospel with Masons. But as important as these are, always remember that the Holy Spirit's role is central to effective evangelism with Masons and everyone else. It is the Holy Spirit who touches their souls; it is He who convinces them of sin and of righteousness and of judgment (John 16:8). And *in His hands* we become effective instruments for the Master's use (see 1 Corinthians 6:19; 12:11; Ephesians 5:18).[10]

Only God can lift the veil of darkness that Freemasonry has cast over the hearts of individual Masons. Our success in bringing a Mason to Christ depends in a big way on the Holy Spirit's work in that person's life. For this reason, *pray fervently* for the Holy Spirit's involvement in *all* your witnessing encounters (1 Corinthians 7:5; Philippians 4:6; 1 Thessalonians 5:17).

Appendix A

An Invitation to Believe

"He who created us without our help will
not save us without our consent."[1]
—*Saint Augustine of Hippo (354–430)*

Do you have a personal relationship with Jesus Christ? Perhaps you are a Mason that somehow came into contact with this book, and, after reading its contents, now desire to truly come into a personal and saving relationship with Jesus Christ. It is for you that I have written this appendix.

A personal relationship with Jesus is the most important decision you will ever make in your life. It is unlike any other relationship because if you die without this one, you will spend eternity apart from God.

So, if you will allow me, I would like to share with you how you can come into this life-changing, uplifting relationship with Jesus.

God Desires a Personal Relationship with You

God created you (Genesis 1:27). And He didn't just create you to exist all alone and apart from Him; He created you to enjoy a personal relationship with Him.

God had face-to-face encounters and fellowship with Adam and Eve, the first couple (Genesis 3:8-19). And just as God fellowshiped with them, so He desires to fellowship with you (1 John 1:5-7). *God loves you* (John 3:16). Never forget that.

The problem is...

Humanity Has a Sin Problem that Blocks Relationship with God

When Adam and Eve chose to sin against God in the Garden of Eden, they catapulted the entire human race—to which they gave birth—into sin. Since the time of Adam and Eve, every human being has been born into the world with a propensity to sin. The apostle Paul affirmed that "sin entered the world through one man, and death through sin" (Romans 5:12). We are also told that "through the disobedience of the one man the many were made sinners" (Romans 5:19). Ultimately this means that "death came through a man...in Adam all die" (1 Corinthians 15:21,22).

Jesus often spoke of sin in metaphors that illustrate the havoc it can wreak in one's life. He described sin as *blindness* (Matthew 23:16-26), *sickness* (Matthew 9:12), being *in bondage* (John 8:34), and living *in darkness* (John 8:12; 12:35-46). Moreover, Jesus taught that this is a *universal condition* and that all people are guilty before God (Luke 7:37-48).

Jesus also revealed that both inner thoughts and external acts render a person guilty (Matthew 5:28). He taught that from within the human heart come evil thoughts, sexual immorality, theft, murder, adultery, greed, malice, deceit, envy, slander, arrogance, and folly (Mark 7:21-23). Moreover, He affirmed that God is fully aware of every person's sins; nothing escapes His notice (Matthew 22:18; Luke 6:8; John 4:17-19).

Some people are more morally upright than others, but *we all fall short* of God's infinite standards (Romans 3:23). In a contest to see who can throw a rock to the moon, I am sure a muscular athlete would be able to throw a rock much farther than I could. But all human beings will ultimately fail at this test. Similarly, all of us fall short of measuring up to God's perfect holy standards. But God has graciously provided a solution.

Jesus Died for Our Sins and Made Salvation Possible

God is so holy that He cannot overlook sin. Indeed, He has no choice but to punish sin. The good news of the gospel, however, is that Jesus has taken this punishment on Himself. God loves us so much that He sent Jesus to bear the penalty for our sins!

Jesus affirmed that it was for the very purpose of dying that He came into the world (John 12:27). Moreover, He perceived His death as being a sacrificial offering for the sins of humanity (Matthew 26:26-28). Jesus took His sacrificial mission with utmost seriousness; He knew that without Him, humanity would certainly perish (Matthew 16:25; John 3:16) and spend eternity apart from God in a place of great suffering (Matthew 10:28; 11:23; 23:33; 25:41; Luke 16:22-28).

Jesus described His mission this way: "The Son of Man did not come to be served, but to serve, and to give his life as a ransom for many" (Matthew 20:28). "The Son of Man came to seek and to save what was lost" (Luke 19:10); "for God did not send his Son into the world to condemn the world, but to save the world through him" (John 3:17).

But the benefits of Christ's death on the cross are not automatically applied to your life. You are required to...

Believe in Jesus Christ

By His sacrificial death on the cross, Jesus took the sins of the entire world on Himself and made salvation available for everyone (1 John 2:2). But this salvation is not automatic. Only those who personally choose to believe in Christ are saved. This is the consistent testimony of the biblical Jesus:

- "For God so loved the world that he gave his one and only Son, that whoever *believes* in him shall not perish but have eternal life" (John 3:16, emphasis added).

- "For my Father's will is that everyone who looks to the Son and *believes* in him shall have eternal life, and I will raise him up at the last day" (John 6:40, emphasis added).

- "I am the resurrection and the life. He who *believes* in me will live, even though he dies" (John 11:25, emphasis added).

Choosing not to believe in Jesus, by contrast, leads to eternal condemnation: "Whoever *believes* in him is not condemned, but whoever *does not believe* stands condemned already because he has not believed in the name of God's one and only Son" (John 3:18, emphasis added).

You need to choose Jesus!

Free at Last: Forgiven of All Sins

When you believe in Christ as Savior, a wonderful thing happens. God forgives you of all your sins. *All of them!* He puts them completely out of His sight. Ponder for a few minutes the following verses that speak of the forgiveness of those who have believed in Christ:

- "In him we have redemption through his blood, the forgiveness of sins, in accordance with the riches of God's grace" (Ephesians 1:7).

- God said, "Their sins and lawless acts I will remember no more" (Hebrews 10:17).

- "Blessed is he whose transgressions are forgiven, whose sins are covered. Blessed is the man whose sin the LORD does not count against him and in whose spirit is no deceit" (Psalm 32:1,2).

- "For as high as the heavens are above the earth, so great is his love for those who fear him; as far as the east is from the west, so far has he removed our transgressions from us" (Psalm 103:11,12).

Such forgiveness is wonderful indeed, for none of us—not even the *very best* Mason—can possibly earn entrance into heaven or be good enough to warrant God's favor. Because of what Jesus has done for us, we can freely receive the gift of salvation. *This gift is provided solely through the grace of God* (see Ephesians 2:8,9). And true freedom is yours by simply believing in Jesus.

Don't Put it Off

It is a highly dangerous thing to put off turning to Christ for salvation, for you do not know the day of your death. What if it happens this evening? "Death is the destiny of every man; the living should take this to heart" (Ecclesiastes 7:2).

If God is speaking to your heart now, then *now* is your door of opportunity to believe. "See the LORD while he may be found; call on him while he is near" (Isaiah 55:6).

Follow Me in Prayer

Would you like to place your faith in Jesus for the forgiveness of sins, thereby guaranteeing your eternal place in heaven by His side? If so, pray the following prayer with me. Keep in mind that it's not the prayer itself that saves you. It is the *faith in your heart* that brings you into God's family. Let the following prayer be a simple expression of the faith that is in your heart:

> *Dear Jesus;*
> *I want to have a relationship with You.*
> *I know I can't save myself, because I know I'm a*
> *   sinner.*
> *Thank You for dying on the cross on my behalf.*

I believe You died for me, and I accept
    Your free gift of salvation.
Thank You, Jesus.

Amen

Welcome to God's Forever Family!

On the authority of the Word of God, I can now assure you that you are a part of God's eternal family. If you prayed the above prayer with a heart of faith, you will spend all eternity by the side of Jesus in heaven. Congratulations and welcome to the family of God!

Now that you are a part of God's family, you will want to take steps to insure steady growth in your spiritual life. The two most important steps are to read your Bible everyday and join a good Bible-believing church. If you have trouble finding a good church, contact me and I'll try to help:

Ron Rhodes
P.O. Box 80087
Rancho Santa Margarita, CA 92688

Appendix B

A Comparison of Yahweh and Jesus

The following chart lists the names, titles, and attributes of Yahweh and Jesus, showing their common identity. What is true of Yahweh is also true of Jesus, which is something Masons desperately need to be aware of.

DESCRIPTION	AS USED OF YAHWEH	AS USED OF JESUS
Yahweh ("I AM")	Exodus 3:14 Deuteronomy 32:39 Isaiah 43:10	John 8:24 John 8:58 John 18:4-6
God	Genesis 1:1 Deuteronomy 6:4 Psalm 45:6-7	Isaiah 7:14; 9:6 John 1:1,14 John 20:28 Titus 2:13 Hebrews 1:8 2 Peter 1:1
Alpha and Omega (First and Last)	Isaiah 41:4 Isaiah 48:12 Revelation 1:8	Revelation 1:17,18 Revelation 2:8 Revelation 22:12-16

DESCRIPTION	AS USED OF YAHWEH	AS USED OF JESUS
Lord	Isaiah 45:22-24	Matthew 12:8 Acts 7:59,60 Acts 10:36 Romans 10:12 1 Corinthians 2:8 1 Corinthians 12:3 Philippians 2:10,11
Savior	Isaiah 43:3 Isaiah 43:11 Isaiah 63:8 Luke 1:47 1 Timothy 4:10	Matthew 1:21 Luke 2:11 John 1:29 John 4:42 Titus 2:13 Hebrews 5:9
King	Psalm 95:3 Isaiah 43:15 1 Timothy 6:14-16	Revelation 17:14 Revelation 19:16
Judge	Genesis 18:25 Psalm 50:4,6 Psalm 96:13 Romans 14:10	John 5:22 2 Corinthians 5:10 2 Timothy 4:1
Light	2 Samuel 22:29 Psalm 27:1 Isaiah 42:6	John 1:4,9 John 3:19 John 8:12 John 9:5
Rock	Deuteronomy 32:3,4 2 Samuel 22:32 Psalm 89:26	Romans 9:33 1 Corinthians 10:3,4 1 Peter 2:4-8
Redeemer	Psalm 130:7,8 Isaiah 48:17 Isaiah 54:5 Isaiah 63:9	Acts 20:28 Ephesians 1:7 Hebrews 9:12

Description	As Used of Yahweh	As Used of Jesus
Our Righteousness	Isaiah 45:24	Jeremiah 23:6 Romans 3:21,22
Husband	Isaiah 54:5 Hosea 2:16	Matthew 25:1 Mark 2:18,19 2 Corinthians 11:2 Ephesians 5:25-32 Revelation 21:2,9
Shepherd	Genesis 49:24 Psalm 23:1 Psalm 80:1	John 10:11,16 Hebrews 13:20 1 Peter 2:25 1 Peter 5:4
Creator	Genesis 1:1 Job 33:4 Psalm 95:5,6 Psalm 102:25,26 Isaiah 40:28	John 1:2,3,10 Colossians 1:15-18 Hebrews 1:1-3,10
Giver of Life	Genesis 2:7 Deuteronomy 32:39 1 Samuel 2:6 Psalm 36:9	John 5:21 John 10:28 John 11:25
Forgiver of Sin	Exodus 34:6,7 Nehemiah 9:17 Daniel 9:9 Jonah 4:2	Mark 2:1-12 Acts 26:18 Colossians 2:13 Colossians 3:13
Lord Our Healer	Exodus 15:26	Acts 9:34
Omnipresent	Psalm 139:7-12 Proverbs 15:3	Matthew 18:20 Matthew 28:20 Ephesians 3:17; 4:10

DESCRIPTION	AS USED OF YAHWEH	AS USED OF JESUS
Omniscient	1 Kings 8:39 Jeremiah 17:9,10,16	Matthew 11:27 Luke 5:4-6 John 2:25 John 16:30 John 21:17 Acts 1:24
Omnipotent	Isaiah 40:10-31 Isaiah 45:5-13	Matthew 28:18 Mark 1:29-34 John 10:18 Jude 24
Preexistent	Genesis 1:1	John 1:15,30 John 3:13,31 John 6:62 John 16:28 John 17:5
Eternal	Psalm 102:26,27 Habakkuk 3:6	Isaiah 9:6 Micah 5:2 John 8:58
Immutable	Isaiah 46:9 Malachi 3:6 James 1:17	Hebrews 13:8
Receiver of Worship	Matthew 4:10 John 4:24 Revelation 5:14 Revelation 7:11 Revelation 11:16	Matthew 14:33 Matthew 28:9 John 9:38 Philippians 2:10,11 Hebrews 1:6
Speaks with Divine Authority	"Thus saith the Lord..." used hundreds of times	Matthew 23:34-37 John 7:46 "Truly, truly, I say..."[1]

Appendix C

Victory over Satan

God had made definite provisions for our defense against Satan and his fallen angels. What does this consist of?

• To begin with we must ever keep in mind that twice in the New Testament we are told that the Lord Jesus lives in heaven to make intercession for us (Romans 8:34; Hebrews 7:25). Jesus prays for us on a regular basis. Certainly Christ's intercession for us includes the kind of intercession He made for His disciples in John 17:15, where He specifically asked the Father to keep them safe from the evil one.

• Beyond this, God has provided spiritual armor for our defense (Ephesians 6:11-18). Each piece of armor is important and serves its own special purpose. But you and I *must choose* to put on this armor. God does not force us to dress in it; we do it by choice. Read Paul's description of this armor:

> Put on the full armor of God so that you can take
> your stand against the devil's schemes. For our

struggle is not against flesh and blood, but against the rulers, against the authorities, against the powers of this dark world and against the spiritual forces of evil in the heavenly realms.

Therefore put on the full armor of God, so that when the day of evil comes, you may be able to stand your ground, and after you have done everything to stand.

Stand firm then, with the belt of truth buckled around your waist, with the breastplate of righteousness in place, and with your feet fitted with the readiness that comes from the gospel of peace. In addition to all this, take up the shield of faith with which you can extinguish all the flaming arrows of the evil one. Take the helmet of salvation and the sword of the Spirit, which is the word of God. And pray in the Spirit on all occasions with all kinds of prayers and requests.

With this in mind, be alert and always keep on praying for all the saints.

Without wearing this spiritual armor, you and I do not stand a chance against the forces of darkness. But with this suit on, victory is ours. "Wearing" this armor means that our lives will be characterized by such things as righteousness, obedience to the will of God, faith in God, and an effective use of the Word of God. These are the things that spell *DEFEAT* for the devil in your life. In effect, putting on the armor of God amounts to putting on Jesus Christ—who defeated the devil (John 12:31). (Good books are available that fully explain how to put on this spiritual armor.)[1]

• Effective use of the Word of God is especially important for spiritual victory. Jesus used the Word of God to defeat the devil during His wilderness temptations (Matthew 4:1-11). We must learn to do the same. Related to this, the late Ray Stedman said, "Obviously, the greater exposure there is to the Scripture the more the Spirit can use this mighty sword in our lives. If you never read or study your Bible, you are terribly exposed to defeat and despair. You have no defense; you have nothing to put up against these forces that are at work. Therefore, learn to read your Bible regularly."[2]

• Of course, Scripture specifically instructs us that each believer must be *informed* and *alert* to the attacks of Satan (1 Peter 5:8). A prerequisite to defeating an enemy is to know as much as possible about him—including his tactics. The apostle Paul says, "We are not to be ignorant of his schemes" (2 Corinthians 2:11 NASB). (One of his schemes is to redefine the key doctrines of Christianity, especially the identity of Jesus Christ and the gospel of grace, which is well illustrated in the Masonic Lodge.) We find all the information we need about this enemy and his schemes in the Word of God.

• We are also instructed to take a decisive stand against Satan. James 4:7 says, "Resist the devil, and he will flee from you." This is not a one-time resistance; on a day-to-day basis we must steadfastly resist the devil. Ephesians 6:13,14 tells us to stand firm against the devil. This we can do not in our own strength but in the strength of Christ. After all, it was Christ who "disarmed the rulers and authorities...[and] made a public display of them, having triumphed over them" (Colossians 2:15 NASB).

• We must not give the devil a foothold by letting sunset pass with unrighteous anger in our hearts toward someone (Ephesians 4:27). An excess of wrath in our heart gives Satan an opportunity to work in our lives.

• We are instructed to rely on the indwelling spirit of God, remembering that "the one who is in you is greater than the one who is in the world" (1 John 4:4).

• We should pray for ourselves and for each other. Jesus set an example for us in the Lord's Prayer by teaching us to pray. "Deliver us from the evil one" (Matthew 6:13). This should be a daily prayer. Jesus also set an example of how to pray for others in His prayer for Peter: "Simon, Simon, Satan has asked to sift you as wheat. But I have prayed for you, Simon, *that your faith may not fail*" (Luke 22:31,32, emphasis added).

• The believer should never dabble in the occult, for this gives the devil opportunity to work in our lives (Deuteronomy 18:10,11; see also Romans 16:19). Masons who have been involved in some of the occultic aspects of Freemasonry must repent of and renounce this activity altogether.

• Finally, we must remember that Satan is on a leash. He cannot go beyond what God will allow him (the book of Job makes this abundantly clear).[3] We can rest secure in the fact that God is in full control of the universe. Satan cannot simply do as he pleases in our lives.

By following disciplines such as those just outlined, we will have increasing victory over Satan and his host of demons who seek to bring us down. Successfully defeating the powers of darkness doesn't rest on what you can do in your own strength. It rests on what Christ has already done. You are more than a conqueror through Him that loved us (Romans 8:37).

Notes

The Masonic Lodge

1. See John J. Robinson, *Born in Blood: The Lost Secrets of Freemasonry* (New York: M. Evans and Company, 1989), pp. 176-77. See also John Ankerberg and John Weldon, *The Secret Teachings of the Masonic Lodge* (Chicago: Moody Press, 1990), p. 25.
2. *Holy Bible: Deluxe Reference Edition* (Wichita: Heirloom Bible Publishers, 1988), p. 9. Heirloom publishes a Bible edition exclusively for Freemasonry.
3. *Holy Bible: Deluxe Reference Edition*, p. 9.
4. See George Mather and Larry Nichols, *Masonic Lodge* (Grand Rapids, MI: Zondervan Publishing House, 1995), p. 27.
5. Ankerberg and Weldon, *Secret Teachings*, p. 22.
6. Henry Wilson Coil, *A Comprehensive View of Freemasonry* (Richmond: Macoy Publishing and Masonic Supply Company, 1973), p. 8.
7. Michael Baigent and Richard Leigh, *The Temple and the Lodge* (New York: Arcade Publishing, 1989), p. xi.
8. Ankerberg and Weldon, *Secret Teachings*, p. 49.
9. Ron Campbell, *Free from Freemasonry* (Ventura, CA: Regal, 1999), p. 29.
10. For a description of Masonic initiation ceremonies, see Robinson, *Born in Blood*, chapters 14–16.
11. *Holy Bible: Deluxe Reference Edition*, p. 9.
12. See Robinson, *Born in Blood*, p. 178.
13. *Holy Bible: Deluxe Reference Edition*, p. 9.
14. See Baigent and Leigh, *The Temple*, p. 126. See also William E. Hammond, *What Masonry Means* (New York: Macoy Publishing and Masonic Supply Co., 1952), pp. 17ff.; and Coil, *Comprehensive View*, p. 5.
15. Baigent and Leigh, *The Temple*, p. 174; Robinson, *Born in Blood*, p. 179; Coil, *Comprehensive Views*, pp. 69, 76-85, 122-31; see also Mather and Nichols, *Masonic Lodge*, p. 8.
16. See Robinson, *Born in Blood*, p. 181.
17. Coil, *Comprehensive View*, p. 378.
18. Ankerberg and Weldon, *Secret Teachings*, p. 258.
19. Alphonse Cerza, *Let There Be Light: A Study in Anti-Masonry* (Silver Spring, MD: The Masonic Service Association, 1983), p. 1.
20. Albert Mackey, *An Encyclopedia of Freemasonry* (New York: The Masonic History Company, 1920), p. 62.
21. Robinson, *Born in Blood*, p. 175.
22. Ibid.
23. Vindex, *Light Invisible: The Freemason's Answer to "Darkness Visible"* (Boston: Masonic Publishers, 1996), p. 4.
24. A case in point is Richard Thorn, *The Boy Who Cried Wolf: The Book that Breaks Masonic Silence* (New York: M. Evans and Company, 1994), p. 22.
25. Ibid.

Chapter 1—Dialoguing with Masons

1. L. James Rongstad, *The Lodge: How to Respond* (Saint Louis: CPH, 1995), p. 7.
2. Walton Hannah, *Darkness Visible: A Christian Appraisal of Freemasonry* (London: The Saint Austin Press, 1998), p. 52.
3. Walter Martin, "Mormons and Biblical Terminology," *Christian Research Newsletter*, vol. 4, is. 5, p. 5.
4. Hannah, *Darkness Visible*, p. 18.
5. Rongstad, *The Lodge*, p. 59.

Chapter 2—Masonic Families

1. L. James Rongstad, *The Lodge: How to Respond* (Saint Louis: CPH, 1995), p. 16.
2. *Holy Bible: Deluxe Reference Edition* (Wichita: Heirloom Bible Publishers, 1988), p. 25.
3. Some Grand Lodges have changed their laws so that black balls are no longer used for balloting. Instead, they use black cubes in order to prevent errors resulting from poor eyesight. The round balls are white and the cubes are black so that someone can know by the sense of touch how he is voting.
4. Henry Wilson Coil, *A Comprehensive View of Freemasonry* (Richmond: Macoy Publishing and Masonic Supply Co., 1973), p. 134.
5. Albert Mackey, *Encyclopedia of Freemasonry* (Chicago: Masonic History, 1946), 1:71.
6. Albert Mackey, *The Manual of the Lodge* (New York: Clark Maynard, 1870), 1:20.
7. Mackey, *Encyclopedia*, 1:263.
8. *Holy Bible: Deluxe Reference Edition*, p. 10.
9. Ibid.
10. Ibid.
11. Ibid.
12. Ibid.
13. Ibid.
14. John J. Robinson, *Born in Blood: The Lost Secrets of Freemasonry* (New York: M. Evans and Company, 1989), p. 253.
15. George Mather and Larry Nichols, *Masonic Lodge* (Grand Rapids, MI: Zondervan Publishing House, 1995), p. 12.
16. Ibid.
17. Ibid.
18. Ibid.
19. Ibid, p. 13.
20. Harold V.B. Voorhis, *Facts for Freemasons* (Richmond: Macoy Publishing and Masonic Supply Company, 1979), p. 91.
21. Mather and Nichols, *Masonic Lodge*, p. 15.
22. Voorhis, *Facts*, pp. 95-102.
23. See Mather and Nichols, *Masonic Lodge*, pp. 15-25.

24. Arthur Edward Waite, *A New Encyclopedia of Freemasonry* (New York: Weathervane Books, 1970), p. xxxiv.
25. *Holy Bible: Deluxe Reference Edition*, p. 21.
26. Ibid., p. 22.
27. Mather and Nichols, *Masonic Lodge*, p. 19.
28. See Coil, *Comprehensive View*, pp. 204-13.

Chapter 3—Understanding Freemasonry

1. Henry Wilson Coil, *A Comprehensive View of Freemasonry* (Richmond: Macoy Publishing and Masonic Supply Co., 1973), pp. 214-15.
2. Ibid.
3. Ibid., p. 232.
4. John J. Robinson, *Born in Blood: The Lost Secrets of Freemasonry* (New York: M. Evans & Company, 1989), p. 175.
5. Albert G. Mackey, *A Manual of the Lodge* (New York: Maynard, Merrill, & Co., 1898), p. 37.
6. *Symbol* may be defined as a visible sign or object with which a spiritual feeling, emotion, or idea is connected.
7. Vindex, *Light Invisible: The Freemason's Answer to "Darkness Visible"* (Boston: Masonic Publishers, 1996), p. 34.
8. Harold V.B. Voorhis, *Facts for Freemasons* (Richmond: Macoy Publishing and Masonic Supply Company, 1979), p. 24.
9. Robinson, *Born in Blood*, p. 177.
10. George Mather and Larry Nichols, *Masonic Lodge* (Grand Rapids, MI: Zondervan Publishing House, 1995), p. 7.
11. J. Blanchard, *Scottish Rite Masonry Illustrated (The Complete Ritual of the Ancient and Accepted Scottish Rite)* (Chicago: Charles T. Powner, 1979), 2:290.
12. *Holy Bible: Deluxe Reference Edition* (Wichita, KA: Heirloom Bible Publishers, 1988), p. 44.
13. Arthur Edward Waite, *A New Encyclopedia of Freemasonry* (New York: Weathervane Books, 1970), p. xxxiii.
14. L. James Rongstad, *The Lodge: How to Respond* (Saint Louis: CPH, 1995), p. 12.
15. *Holy Bible: Deluxe Reference Edition*, p. 9.
16. Voorhis, *Facts*, p. 17.
17. Robinson, *Born in Blood*, p. xiii.
18. Michael Baigent and Richard Leigh, *The Temple and the Lodge* (New York: Arcarde Publishing, 1989), p. 123.
19. See ibid., p. 126; see also William E. Hammond, *What Masonry Means* (New York: Macoy Publishing and Masonic Supply Co., 1952), pp. 17ff.; and Coil, *Comprehensive View*, p. 5.
20. Rongstad, *The Lodge*, p. 14.
21. Voorhis, *Facts*, p. 10.
22. Rongstad, *The Lodge*, p. 14.

23. John Ankerberg and John Weldon, *The Secret Teachings of the Masonic Lodge* (Chicago: Moody Press, 1990), p. 35.
24. Rongstad, *The Lodge*, p. 14.
25. Voorhis, *Facts*, p. 9.
26. Rongstad, *The Lodge*, p. 14.
27. Robert Morey, *The Origins and Teachings of Freemasonry* (Southbridge, MA: Crowne Publications, 1990), p. 69.
28. Others have claimed, however, that the operative Masons had developed secret signs and words for professional purposes. Ron Campbell writes: "As the theory goes, the skill levels of the operative masons of these builders' guilds varied greatly. A Master Mason knew considerably more than an Entered Apprentice and thus his wages were commensurate with his skill. As these masons traveled from site to site, building the Gothic cathedrals, they needed a method of communicating their skill level to the foreman of the new job site. These traveling masons developed an elaborate mode of recognition involving secret signs, words, tokens and grips. According to some Masonic writers, these are the mystical roots of modern Freemasonry." (Ron Campbell, *Free from Freemasonry* [Ventura, CA: Regal, 1999], p. 43).
29. See Ed Decker, *What You Need to Know About Masons* (Eugene, OR: Harvest House Publishers, 1992), p. 74.
30. Voorhis, *Facts*, p. 11.
31. Mackey, *Manual*, p. 35.
32. Campbell, *Free*, p. 20.
33. Voorhis, *Facts*, p. 69.
34. Mackey, *Manual*, p. 58.
35. *Holy Bible: Deluxe Reference Edition*, p. 35.
36. Ibid.
37. Albert Mackey, *An Encyclopedia of Freemasonry* (New York: The Masonic History Company, 1920), p. 121.
38. *Holy Bible: Deluxe Reference Edition*, p. 35.
39. *Zondervan NIV Bible Commentary*, Kenneth L. Barker and John Kohlenberger III, eds. (Grand Rapids, MI: Zondervan Publishing House, 1994), p. 1008.
40. Richard Thorn, *The Boy Who Cried Wolf: The Book that Breaks Masonic Silence* (New York: M. Evans and Company, 1994), p. 27.

Chapter 4—Becoming a Mason

1. Vindex, *Light Invisible: The Freemason's Answer to "Darkness Visible"* (Boston: Masonic Publishers, 1996), p. 16.
2. John Ankerberg and John Weldon, *The Secret Teachings of the Masonic Lodge* (Chicago: Moody Press, 1990), p. 15.
3. Malcolm Duncan, *Duncan's Masonic Ritual and Monitor* (New York: David McKay Company, Inc., n.d.), p. 19.
4. Bernard E. Jones, *Freemasons' Guide and Compendium* (London: Harrap, 1950), p. 259.

5. Duncan, *Duncan's*, p. 24.
6. John J. Robinson, *Born in Blood: The Lost Secrets of Freemasonry* (New York: M. Evans & Company, 1989), p. 202.
7. Duncan, *Duncan's*, p. 9.
8. Ron Carlson and Ed Decker, *Fast Facts on False Teachings* (Eugene, OR: Harvest House Publishers, 1994), pp. 74-75.
9. William E. Hammond, *What Masonry Means* (New York: Macoy Publishing and Masonic Supply, 1952), p. 68.
10. Robinson, *Born in Blood*, pp. 206-07.
11. Ibid.
12. Ibid.
13. George Mather and Larry Nichols, *Masonic Lodge* (Grand Rapids, MI: Zondervan Publishing House, 1995), p. 11. See also Carlson and Decker, *Fast Facts*, p. 75.
14. Robinson, *Born in Blood*, p. 217.
15. Duncan, *Duncan's*, p. 230.
16. Robinson, *Born in Blood*, p. 207.
17. Ibid., pp. 207-08.
18. Duncan, *Duncan's*, p. 40.
19. Ibid.
20. Ibid.
21. Ibid., p. 35.
22. *Holy Bible: Deluxe Reference Edition* (Wichita: Heirloom Bible Publishers, 1988), p. 39.
23. Ibid.
24. *Adam Clarke's Commentary*, electronic database, 1996, Biblesoft.
25. *Holy Bible: Deluxe Reference Edition*, p. 52.
26. Ibid.
27. Ibid.
28. Cited in Mather and Nichols, *Masonic Lodge*, p. 11.
29. F.F. Bruce, *The Hard Sayings of Jesus* (Downers Grove, IL: InterVarsity Press, 1983), p. 67.
30. Walton Hannah, *Darkness Visible: A Christian Appraisal of Freemasonry* (London: The Saint Austin Press, 1998), pp. 26-27.
31. Jim Tresner, "Conscience and the Craft," *Scottish Rite Journal*, Feb. 1993: 21.
32. Ankerberg and Weldon, *Secret Teachings*, p. 185.
33. Hannah, *Darkness Visible*, p. 21.
34. Robinson, *Born in Blood*, p. 250.
35. Ibid., p. 247.
36. Ibid., p. 248.
37. *Holy Bible: Deluxe Reference Edition*, p. 48.
38. Ibid.
39. Ibid.
40. Ibid.
41. Albert G. Mackey, *A Manual of the Lodge* (New York: Maynard, Merrill, & Co., 1898), p. 41.

42. Harold V.B. Voorhis, *Facts for Freemasons* (Richmond: Macoy Publishing and Masonic Supply Company, 1979), p. 231.
43. *Adam Clarke's Commentary*, electronic database.

Chapter 5—Is Masonry a Religion?

1. Albert Mackey, *An Encyclopedia of Freemasonry* (Chicago: Masonic History, 1946), 2:847.
2. Henry Wilson Coil, *Coil's Masonic Encyclopedia* (New York: Macoy Publishing and Masonic Supply Co., 1961), p. 158.
3. Ibid., p. 13.
4. Henry Wilson Coil, *A Comprehensive View of Freemasonry* (Richmond: Macoy Publishing and Masonic Supply Co., 1973), p. 234.
5. Coil, *Coil's Masonic Encyclopedia*, p. 512.
6. Cited in L. James Rongstad, *The Lodge: How to Respond* (Saint Louis: CPH, 1995), p. 23.
7. Cited in ibid., p. 23.
8. Ibid.
9. *Liturgy of the Ancient and Accepted Scottish Rite of Freemasonry for the Southern Jurisdiction of the United States*, part 2 (Washington, D.C.: The Supreme Council, 1982), pp. 198-99.
10. Albert Pike, *Morals and Dogma of the Ancient and Accepted Scottish Rite of Freemasonry* (Kila, MT: Kessinger Publishing Company, n.d.), p. 219.
11. Ibid., p. 219.
12. Mackey, *Encyclopedia*, p. 619.
13. Ibid., p. 50.
14. Joseph Fort Newton, *The Religion of Masonry: An Interpretation* (Richmond: Macoy Publishing and Masonic Supply Co., 1969), pp. 58-59.
15. Martin Wagner, *Freemasonry: An Interpretation* (Columbiana, OH: Missionary Service and Supply, n.d.), pp. 292-93.
16. Carl Claudy, *Foreign Countries: Our Gateway to the Interpretation and Development of Certain Symbols of Freemasonry* (Richmond: Macoy Publishing and Masonic Supply, 1971), p. 23.
17. Vindex, *Light Invisible: The Freemason's Answer to "Darkness Visible"* (Boston: Masonic Publishers, 1996), p. 20.
18. Manly P. Hall, *The Lost Keys of Freemasonry* (Richmond: Macoy Publishing and Masonic Supply Co., 1976), p. 33.
19. See John J. Robinson, *Born in Blood: The Lost Secrets of Freemasonry* (New York: M. Evans and Company, 1989), p. 255, emphasis added.
20. Alphonse Cerza, *Let There Be Light: A Study in Anti-Masonry* (Silver Spring, MD: The Masonic Service Association, 1983), p. 41.
21. *Little Masonic Library* (Richmond: Macoy Publishing and Masonic Supply Co., 1977), 1:138.
22. Charles H. Lacquement, "Freemasonry and Organized Religions," *The Pennsylvania Freemason*, February 1989 : 7.
23. Richard Thorn, *The Boy Who Cried Wolf: The Book that Breaks Masonic Silence* (New York: M. Evans and Company, 1994), p. 83.

24. Robinson, *Born in Blood*, p. 255.
25. Ibid.
26. Norman Vincent Peale, "What Freemasonry Means to Me," *Scottish Rite Journal*, February 1993 : 40, cited in George Mather and Larry Nichols, *Masonic Lodge* (Grand Rapids, MI: Zondervan Publishing House, 1995), p. 31.
27. William E. Hammond, *What Masonry Means* (New York: Macoy Publishing, 1952), p. 99.
28. See Ibid., p. 15.
29. Thorn, *Boy Who Cried Wolf*, p. 22.
30. Ibid., p. 83.
31. *Liturgy of the Ancient and Accepted Scottish Rite*, pp. 198-99.
32. Pike, *Morals and Dogmas*, p. 161.
33. *Holy Bible: Deluxe Reference Edition* (Wichita: Heirloom Bible Publishers, 1988), p. 10.
34. George Mather and Larry Nichols, *Masonic Lodge* (Grand Rapids: Zondervan Publishing House, 1995), p. 32.
35. Coil, *Comprehensive View*, p. 234.
36. See Malcolm Duncan, *Duncan's Masonic Ritual and Monitor* (New York: David McKay Company, Inc., n.d.), pp. 7-57.
37. Ibid.
38. Mather and Nichols, *Masonic Lodge*, pp. 34-35. See also John Ankerberg and John Weldon, *The Secret Teachings of the Masonic Lodge* (Chicago: Moody Press, 1990), pp. 44-45.
39. Mather and Nichols, *Masonic Lodge*, p. 31.
40. Ibid.
41. Coil, *Comprehensive View*, p. 186.
42. John Ankerberg and John Weldon, *The Secret Teachings of the Masonic Lodge* (Chicago: Moody Press, 1990), p. 20.
43. Walton Hannah, *Darkness Visible: A Christian Appraisal of Freemasonry* (London: The Saint Austin Press, 1998), p. 28.
44. Ibid., p. 31.

Chapter 6—The Bible: A "Great Light"

1. Vindex, *Light Invisible: The Freemason's Answer to "Darkness Visible"* (Boston: Masonic Publishers, 1996), p. 40.
2. Ibid.
3. John J. Robinson, *Born in Blood: The Lost Secrets of Freemasonry* (New York: M. Evans and Company, 1989), p. 255.
4. Henry Wilson Coil, *Coil's Masonic Encyclopedia* (New York: Macoy Publishing and Masonic Supply Co., 1961), p. 520.
5. Albert Mackey, *An Encyclopedia of Freemasonry* (New York: The Masonic History Company, 1920), p. 672.
6. Albert Pike, *Morals and Dogma of the Ancient and Accepted Scottish Rite of Freemasonry* (Kila, MT: Kessinger Publishing Company, n.d.), p. 11.
7. Mackey, *Encyclopedia*, p. 104.

8. Albert G. Mackey, *A Manual of the Lodge* (New York: Maynard, Merrill, & Co., 1898), p. 30.
9. William E. Hammond, *What Masonry Means* (New York: Macoy Publishing and Masonic Supply Co., 1952), p. 159.
10. Ibid., p. 100.
11. Pike, *Morals and Dogmas,* pp. 744-45.
12. Vindex, *Light Invisible,* p. 38.
13. Martin Wagner, *Freemasonry: An Interpretation* (Columbiana, OH: Missionary Service and Supply, n.d.), p. 335.
14. Richard Thorn, *The Boy Who Cried Wolf: The Book that Breaks Masonic Silence* (New York: M. Evans and Company, 1994), p. 70.
15. Cited in ibid., pp. 69-70.
16. Norman Geisler and William Nix, *A General Introduction to the Bible* (Chicago: Moody Press, 1978), p. 28.
17. Donald J. Wiseman, "Archaeological Confirmation of the Old Testament," in Norman L. Geisler, *Christian Apologetics* (Grand Rapids, MI: Baker Book House, 1976), p. 322.
18. Nelson Glueck, *Rivers in the Desert* (Philadelphia: Jewish Publications Society of America, 1969), p. 31.
19. William F. Albright, cited in Josh McDowell, *Evidence that Demands a Verdict* (San Bernardino, CA: Campus Crusade for Christ, 1972), p. 68.
20. Norman L. Geisler, *Explaining Hermeneutics: A Commentary* (Oakland, CA: International Council on Biblical Inerrancy, 1983), p. 6.
21. Geisler, *Explaining Hermeneutics,* p. 7.
22. Douglas Groothuis, *Confronting the New Age* (Downers Grove, IL: InterVarsity Press, 1988), p. 85.
23. Geisler, *Explaining Hermeneutics,* p. 7.
24. Tal Brooke, *When the World Will Be as One* (Eugene, OR: Harvest House Publishers, 1989), p. 118.
25. Robert P. Lightner, *The Savior and the Scriptures* (Grand Rapids, MI: Baker Book House, 1966), p. 30.

Chapter 7—God: The Great Architect of the Universe

1. See Henry Wilson Coil, *Coil's Masonic Encyclopedia* (New York: Macoy Publishing and Masonic Supply Co., 1961), p. 104.
2. Jim Tresner, "Conscience and the Class: Questions on Religion and Freemasonry," *The Northern Lights,* Feb. 1993, p. 18, cited in George Mather and Larry Nichols, *Masonic Lodge* (Grand Rapids, MI: Zondervan Publishing House, 1995), p. 41.
3. Carl Claudy, *Introduction to Freemasonry* (Washington D.C.: Temple Publishers, 1984), 2:110.
4. Vindex, *Light Invisible: The Freemason's Answer to "Darkness Visible"* (Boston: Masonic Publishers, 1996), p. 4.
5. William E. Hammond, *What Masonry Means* (New York: Macoy Publishing and Masonic Supply Co., 1952), p. 159.

6. H.L. Haywood, *Great Teachings of Masonry* (Kingsport, TN: Southern Publishers, 1923), pp. 119-20.
7. Albert Mackey, *An Encyclopedia of Freemasonry* (New York: The Masonic History Company, 1920), p. 48.
8. Ibid.
9. Ibid.
10. Henry Wilson Coil, *A Comprehensive View of Freemasonry* (Richmond: Macoy Publishing and Masonic Supply Co., 1973), p. 192.
11. Albert Mackey, *Mackey's Revised Encyclopedia of Freemasonry* (Richmond: Macoy Publishing and Masonic Supply Co., 1966), 1:409-10.
12. Martin Wagner, *Freemasonry: An Interpretation* (Columbiana, OH: Missionary Service and Supply, n.d.), p. 330.
13. John Ankerberg and John Weldon, *The Secret Teachings of the Masonic Lodge* (Chicago: Moody Press, 1990), pp. 112-13.
14. J.W. Acker, *Strange Altars: A Scriptural Appraisal of the Lodge* (St. Louis: Concordia, 1959), p. 37.
15. Coil, *Coil's Masonic Encyclopedia*, p. 516.
16. Wagner, *Freemasonry,* pp. 338-39.
17. Mackey, *Encyclopedia*, p. 301.
18. Ibid., p. 149.
19. Vindex, *Light Invisible*, p. 28.
20. Lewis M. Hopfe, *Religions of the World* (New York: Macmillan Publishing Company, 1991), p. 91.
21. Ibid., p. 98. See also John Ankerberg and John Weldon, *The Facts on Hinduism in America* (Eugene, OR: Harvest House Publishers, 1991), pp. 9-10.
22. Walter Martin, *The New Cults* (Ventura, CA: Regal Books, 1980), p. 82.
23. J. Isamu Yamamoto, *Hinduism, TM & Hare Krishna* (Grand Rapids, MI: Zondervan Publishing House, 1995), p. 11.
24. Dean C. Halverson, "Hinduism," in *The Compact Guide to World Religions* (Minneapolis: Bethany House Publishers, 1996), p. 89.
25. Hopfe, *Religions,* p. 99.
26. Yamamoto, *Hinduism,* p. 11.
27. Hopfe, *Religions,* p. 99.
28. Mark Albrecht, "Hinduism," in *Evangelizing the Cults*, Ronald Enroth, ed. (Ann Arbor, MI: Servant Publications, 1990), p. 22.
29. Hopfe, *Religions,* p. 98.
30. Ibid.
31. Martin, *New Cults,* p. 80.
32. Ibid., p. 86, inserts added.
33. For more on Islam, see Ron Rhodes, *Islam: What You Need to Know* (Eugene, OR: Harvest House Publishers, 2000).
34. Christopher Haffner, *Workman Unashamed: The Testimony of a Christian Freemason*, p. 39, cited in "Why Does Freemasonry Call Its God the Great Architect of the Universe?" Ex-Masons for Jesus, Box 4372, Laurel, MS 39441.
35. *Holy Bible: Deluxe Reference Edition* (Wichita: Heirloom Bible Publishers, 1988), p. 41.

36. *International Standard Bible Encyclopedia,* "Father, God the," electronic database, Biblesoft, 1996.
37. Cited in Walton Hannah, *Darkness Visible: A Christian Appraisal of Freemasonry* (London: The Saint Austin Press, 1998), p. 35. According to John Robinson, the name *Jabulon* is not interpreted by all Masons in the same way. He notes that some Masons trying to "break the code" of the name arrived at the conclusion that the name is made up of three syllables standing for Jehovah, Baal, and On, or Osiris, but this interpretation is by no means universally accepted by all Masonic historians (*Born in Blood: The Lost Secrets of Freemasonry* [New York: M. Evans & Company, 1989], p. 311). Robinson also notes that "the assumption that Jabulon means Jehovah, Baal, and Osiris is itself pure conjecture. No one knows for certain what it means" (p. 313).
38. Hannah, *Darkness Visible,* p. 34.
39. Cited in Benjamin B. Warfield, *The Person and Work of Christ* (Philadelphia: Presbyterian and Reformed, 1950), p. 66, brackets and emphasis in original.
40. Ankerberg and Weldon, *Secret Teachings,* pp. 168-73.
41. Ibid.
42. Hannah, *Darkness Visible,* p. 42.

Chapter 8—Masonry's Connection to Paganism
1. Albert Mackey, *An Encyclopedia of Freemasonry* (New York: The Masonic History Company, 1920), pp. 233, 364-65, 587.
2. See, for example, Albert Pike, *Morals and Dogma of the Ancient and Accepted Scottish Rite of Freemasonry* (Kila, MT: Kessinger Publishing Company, n.d.), pp. 255, 290-91, 364-65, 376, 406, 460, 469, 477, 587.
3. See, for example, ibid., p. 255.
4. Ibid., p. 460.
5. Ibid., pp. 22, 23.
6. Vindex, *Light Invisible: The Freemason's Answer to "Darkness Visible"* (Boston: Masonic Publishers, 1996), p. 10.
7. Ibid., p. 9.
8. Cited in L. James Rongstad, *The Lodge: How to Respond* (Saint Louis: CPH, 1995), p. 12.
9. John Ankerberg and John Weldon, *The Secret Teachings of the Masonic Lodge* (Chicago: Moody Press, 1990), p. 37.
10. Martin Wagner, *Freemasonry: An Interpretation* (Columbiana, OH: Missionary Service and Supply, n.d.), p. 253.
11. Ankerberg and Weldon, *Secret Teachings,* p. 253.
12. Ron Campbell, *Free from Freemasonry* (Ventura, CA: Regal Book Publishers, 1999), p. 48.
13. Ibid., p. 51.
14. Ron Rhodes, *Miracles Around Us: How to Recognize God at Work Today* (Eugene, OR: Harvest House Publishers, 2000).
15. John J. Davis, *Moses and the Gods of Egypt: Studies in Exodus* (Grand Rapids, MI: Baker Book House, 1986), p. 94.
16. Ibid., p. 97.

17. Ibid., pp. 59, 81.
18. Ibid., p. 100.
19. Pierre Montet, *Eternal Egypt* (New York: The New American Library, 1964), p. 57.
20. God accomplished several purposes in the plagues. First, He showed the *Egyptians* that He is the Lord (Exodus 7:5). Second, He showed the *Israelites* that He is the Lord (10:2). And third, He judged the many false gods of Egypt by the plagues, showing Himself superior to them all (Numbers 33:4).
21. Alan Cole, *Exodus: An Introduction and Commentary* (Downers Grove, IL: InterVarsity Press, 1973), p. 90.
22. *Ancient Near Eastern Texts*, edited by James B. Pritchard, "Hymn to the Nile," translated by John Wilson (Princeton: Princeton University Press, 1969), p. 272.
23. Old Testament scholar Merrill F. Unger tells us: "Moses appears in the OT as the first great miracle worker. And the reason for that is evident when we remember his unique position in the religious history of mankind, the greatness of his work, and the obstacles he encountered (Exodus 10:1,2; 14:21–31; 20:1–21; etc.)" (*The New Unger's Bible Dictionary*, electronic database, PC Study Bible, Biblesoft, 1999.)
24. Norman L. Geisler, *A Popular Survey of the Old Testament* (Grand Rapids, MI: Baker Book House, 1977), p. 56.
25. Davis, *Moses and the Gods of Egypt*, p. 102.
26. Ibid., p. 103.
27. Ibid., p. 107.
28. Ibid., p. 108.
29. Ibid.
30. C.F. Keil and F. Delitzsch, *The Pentateuch: Biblical Commentary on the Old Testament* (Grand Rapids, MI: Eerdmans, 1949), p. 483.
31. Montet, *Eternal Egypt*, p. 177.
32. Cole, *Exodus*, p. 93.
33. Davis, *Moses and the Gods of Egypt*, p. 114.
34. Geisler, *Popular Survey*, p. 56.
35. Cole, *Exodus*, p. 95.
36. See John B. Noss, *Man's Religions* (New York: Macmillan Publishing Co., 1974), pp. 35-37.
37. Montet, *Eternal Egypt*, p. 172.
38. Davis, *Moses and the Gods of Egypt*, pp. 122-23.
39. Cole, *Exodus*, p. 96.
40. Davis, *Moses and the Gods of Egypt*, p. 123.
41. Ibid., p. 124; Walton Hannah, *Darkness Visible: A Christian Appraisal of Freemasonry* (London: Saint Austin Press, 1998), p. 120.
42. Geisler, *Popular Survey*, p. 56.
43. Noss, *Man's Religions*, p. 38.
44. Davis, *Moses and the Gods of Egypt*, p. 128.
45. Notice that some of the plagues—such as the plague of gnats, the hail, and the locusts—involved natural conditions which, in less extreme forms, have

prevailed in the Nile valley from time to time. The miraculous element in the plagues is to be found in their timing (*when* Moses said so), their intensity (worse than ever), and the location *(in Egypt alone* and not in neighboring Goshen, where the Israelites were).

46. Davis, *Moses and the Gods of Egypt,* p. 130.
47. Montet, *Eternal Egypt,* pp. 39,169.
48. C.J. Labuschagne, *The Incomparability of Yahweh in the Old Testament,* Pretoria Oriental Series (Leiden, Netherlands: Brill, 1966), p. 58.
49. Davis, *Moses and the Gods of Egypt,* p. 134.
50. *Ancient Near Eastern Texts,* pp. 367-68.
51. Davis, *Moses and the Gods of Egypt,* p. 134.
52. Ibid., p. 141.
53. Ibid., p. 149.
54. Geisler, *Popular Survey,* p. 56.
55. Davis, *Moses and the Gods of Egypt,* p. 149.
56. Cited in Ankerberg and Weldon, *Secret Teachings,* p. 242.

Chapter 9—Whatever Happened to Jesus?

1. There are some Masonic Lodges that acknowledge Jesus, but they are few in number. One example is the Masonic Code of the Grand Lodge of Alabama, which states: "It is therefore proper and in accordance with Masonic law and tenets for a Mason who believes in Christ Jesus to offer prayers in the Lodge in His Name" (*Masonic Code* [Grand Lodge of Alabama, 1963], p. 141, cited in "Freemasonry Report," prepared by David W. Atchison, Executive Committee, Southern Baptist Convention, June 15-17, 1993).
2. Jack Harris, *Freemasonry: The Invisible Cult in Our Midst* (Chattanooga, TN: Global, 1983), p. 112.
3. Albert Mackey, *Encyclopedia of Freemasonry* (Chicago: Masonic History, 1946), vol. 1, p. 149.
4. Albert Pike, *Morals and Dogma of the Ancient and Accepted Scottish Rite of Freemasonry;* cited in L. James Rongstad, *The Lodge: How to Respond* (Saint Louis: CPH, 1995), p. 40.
5. Albert Pike, *Morals and Dogma of the Ancient and Accepted Scottish Rite of Freemasonry* (Kila, MT: Kessinger Publishing Company, n.d.), p. 540.
6. Ibid., p. 308.
7. Ibid., p. 310.
8. Richard Thorn, *The Boy Who Cried Wolf: The Book that Breaks Masonic Silence* (New York: M. Evans and Company, 1994), p. 25.
9. Pike, *Morals and Dogma,* p. 18.
10. John Ankerberg and John Weldon, *The Secret Teachings of the Masonic Lodge* (Chicago: Moody Press, 1990), p. 127.
11. Ibid.
12. Ibid.
13. J. Isamu Yamamoto, *Hinduism, TM & Hare Krishna* (Grand Rapids, MI: Zondervan Publishing House, 1995), p. 32.

14. See George A. Mather and Larry A. Nichols, *Dictionary of Cults, Sects, Religions and the Occult* (Grand Rapids, MI: Zondervan Publishing House, 1993), p. 119.
15. Yogi, *Meditations of Maharishi Mahesh Yogi*, pp. 123-24, cited in Yamamoto, *Hinduism*, p. 48.
16. C.S. Lewis, *Mere Christianity* (New York: Macmillan, 1960), pp. 40-41.
17. Robert L. Reymond, *Jesus, Divine Messiah: The Old Testament Witness* (Geanies House, Scotland: Christian Focus Publications, 1990), pp. 78-84.
18. Jon A. Buell and O. Quentin Hyder, *Jesus: God, Ghost or Guru?* (Grand Rapids, MI: Zondervan Publishing House, 1978), p. 27; cf. Josh McDowell and Bart Larson, *Jesus: A Biblical Defense of His Deity* (San Bernardino, CA: Here's Life Publishers, 1983), pp. 21-24.
19. Robert L. Reymond, *Jesus, Divine Messiah: The New Testament Witness* (Phillipsburg, NJ: Presbyterian and Reformed, 1990), pp. 92-94.
20. Millard J. Erickson, *The Word Became Flesh: A Contemporary Incarnational Christology* (Grand Rapids, MI: Baker Book House, 1991), pp. 28-29.
21. David F. Wells, *The Person of Christ* (Westchester, IL: Crossway Books, 1984), pp. 64-65.
22. I am sometimes asked where the name *Jehovah* came from. This name is not found in the Hebrew and Greek manuscripts, from which English translations of the Bible are derived. (The Old Testament contains the name *Yahweh*—or, more literally, *YHWH* [the original Hebrew had only consonants].) This being so, then, where did the name *Jehovah* come from?

   The ancient Jews had a superstitious dread of pronouncing the name YHWH. They felt that if they uttered this name, they might violate the Third Commandment, which deals with taking God's name in vain (Exodus 20:7). So, to avoid the possibility of breaking this commandment, the Jews for centuries substituted the name *Adonai* (Lord) or some other name in its place whenever they came across it in public readings of Scripture.

   Eventually, the fearful Hebrew scribes decided to insert the vowels from Adonai (a-o-a) within the consonants, YHWH. The result was *Yahowah*, or Jehovah. The word *Jehovah* is derived from a consonant-vowel combination from the words YHWH and Adonai. Jehovah is thus not a *biblical* term. It is a *man-made* term.
23. Cited in E.M. Storms, *Should a Christian Be a Mason?* (Kirkwood, MO: Impact Christian Books, 1999), p. 86.
24. Cited in ibid., p. 86.
25. Walton Hannah, *Darkness Visible: A Christian Appraisal of Freemasonry* (London: The Saint Austin Press, 1998), p. 38.
26. Ibid., p. 42.

Chapter 10—Redefining Sin and Salvation: Part 1

1. Vindex, *Light Invisible: The Freemason's Answer to "Darkness Visible"* (Boston: Masonic Publishers, 1996), p. 53.
2. H.L. Haywood, *The Great Teachings of Masonry* (Richmond: Macoy Publishing and Masonic Supply Co., 1971), pp. 138-39.

3. Ibid., p. 140.
4. Ibid., p. 138.
5. L. James Rongstad, *The Lodge: How to Respond* (Saint Louis: CPH, 1995), p. 22.
6. Ibid., p. 47.
7. Grand Lodge of Texas, *Monitor of the Lodge* (Fort Worth: Grand Lodge of Texas, 1982), p. 19.
8. W.L. Wilmhurst, *The Masonic Initiation* (London: John M. Watkins, 1957), pp. 27-28.
9. Jack Harris, *Freemasonry: The Invisible Cult in Our Midst* (Chattanooga, TN: Global, 1983), p. 132.
10. Albert Mackey, *Encyclopedia of Freemasonry* (Chicago: Masonic History, 1946), 1:269.
11. Haywood, *Great Teachings*, p. 137.
12. Ibid., pp. 138-39.
13. Albert G. Mackey, *A Manual of the Lodge* (New York: Maynard, Merrill, & Co., 1898), p. 21.
14. Mackey, *Manual*, pp. 20-21.
15. Haywood, *Great Teachings*, p. 31.
16. Ibid., p. 43.
17. Arthur Edward Waite, *A New Encyclopedia of Freemasonry* (New York: Weathervane Books, 1970), p. 332.
18. Haywood, *Great Teachings*, p. 139, emphasis added.
19. William E. Hammond, *What Masonry Means* (New York: Macoy Publishing and Masonic Supply, 1952), p. 165.
20. John J. Robinson, *Born in Blood: The Lost Secrets of Freemasonry* (New York: M. Evans & Company, 1989), p. 256.
21. Cited in John Ankerberg, et al., *The Masonic Lodge: What Goes on Behind Closed Doors?* (Chattanooga, TN: The John Ankerberg Evangelistic Association, 1986), p. 35.
22. Mackey, *Manual*, p. 16, emphasis added.
23. Cited in Rongstad, *The Lodge*, pp. 33-34, emphasis added.
24. Raymond Lee Allen, *Tennessee Craftsmen or Masonic Textbook* (Nashville: Tennessee Board of Custodians Members, 1963), p. 17.
25. Hammond, *What Masonry Means*, p. 50.
26. Cited in E.K. Simpson and F.F. Bruce, *Commentary on the Epistles to the Ephesians and Colossians* (Grand Rapids, MI: Eerdmans, 1975), p. 50.
27. John Ankerberg and John Weldon, *The Secret Teachings of the Masonic Lodge* (Chicago: Moody Press, 1990), p. 142.
28. To *impute* means "to credit," "to attribute," or "to transfer." Christ's righteousness is *credited* to the believer's life.
29. Wayne Grudem, *Systematic Theology: An Introduction to Biblical Doctrine* (Grand Rapids, MI: Zondervan Publishing House, 1994), p. 723.
30. Martin Luther, cited in J.I. Packer, *Knowing Christianity* (Wheaton, IL: Harold Shaw Publishers, 1995), p. 94.

31. Cited in John R. Rice, *Lodges Examined by the Bible* (Murfreesboro, TN: Sword of the Lord Publishers, 1943), p. 55.
32. Josh McDowell, *A Ready Defense* (Nashville: Thomas Nelson Publishers, 1993), p. 272. See also John B. Noss, *Man's Religions* (New York: Macmillan Publishing Co., 1974), pp. 104, 186.

Chapter 11—Redefining Sin and Salvation: Part 2

1. Albert Pike, *Morals and Dogma of the Ancient and Accepted Scottish Rite of Freemasonry* (Kila, MT: Kessinger Publishing Company, n.d.), p. 36.
2. Vindex, *Light Invisible: The Freemason's Answer to "Darkness Visible"* (Boston: Masonic Publishers, 1996), p. 48.
3. *The Bible Knowledge Commentary*, New Testament, eds. John F. Walvoord and Roy B. Zuck (Wheaton, IL: Victor Books, 1989), p. 825.
4. Richard Thorn, *The Boy Who Cried Wolf: The Book that Breaks Masonic Silence* (New York: M. Evans and Company, 1994), p. 39.
5. Ibid., p. 23.
6. Ibid., p. 8, emphasis added.
7. Ibid., p. 24.
8. Vindex, *Light Invisible,* p. 50.
9. *Bible Knowledge Commentary*, p. 80, emphasis added.
10. *Holy Bible: Deluxe Reference Edition* (Wichita: Heirloom Bible Publishers, 1988), p. 32.
11. Albert Mackey, *An Encyclopedia of Freemasonry* (New York: The Masonic History Company, 1920), p. 361.
12. *Holy Bible: Deluxe Reference Edition,* p. 46.
13. Donald Grey Barnhouse, *Genesis: A Devotional Exposition* (Grand Rapids, MI: Zondervan Publishing House, 1973), 2:84.
14. *Treasury of Scripture Knowledge*, electronic edition, Parsons Technology, 1998.
15. Albert G. Mackey, *A Manual of the Lodge* (New York: Maynard, Merrill, & Co., 1898), p. 66.
16. *NIV Study Bible* (Grand Rapids, MI: Zondervan Publishing House, 1985), p. 1356.
17. *Holy Bible: Deluxe Reference Edition,* p. 54.
18. Mackey, *Manual*, p. 88.
19. *Holy Bible: Deluxe Reference Edition,* p. 55.

Chapter 12—Masonry's Great Omission

1. H.L. Haywood, *Great Teachings of Masonry* (Kingsport, TN: Southern Publishers, 1923), p. 127.
2. Albert Mackey, *An Encyclopedia of Freemasonry* (New York: The Masonic History Company, 1920), p. 198.
3. Albert G. Mackey, *A Manual of the Lodge* (New York: Maynard, Merrill, & Co., 1898), p. 96.
4. J.I. Packer, *Knowing God* (Downers Grove, IL: InterVarsity Press, 1983), p. 126.

5. Douglas Connelly, *What the Bible Really Says: After Life* (Downers Grove, IL: InterVarsity Press, 1995), p. 119.
6. Ibid., p. 118.
7. Merrill F. Unger, *Beyond the Crystal Ball* (Chicago: Moody Press, 1973), p. 63.
8. John Wesley, *The Nature of Salvation* (Minneapolis: Bethany House Publishers, 1987), p. 135.
9. Ibid.
10. John Blanchard, *Whatever Happened to Hell?* (Durham, England: Evangelical Press, 1993), p. 116.
11. Ibid., p. 156.
12. Ibid.
13. Robert L. Thomas, "2 Thessalonians," *The Expositors Bible Commentary*, Frank E. Gaebelein, ed. (Grand Rapids, MI: Zondervan Publishing House, 1978), p. 313.
14. Robert A. Morey, *Death and the Afterlife* (Minneapolis: Bethany House Publishers, 1984), p. 138.

Chapter 13—Occultism in Masonry

1. H.L. Haywood, *Great Teachings of Masonry* (Kingsport, TN: Southern Publishers, 1923), p. 94.
2. See John Ankerberg and John Weldon, *The Secret Teachings of the Masonic Lodge* (Chicago: Moody Press, 1990), pp. 216-18.
3. I recommend ibid., pp. 215-43. See also E.M. Storms, *Should a Christian Be a Mason?* (Kirkwood, MO: Impact Christian Books, 1999).
4. Elliot Miller, "Cabala," fact sheet published by Christian Research Institute, P.O. Box 7000, Rancho Santa Margarita, CA 92688.
5. Ibid.
6. *The Sorcerer's Handbook*, cited in E.M. Storms, *Should a Christian Be a Mason?* (Kirkwood, MO: Impact Christian Books, 1999), p. 20.
7. Cited in Storms, *Should a Christian*, p. 20.
8. Ibid.
9. Ibid., pp. 20-21.
10. Ankerberg and Weldon, *Secret Teachings*, p. 219.
11. Ibid.
12. Albert Pike, *Morals and Dogma* (Kila, MT: Kessinger Publishing Co., n.d.), p. 741.
13. Ibid., p. 625.
14. Ibid., p. 266.
15. Ibid., p. 745.
16. Albert Mackey, *Mackey's Revised Encyclopedia of Freemasonry* (Richmond: Macoy Publishing and Masonic Supply Co., 1966), p. 375.
17. Vindex, *Light Invisible: The Freemason's Answer to "Darkness Visible"* (Boston: Masonic Publishers, 1996), p. 11.
18. Ibid.
19. *Liturgy of the Ancient and Accepted Scottish Rite of Freemasonry for the Southern Jurisdiction of the United States* (Washington D.C.: The Supreme Council, 1982), p. 166.

20. Ankerberg and Weldon, *Secret Teachings*, p. 215.
21. Ibid., p. 220.
22. R.D. Clements, *God & the Gurus* (Downers Grove, IL: InterVarsity Press, 1975), pp. 38-39.
23. Miller, "Cabala."
24. Charles C. Ryrie, *A Survey of Bible Doctrine* (Chicago: Moody Press, 1980), p. 94.
25. Charles Ryrie, *Basic Theology* (Wheaton, IL: Victor Books, 1985), p. 147.
26. Charles Ryrie, *Balancing the Christian Life* (Chicago: Moody Press, 1980), p. 124.

Chapter 14—Should Christians Be Masons?

1. "Freemasonry Report," prepared by David W. Atchison, Executive Committee, Southern Baptist Convention, Augusta, GA, presented in Houston, TX, June 15-17, 1993.
2. Ibid.
3. Ibid.
4. Cited in Eddy D. Field II and Eddy D. Field III, "Freemasonry and the Christian," *The Master's Seminary Journal*, Fall 1994, pp. 141-57.
5. George A. Mather and Larry A. Nichols, *Masonic Lodge* (Grand Rapids, MI: Zondervan Publishing House, 1995), p. 26.
6. Field and Field, "Freemasonry," pp. 141-57.
7. Walton Hannah, *Darkness Visible: A Christian Appraisal of Freemasonry* (London: The Saint Austin Press, 1998), p. 76.
8. L. James Rongstad, *The Lodge: How to Respond* (Saint Louis: CPH, 1995), p. 57.
9. John Ankerberg and John Weldon, *The Secret Teachings of the Masonic Lodge* (Chicago: Moody Press, 1990), p. 45.
10. Walter Martin, *The Rise of the Cults* (Ventura, CA: Regal Books, 1983), p. 24.
11. George Barna, *The Barna Report 1992–93* (Ventura, CA: Regal Books, 1993), p. 50.
12. Cited in Karl Menninger, *What Ever Became of Sin?* (New York: Hawthorne Books, 1973).
13. Barna, *Barna Report*, pp. 43, 50.
14. Ron Carlson and Ed Decker, *Fast Facts on False Teachings* (Eugene, OR: Harvest House Publishers, 1994), pp. 74-75.
15. John J. Robinson, *Born in Blood: The Lost Secrets of Freemasonry* (New York: M. Evans & Company, 1989), pp. 206-07.
16. Ibid., p. 255.
17. Henry Wilson Coil, *A Comprehensive View of Freemasonry* (Richmond: Macoy Publishing and Masonic Supply Co., 1973), p. 192.
18. See, for example, Albert Pike, *Morals and Dogma of the Ancient and Accepted Scottish Rite of Freemasonry* (Kila, MT: Kessinger Publishing Company, n.d.), p. 255.
19. Hannah, *Darkness Visible*, pp. 18-19.
20. Ibid., p. 39.

21. Cited in Arthur Pruess, *Dictionary of Secret and Other Societies* (St. Louis: B. Herder Company, 1924), p. 143.

Chapter 15—Evangelism Among Masons

1. Walter Martin, "The Do's and Don'ts of Witnessing to Cultists," *Christian Research Newsletter*, Jan.-Feb. 1992, p. 4.
2. Ibid.
3. Ibid.
4. Ibid.
5. Ibid.
6. Ibid.
7. David Reed, *Jehovah's Witnesses Answered Verse by Verse* (Grand Rapids, MI: Baker Book House, 1992), pp. 115-16.
8. Martin, "Do's and Don'ts," p. 4.
9. Ibid.
10. Ibid.

Appendix A

1. Edythe Draper, *Draper's Book of Quotations for the Christian World* (Wheaton, IL: Tyndale House Publishers, 1992), p. 539.

Appendix B

1. Adapted from Josh McDowell and Bart Larson, *Jesus: A Biblical Defense of His Deity* (San Bernardino, CA: Here's Life Publishers, 1983), pp. 62-64.

Appendix C

1. See, for example, Thomas Ice and Robert Dean, *A Holy Rebellion* (Eugene, OR: Harvest House Publishers, 1995), ch. 8.
2. Ray Stedman, *Spiritual Warfare* (Waco, TX: Word Books, 1976), p. 114.
3. Millard Erickson, *Christian Theology* (Grand Rapids, MI: Baker Book House, 1987), p. 449.

Bibliography

Abanes, Richard. *Cults, New Religious Movements, and Your Family*. Wheaton, IL: Crossway, 1998.

Acker, J.W. *Strange Altars: A Scriptural Appraisal of the Lodge*. St. Louis: Concordia, 1959.

Allen, Raymond Lee. *Tennessee Craftsmen or Masonic Textbook*. Nashville: Tennessee Board of Custodians Members, 1963.

Ankerberg, John and John Weldon, *Cult Watch: What You Need to Know About Spiritual Deception*. Eugene, OR: Harvest House Publishers, 1991.

———. *Encyclopedia of Cults and New Religions*. Eugene, OR: Harvest House Publishers, 1999.

———. *The Secret Teachings of the Masonic Lodge*. Chicago: Moody Press, 1990.

Baigent, Michael, and Richard Leigh. *The Temple and the Lodge*. New York: Arcade, 1989.

Beliefs of Other Kinds: A Guide to Interfaith Witness in the United States. Atlanta: Baptist Home Mission Board, 1984.

Blanchard, J. *Scottish Rite Masonry Illustrated (The Complete Ritual of the Ancient and Accepted Scottish Rite)*. Chicago: Charles T. Powner, 1979.

Boa, Kenneth. *Cults, World Religions, and You*. Wheaton, IL: Victor Books, 1979.

Bradley, Don. *Freemasonry in the 21st Century*. Burbank, CA: Native Planet Publishing, 1997.

Campbell, Ron G. *Free from Freemasonry*. Ventura, CA: Regal, 1999.

Carlson, Ron and Ed Decker. *Fast Facts on False Teachings*. Eugene, OR: Harvest House Publishers, 1994.

Cerza, Alphonse. *Let There Be Light: A Study in Anti-Masonry*. Silver Spring, MD: The Masonic Service Association, 1983.

Coil, Henry Wilson. *A Comprehensive View of Freemasonry*. Richmond: Macoy Publishing and Masonic Supply Co., 1973.

Decker, Ed. *What You Need to Know About Masons*. Eugene, OR: Harvest House Publishers, 1992.

Duncan, Malcolm. *Duncan's Masonic Ritual and Monitor*. New York: David McKay Company, Inc., n.d.

Enroth, Ronald. *A Guide to Cults and New Religions*. Downers Grove, IL: InterVarsity Press, 1983.

———. *The Lure of the Cults*. Downers Grove, IL: InterVarsity Press, 1987.

Gerstner, John H. *The Theology of the Major Sects*. Grand Rapids, MI: Baker Book House, 1980.

Gomes, Alan. *Unmasking the Cults*. Grand Rapids, MI: Zondervan Publishing House, 1995.

Halverson, Dean C., ed. *The Compact Guide to World Religions*, Minneapolis: Bethany House Publishers, 1996.

Hammond, William E. *What Masonry Means*. New York: Macoy Publishing and Masonic Supply Co., 1952.

Hannah, Walton. *Darkness Visible: A Christian Appraisal of Freemasonry*. London: Saint Austin Press, 1998.

Harris, Jack. *Freemasonry: The Invisible Cult in Our Midst*. Chattanooga, TN: Global, 1983.

Haywood, H.L. *Great Teachings of Masonry*. Kingsport, TN: Southern Publishers, n.d.

Hoekema, Anthony A. *The Four Major Cults*. Grand Rapids, MI: Eerdmans, 1978.

Holy Bible: Deluxe Reference Edition. Wichita: Hierloom Bible Publishers, 1988.

Holy Bible (Temple Illustrated Edition). Nashville: Holman, 1968.

Jones, Bernard E. *Freemason's Guide and Compendium*. London: Harrap, 1973.

Liturgy of the Ancient and Accepted Scottish Rite of Freemasonry for the Southern Jurisdiction of the United States. Washington D.C.: The Supreme Council, 1982.

Mackey, Albert. *Encyclopedia of Freemasonry*. Chicago: Masonic History, 1946.

_____. *A Manual of the Lodge*. New York: Maynard, Merrill, & Co., 1898.

Martin, Paul. *Cult-Proofing Your Kids*. Grand Rapids, MI: Zondervan Publishing House, 1993.

Martin, Walter. *The Kingdom of the Cults*. Minneapolis: Bethany House Publishers, 1999.

_____. *Martin Speaks Out on the Cults*. Ventura, CA: Regal Books, 1983.

_____. *The New Cults*. Ventura, CA: Regal Books, 1980.

_____. *The Rise of the Cults*. Ventura, CA: Regal Books, 1983.

Mather, George A., and Larry A. Nichols. *Dictionary of Cults, Sects, Religions and the Occult*. Grand Rapids, MI: Zondervan Publishing House, 1993.

McDowell, Josh, and Don Stewart. *Handbook of Today's Religions*. San Bernardino, CA: Here's Life Publishers, 1989.

_____. *Understanding the Cults*. San Bernardino, CA: Here's Life Publishers, 1983.

Morey, Robert A. *The Origins and Teachings of Freemasonry*. Southbridge, MA: Crowne Publications, 1990.

Pement, Eric, ed. *Contend for the Faith*. Chicago: EMNR, 1992.

Pike, Albert. *Morals and Dogma of the Ancient and Accepted Scottish Rite of Freemasonry*. Charleston, S.C.: The Supreme Council, 1906.

Robertson, Irvine. *What the Cults Believe*. Chicago: Moody Press, 1983.

Robinson, John J. *Born in Blood: The Lost Secrets of Freemasonry*. New York: M. Evans, 1989.

Rongstad, L. James. *The Lodge: How to Respond*. Saint Louis: CPH, 1995.

Saliba, John A. *Understanding New Religious Movements*. Grand Rapids, MI: Eerdmans, 1995.

Sire, James. *Scripture Twisting*. Downers Grove, IL: InterVarsity Press, 1980.

Storms, E.M. *Should a Christian Be a Mason?* Kirkwood, MO: Impact Christian Books, 1999.

Swenson, Orville. *The Perilous Path of Cultism*. Caronport, Saskatchewan: Briercrest Books, 1987.

Thorn, Richard. *The Boy Who Cried Wolf: The Book that Breaks Masonic Silence*. New York: M. Evans and Company, 1994.

Tucker, Ruth. *Another Gospel: Alternative Religions and the New Age Movement*. Grand Rapids, MI: Zondervan Publishing House, 1989.

Vindex. *Light Invisible: The Freemason's Answer to Darkness Visible*. Boston: Masonic Publishers, 1996.

Voorhis, Harold V.B. *Facts for Freemasons*. Richmond: Macoy Publishing and Masonic Supply Co., 1979.

Waite, Arthur Edward. *A New Encyclopedia of Freemasonry*. New York: Weathervane Books, 1970.

Subject Index

A

Acceptable religion requires works — 192
Adam and Eve — 34
Adoption into God's family — 117
African Americans — 29
All-seeing eye (God) — 106
Allegories and symbols — 33
Almsgiving required — 199
Ancient Arabic Order of the Nobles of the Mystic Shrine — 26
Archeological support for Bible — 95
Authority of Bible — 95

B

Bible interpretation
    Context important — 102
    History important — 103
Bible
    Archeological support for — 95
    Authority of — 95
    Contradicts other "holy books" — 89
    Esotericism unreliable — 98
    Great light — 87
    Inspiration of — 92
    Should not be added to — 97
    Symbol of Divine will — 87
    Volume of Sacred Law — 87
Biblical illiteracy, problem of — 239
Black ball — 22, 55
Blasphemy — 128
Blood oaths
    Entered Apprentice degree — 56
    Fellow Craft degree — 57
    Master Mason degree — 58
    Royal Arch Mason — 58
Blue Lodge
    Entrance into — 22
    Meaning of — 21
Brotherly love
    In Masonic Lodge — 42
    True basis of — 51

G

Scripture Index

index.

Other Good Books
by *Ron Rhodes*

Angels Among Us
The Complete Book of Bible Answers
Find It Fast in the Bible
Miracles Around Us
What Did Jesus Mean

QUICK REFERENCE GUIDES

Angels: What You Need to Know
Believing in Jesus: What You Need to Know
Bible Translations: What You Need to Know
Islam: What You Need to Know
Jehovah's Witnesses: What You Need to Know

Contacting the Author

REASONING FROM THE SCRIPTURES MINISTRIES is a teaching ministry that will help you grow strong in the Word of God and equip you to become knowledgeable in the application of biblical wisdom.

We publish a free newsletter and offer numerous materials (many free) on a variety of relevant issues. If you would like to be on our mailing list, or if we can be of service to you in any way, please do not hesitate to write:

Ron Rhodes
Reasoning from the Scriptures Ministries
P.O. Box 80087
Rancho Santa Margarita, CA 92688

We also have a free Internet newsletter that goes out to thousands of Christians in over 45 countries. If you would like to subscribe, send an e-mail to ronrhodes@aol.com and put put "Subscribe" in the body of your e-mail.

Other Good Harvest House Reading

Bruce and Stan's™ Guide to God
by *Bruce Bickel and Stan Jantz*

Bruce and Stan explain Christian lingo and provide key verses, suggested readings, questions for group or personal study, and much more. Discovering new ideas and reviewing what you already know isn't boring—as long as you're using *Bruce and Stan's™ Guide to God!*

How to Study the Bible for Yourself
by *Tim LaHaye*

This book will give you some fascinating study helps and charts that will make the Bible come alive! Personal Bible study will become an interesting and rewarding daily experience. The three year program outlined will give you the working knowledge of the Bible that you've always wanted to have.

The Stones Cry Out
by *Randall Price*

Discover what new archaeological finds have to tell us about Israel's journey to the Promised Land, the fall of Jericho's walls, the Ark of the Covenant, the kings and prophets of Israel, the Assyrian and Babylonian invasions, the Dead Sea Scrolls, the time and people of Jesus, and more. Includes testimonies and interviews from leading archaeologists and exciting pictures features the latest finds made in the lands of the Bible.

What a Hunter Brings Home
by *Steve Chapman*

Have you searched for the elusive whitetail? Experienced the thundering charge of a bull elk? Tried to outsmart an old gobbler? Whether reminiscing or dreaming of the hunt, you'll savor these true tales of heart-stopping action and life changing encounters with God.

What a Hunter Brings Home captures the joy of the hunt and demonstrates how God uses solitude of the woods to reveal His eternal truths.